MOLYVOS

MOLYVOS

A Greek Village's Heroic Response to
the Global Refugee Crisis

JOHN WEBB

POTOMAC BOOKS
An imprint of the University of Nebraska Press

All rights reserved. Potomac Books is an imprint
of the University of Nebraska Press.
Manufactured in the United States of America.

Library of Congress Cataloging-in-Publication Data
Names: Webb, John, author.
Title: Molyvos: a Greek village's heroic response
to the global refugee crisis / John Webb.
Description: Lincoln: Potomac Books, an imprint
of the University of Nebraska Press, [2023] |
Includes bibliographical references and index.
Identifiers: LCCN 2023003703
ISBN 9781640125704 (hardback)
ISBN 9781640126091 (epub)
ISBN 9781640126107 (pdf)
Subjects: LCSH: Refugees—Greece—
Mēthymna. | Emigration and immigration.
Classification: LCC HV640.4.G8 W43 2023 | DDC
325/.210949582—dc23/eng/20230607
LC record available at https://lccn.loc.gov/2023003703

Set in Arno.
Designed by N. Putens.

Many people do not realize exactly what happened here. It was massive, and people don't have any concept of it.

—MELINDA MCROSTIE, co-owner of the Captain's Table and founder of the Starfish Foundation

CONTENTS

ILLUSTRATIONS

MOLYVOS

Prologue

Introduction to the Story of Molyvos

Molyvos is a uniquely picturesque and captivating village nestled on the north shore of Lesvos, Greece's northernmost island. Built on the slopes and along the cliffs of an escarpment that rises abruptly from the water's edge to the 650-year-old castle at the top, it looks like those medieval towns illustrated in storybooks. Its steep cobblestone streets that wind their way up to the castle are so narrow that, halfway up, only pedestrians, bicycles, and small motorbikes can get through. Even garbage on those upper streets must be collected with a donkey carrying large baskets strapped to its back. Village residents do much of their shopping in small family-owned stores and markets that display the day's fresh produce under awnings that protect the front entrances from sun and rain. In midmorning, fishmongers can be heard announcing their catch over the loudspeakers of their trucks as they slowly move through the village streets stopping for housewives and restaurant owners who hurry out to buy fresh fish for the evening meal. Restaurants with their daily menus handwritten on signboards and specialty gift shops, many of them family-owned, are located in the harbor and along the side streets frequented by pedestrian tourists exploring the village or making their way on foot up to the castle. Some streets have been turned into covered passageways with wisteria vines hanging from wires that stretch between buildings. The vines flower profusely in April, and their broad leaves provide cool shade where many local residents, particularly the elderly, sit protected from the summer's afternoon heat. Sycamore trees shade public squares where tourists and locals can all take a break, particularly if they are making the steep climb up one of the streets.

There was a time when most of the residents of Molyvos were fishermen who plied the waters of the Mytilene Strait—the channel of the northern Aegean Sea that separates Lesvos from Turkey—and shepherds who pastured their flocks of sheep on the neighboring fields and hillsides. When Greece joined the European Union (EU) in 1981, Molyvos gradually became a destination for increasing numbers of summer tourists, drawn there from all parts of Europe by its quiet way of life, its warm sun and beaches, its harbor lined with colorful fishing boats and artisan shops, and its inviting restaurants featuring the day's catch of fresh fish and authentic Greek dishes made from locally grown ingredients.

In September 2013 my husband, Nelson Mondaca, and I traveled to Molyvos to spend some vacation time there with our friends, Michael Honegger and Timothy Jay Smith. Molyvos is one of their favorite destinations, and they had urged us many times to join them. For them it is a kind of second home, and they have spent every May and September there for the past fifteen years. At the time, Michael had just started a new career as a fine art and documentary photographer. Tim had just published his first novel and was beginning work on his second one. Over the years, they always found inspiration for their creative work in Molyvos, its sunshine, the water, and through the many friendships they had built with the people there.

Our flight from Athens to Mytilene, the island's capital located on Lesvos's southern coast, landed in the late afternoon, and when Michael picked us up at the airport, he wanted to start the trip back right away so there would be enough daylight for us to enjoy the impressive and often breathtaking drive north over the two mountain ranges that separate Molyvos from Mytilene. By the time we arrived in Molyvos, the sun had begun its descent behind the hills of Turkey only four miles away across the Mytilene Strait. Before long, just like everyone, residents and visitors, we found ourselves mesmerized by the glorious Molyvos sunset, with its brilliant pallet of red, orange, and blue rays filling the sky and reflecting like a mirror on the entire span of water. The sunset is an indelible part of life along that coast and is part of what beckons visitors to return to Molyvos year after year. It certainly captured us.

It is a long-standing tradition for Michael and Tim to have dinner on their first night back in Molyvos at the Captain's Table, a popular and charming restaurant in the harbor that lies at the bottom of the steep slope on which the village of Molyvos is built. Our friends wanted us to experience that tradition, so as darkness settled over the village, we made our way down the main road, a cobblestone street that runs along the edge of the cliff as it descends directly to the harbor. We passed under the colorful canopies of the harbor's restaurants, all festively lit with strings of hanging lights and filled with diners seated at tables covered with platters of food. As we neared the other end of the harbor, we were greeted by a young server who obviously knew Michael and Tim very well and was expecting us. Within moments we were seated at one of the tables draped with the restaurant's signature muted blue-and-gold-checkered tablecloths under gentle white canopies and hanging lights. Our table was right next to the water's edge where surprisingly small, multicolored fishing boats were moored, the very ones that had brought in the sardines—a Molyvos specialty—that we would have as one of our appetizers that evening.

"I carry my own bottle of wine with me, but Michael and Tim know that I always share," the server who approached our table said jokingly as she set glasses in front of the four of us and poured a generous serving of white wine from a bottle that bore the restaurant's label. Right behind her came a man with a sparkling smile and a sporty pigtail carrying a platter of sardines that he placed on the table. With that gesture of warm welcome and hospitality, what the Greeks call *philoxenia*—the art of expressing love and friendship to strangers—we met Melinda McRostie and Theo Kosmetos, the delightfully affable chef-owners of the Captain's Table.[1] As the evening wore on, lasting until nearly two in the morning, the number of people at our table grew, and more tables were added to accommodate Michael's and Tim's many friends, expats who live in Molyvos, locals from the village and the surrounding area, longtime seasonal residents, shop owners, and artists, all gathered to share food, wine, and laughter-filled conversation. Any jet lag that we might have felt from the ten-hour flight from the United States to Athens, the hour-long flight from there to Mytilene, and the car trip over the mountains to Molyvos was long forgotten. We already knew that when our stay ended it was going to be hard to leave.

The nightly gatherings continued with many of the same friends. On some evenings, a whole new group of people would join us, some from the United Kingdom, a few from the United States, and some from as far away as Australia. They were all frequent visitors to the island, and some spend every summer in Molyvos or out at Eftalou, a beachside area just a few kilometers to the east of Molyvos.

Nelson and I shared the same passion for good food as Michael and Tim and their friends, so every meal was a delight, whether we ate at the Captain's Table or another restaurant in Molyvos—the day's fresh catch of fish; the colorful salads filled with ripe red tomatoes, locally grown cucumbers, and kalamata olives; creamy fava, a puree of split peas topped with sliced red onion and generously sprinkled with olive oil pressed in nearby Stypsie, a mountain village south of Petra on the road to Mytilene; stuffed zucchini blossoms served with tzatziki—the Greek cucumber yogurt sauce—and warm pita bread; beetroots and a side order of skordalia, the Greek garlic mashed potato dip; ladotyri, the delectable Lesvos cheese that we ended up also having fried for breakfast almost every morning along with a large Greek salad. The list could go on much longer.

Road trips on the island invariably included lunch under the grape arbor of a roadside restaurant overlooking a hillside panorama of olive trees or on a secluded beach where the owner prepared fish that had been caught that morning along with, perhaps, his homemade vegetable stifada, a Greek stew whose ingredients came fresh from his own garden. Good food was everywhere, as was the feeling of warm hospitality—philoxenia—which we quickly learned is how people there prefer to live and what makes tourism such an important part of the area's economy.

Several of our evening dining companions organized daytime outings for us to travel to places such as Mantamados, a hill town located in northeast Lesvos—slightly less than an hour's drive from Molyvos—that is known for its pottery and its monastery of the Archangel Michael of Mantamados, a site of religious pilgrimage. Nelson and I rented a car so we could explore the coast between Eftalou and Skala Sykaminias, a charming little fishing village to the east of Molyvos. We also discovered several inviting beaches, where we crossed the pebbles and the sand to swim in the bracing and stunningly clear blue water of the Aegean. We climbed the cobblestone streets all the way up to the castle, where we could look out over the entire village of Molyvos down to the harbor and, on clear days, all the way to the far reaches of the island's northwest point.

Before our stay in Molyvos ended, we had savored every dish on the menu of the Captain's Table, and we had become well acquainted with Melinda and Theo, their children Afrodite, Kimon, and Rhea, and with Jennifer, Melinda's fun-loving mother. We even liked to think that the family cat enjoyed our presence. In short we fell totally in love with Molyvos and, like so many of the tourists who go there, wanted to maintain our ties with the place and the people we met. It was hard to leave, but after hugs all around and promises to return as soon as possible, Michael drove us back over the mountains to Mytilene for our flight to the United States. Little did we know, nor could we ever have imagined, that before we would return, the enchanting and seemingly unspoiled way of life that we had so enjoyed during our stay would be completely upended and that the lives of Melinda, her family, and the people we met would be permanently reshaped by a massive refugee crisis that would reverberate throughout Europe and the rest of the Western world.

Our plan was to return to Molyvos in September 2015. Unfortunately, intervening personal circumstances early that year forced us to cancel the trip, but we stayed in touch with Melinda, Michael and Tim, and a few others as best we could through Facebook. At some point in late April, we started to notice postings in which Melinda asked for donations of money and clothing "for the refugees." Before long, her postings became more frequent and her tone more urgent. We were puzzled because she had never mentioned anything about refugees in Molyvos before. Then in May, after Michael and Tim arrived in Molyvos for their spring stay, Michael began to post pictures every day that he had taken of refugees in the village and harbor of Molyvos and out on the beach at Eftalou. The pictures showed what appeared to be flimsy gray or black rubber rafts approaching the shore, all looking as if they would capsize immediately if a wave, even one moderate in size, hit them, and every one was crammed so full that many of the passengers were forced to sit on the edges of the vessel, perilously close to the water.

Michael's postings were like a newsreel. There were women and children on the beach getting wrapped in silver-colored emergency blankets, people lying unconscious on the sand, some bleeding, many weeping. He captured vivid images of babies clasped in the arms of their parents and young men supporting elderly people as they made their way through the water toward the beach together. Other photos revealed refugees on their knees praying or, in total contrast, taking selfies in which they were smiling broadly, even triumphantly, for having landed safely. In Michael's pictures, the harbor of Molyvos was almost unrecognizable because of the number of refugees gathered there and because the harbor walls were at least partially concealed by clothing and blankets hanging out to dry. Even the stones of the harbor pavement were covered with pieces of cardboard where refugee families were sitting or sleeping.

Then Tim began posting text in which he described how desperate refugees, mostly Syrians and Afghans at that time, were fleeing the wars in their homelands and heading for the Turkish coast where they boarded flimsy vessels to make the crossing to the beach of Eftalou and the harbor of Molyvos, their shortest route to the safety of Europe. Those who survived the crossing, especially in bad weather, often arrived in pitiful condition, either from exposure to the cold water and high waves during the crossing itself, from wounds they had sustained during the fighting in their home countries, or from the thousand-mile treks that they had made just to get to the Turkish coast. Tim's pleas were really made on behalf of Melinda and Theo, along with their friends and acquaintances who exhausted their personal financial resources to provide for the refugees once they had landed in Molyvos. Dry clothes, shoes in particular, were in seriously short supply because the refugees all arrived wet and cold, and many of them had lost their shoes along the way. All monetary donations, Tim told everyone, would go to purchase not only clothing but also food and other essential supplies. He posted his appeals on Facebook, but he also made direct contact with friends and acquaintances, providing them with the information they would need to ensure that the donations ended up in the specially designated account that he had created. Michael's pictures and Tim's appeals were all so striking that we couldn't believe what we were seeing, and we remained baffled because nothing about any such crisis was being reported in the United States.

It wasn't until September that we began to see reports and then, all at once, Molyvos was on the nightly news and in the newspapers. Celebrities like Anderson Cooper were there reporting from spots on the beach at Eftalou that we recognized. Once, we even saw Melinda in the background of one of the videos. She was helping to wrap a refugee child in a silver emergency blanket. Gradually what Michael and Tim had been portraying on Facebook since May all started to become gruesomely palpable for us.

Tim's pleas for assistance continued throughout the summer and fall of 2015. Michael's pictures resumed in September when the two of them returned to Molyvos. By that time they were able to report, gratefully, that the response to their appeals had been generous and that the money was being used to buy shoes, thousands of them; caps to protect refugees from the summer sun, also thousands of them; and thousands of ponchos for when the fall weather turned cold and wet. At the end of September, when Michael and Tim returned to their home in Paris, the personal reporting slowed down, and the news out of Molyvos became more sporadic. Early in 2016 we learned of the agreement that the EU signed with Turkey to stop the deluge of refugees entering Europe, and come spring, we saw postings from Melinda on Facebook urging tourists to return to Molyvos because the refugees were no longer arriving as they had been.

When we were finally able to return to Molyvos in September 2017, Melinda arranged for one of her friends who operated a taxi service to pick us up at the airport in Mytilene. Needless to say, as our taxi headed toward the route north, we immediately asked our driver to tell us all about what had happened since our last trip. He appeared eager to talk, and when we passed the turnoff to Moria, the largest of the refugee camps, where thousands of refugees were still being held, he began to describe what had taken place along the very roadway on which we were traveling. He pointed to places where he had seen scores of refugees walking, forced to make the long trip from Molyvos to Moria on foot because it was against the law for them to be transported. As a taxi driver he could not give any of them a ride for fear of being fined. Instead he carried bottles of water with him to hand out to the refugees as he passed by. His wife had worked closely alongside Melinda in Molyvos, helping to collect and distribute clothing and prepare food. We sat in the back seat, hanging on his every word. This time, unlike our first trip from the airport to Molyvos four years before, the dramatic scenery passed largely unnoticed while we listened raptly to his firsthand account of what had happened in 2015.

By the time we reached the house that we had rented from Melinda and Theo, with its sweeping view of the village and the sea, we were so taken by what we had heard that we dropped our luggage and sat almost motionless in the chairs on the balcony, watching the glorious Molyvos sunset in silence. Then we did what Michael and Tim had always done on their first night back. We walked down the street to the harbor, passed under the lights of the canopies, and, when we reached the far end of the harbor, the same server welcomed us to the Captain's Table and seated us right next to where the fishing boats were moored.

It was mid-September, and the tourist season was just starting to wind down, but it was far quieter than it had been in 2013 on our first visit. The refugee crisis that enveloped Lesvos, Molyvos in particular, was still hurting the tourist business, even well into the 2017 season, and we could tell from our conversations with almost everyone that business owners were already worried about what would happen if the downturn were to continue into 2018. One afternoon we went back to the harbor hoping to have a chance to talk with Melinda and Theo so we could catch up a bit and renew our friendship after four years. As chance would have it, the lunch hour at the Captain's Table had ended, most of the diners had left, and the two were sitting alone at the table on the porch just to the right of the front door, where we knew they always sat in the evening after meal service winds down. They invited us to join them. We gently brought up the whole refugee story, not knowing how much they'd want to talk about it two years later. Theo had been deeply affected by everything that had happened and remained rather quiet. Melinda, on the other hand, seemed

willing to share and began to tell us how the crisis had engulfed the village, how literally hundreds of thousands of refugees had crossed the four
miles from Turkey in frail vessels, many perishing en route, and how the
vast majority of those who survived that crossing ended up in the harbor
right in front of the very porch where we were sitting.

She told us how the two of them and their children, along with a small
group of their friends, suddenly found themselves at the center of the
crisis and how they labored incessantly, even when they were completely
exhausted. For them to stop was unthinkable because they were the only
ones on the ground helping these masses of people with overwhelming
needs and had experienced equally overwhelming tragedies. The gravity of
what had taken place was brought home to us when Melinda described in
detail a scene where a young mother, having lost her husband and children
when their boat broke apart during the crossing, lay on the harbor floor,
banging her head on the pavement and wailing for hours. Her eyes welling
up with tears, Melinda told us, "I can still hear her screams, and I have been
very much affected by them."

The afternoon's conversation was stirring for me personally, not only
because of the magnitude of the crisis that Melinda described and her role
in it but because it also invoked vivid memories of a time, fifty years earlier,
when I, too, had to act in response to a large migration of people—adults
and children—fleeing their homeland in search of refuge from a brutal
dictatorship. It was in 1968. I was fresh out of college and had just begun
my first job as a French teacher in Spring Valley, New York, a suburban
community in Rockland County just north of New York City. That year,
the area was starting to experience a significant increase in the arrival of
families from Haiti.

Small numbers of Haitians had been moving to Spring Valley and its
neighboring Hudson River village of Nyack since the late 1950s, when Ford
Motor Company went to Haiti to recruit workers for its newly opened
assembly plant in nearby Mahwah, New Jersey. What started as an orderly
migration became a chaotic flood by the end of the 1960s and the beginning
of the 1970s, when Haiti's turbulent political, economic, and social climate
began to deteriorate under the murderous reign of its president, François

"Papa Doc" Duvalier. After his rise to power in 1957, Duvalier, with the help of his brutal special militia known as the Tontons Macoutes, unleashed a reign of terror, torturing and murdering anyone suspected of opposing his rule. This lasted for the next three decades until his son, Jean-Claude, who succeeded him upon his death, was overthrown and forced to flee the country in 1986. During that time, thousands of Haitians left their homeland to seek refuge and asylum abroad. Many went to France and the eastern Canadian province of Quebec, but the vast majority headed to the United States and, once in the country, made their way to areas where they had relatives or where there was already a community of Haitians. Rockland County was one of those places, and Spring Valley became one of their primary destinations.

There was a ten-year period beginning in 1972 when thousands also boarded flimsy vessels, just like the refugees coming into Molyvos, many at the mercy of smugglers, to make the treacherous and often deadly seven-hundred-mile crossing from the northern coast of Haiti to the Bahamas or the coast of South Florida. All of my students shared the trauma of forced migration and resettlement in a new community and school. Many were firsthand witnesses to the murder of family members, friends, and neighbors at the hands of the Tontons Macoutes. Some endured ocean crossings in which fellow migrants or family members drowned. I was a young, enthusiastic teacher and more than willing to accept the responsibility of tending to the needs of the Haitian immigrant students. As a result, almost from my first day of teaching, I found myself engrossed in the myriad linguistic, cultural, social, and psychological challenges that the students and their families faced when circumstances forced them to flee for their lives and settle in what they hoped was the safety of the United States.

Nothing I experienced in Spring Valley, as dramatic and gripping as it was at times, ever came near to what Melinda saw and had to do in Molyvos during the refugee crisis of 2015–16. Nevertheless when she shared her stories that afternoon at the restaurant, I could sense how she felt, why she chose to assume such enormous responsibility, and what had prompted her to devote so much of her life to the refugees. In a way, I had walked in Melinda's shoes.

That afternoon in 2017, Melinda also told me that she was starting to forget events that had occurred and that this forgetting troubled her deeply. She believed that the story needed to be more than just remembered—people had to know what had happened in Molyvos; people needed to know that thousands were driven to such desperation that they had no choice but to flee the homes they loved, the countries of their birth, and face a life-altering trek into a terrifying unknown. Their desperation was so intense that they were willing to face the gravest dangers and endure unfathomable hardships before they found safety and freedom, if they ever could. Melinda also felt strongly that it was important for people to understand what it was really like in Molyvos and on the neighboring beaches when the refugees landed, particularly during the period before there was any help from the outside and they were alone facing the growing crisis. She wanted people to know what the volunteers actually saw, did, and felt as they attempted to provide for the critical needs of such large numbers of people and assist with their movement through the community and across their island.

During his affiliation with the Humanitarian Academy at Harvard University, Joel Hernandez wrote and published an article titled "Humanitarianism without Humanitarians: Refugee Relief in Lesvos, Greece." The "humanitarians" whom he refers to in the article are the professionals from all the non-governmental organizations (NGOs) that deal in humanitarianism worldwide.[2] However, in the ten months between November 2014 and the fall of 2015, the period that is the primary focus of this book, those particular humanitarians were nowhere to be seen. Yet in their absence there was a large and powerful measure of humanitarianism—the earnest and instinctive generosity of local people and volunteers in Molyvos and on the beaches of nearby Eftalou. When Melinda shared her concern about forgetting events that occurred, I believe that their "humanitarianism" was foremost in her mind, and I couldn't help myself; I had to offer to write the story. I felt that I owed it to her, to the people of Molyvos who stepped forward to help, and to my colleagues from back in Spring Valley some fifty years ago who also stepped in to ensure that all the immigrant children who came to us had a safe harbor where they and their families could find respect, care, and an opportunity to learn.

When we arrived back in the United States at the end of our stay that September, I began my research to locate everything that had been written about the refugee crisis, specifically between November 2014, when Melinda first became involved, and the fall of 2015, when NGOs, the EU, and the Greek government finally stepped in to help. She and I agreed to have regularly scheduled conversations via Skype that I would then transcribe and use as the basis for telling the story.

I soon learned that very little material existed about the crisis in Molyvos prior to September 2015, when reporters finally started going there after pictures of the lifeless body of Alan Kurdi, a young Syrian boy, lying dead on a Turkish beach, were shown on media all over the world. Almost everyone on his boat had died when it was shipwrecked shortly after leaving Turkey on its way to the Greek island of Kos; only his father survived. Before that, there were no reporters on the north coast of Lesvos. The only substantial information that I could find came from videos that had been posted on YouTube by Eric Kempson, a British expat and artist, who lived in Eftalou with his wife, Philippa, and their daughter, Elleni. Like Melinda and Theo, the Kempsons helped refugees who landed on the beach just down the road from their home; whenever Eric went to the beach, he carried his cell phone to record videos and narrate what was happening. It soon became evident that I needed to speak with others in addition to Melinda, specifically the people who helped her, and it was also essential to speak with the Kempsons. Melinda suggested that I return to Molyvos for that purpose, and she offered to establish some initial contacts for me.

In April 2018 Nelson and I returned to Molyvos, and I conducted a series of interviews with Eric and Philippa Kempson, Melinda and Theo, and Melinda's friends and colleagues. During the sixteen months between November 2014 and March 2016, they were the backbone of what became the area's major, bespoke, and highly effective response to the crisis in Molyvos and all along the north coast. While we were there we also walked the beaches of Eftalou, drove on both the coastal road and the upper road to Skala Sykaminias, and visited with the volunteers for Lighthouse Relief at their spot high on the upper road, from which they watched for refugee boats. Before our time there was over, we made the trip up to the "dump," where all the boats and life vests left behind from the refugee landings were deposited. From all of this, I have constructed the story of what happened in Molyvos, hoping to—as Joel Hernandez suggested—offer insights that might better prepare us to meet the challenges posed by the millions of displaced people on our planet that will preoccupy this generation and beyond.

In the process I learned that empathy was what motivated Melinda and her friends, as well as Eric and Philippa Kempson, and what eventually became an army of volunteers, to become so passionately involved. It seemed to me then, as it does now, that knowing what happened also compels us to consider what prompts people to come forward and help, even when faced with frightening and overwhelming situations that can change lives forever and leave permanent scars. After all, the empathy and compassion of a relative few, while seemingly minuscule or even negligible, can in the end be an actual force that changes the world by showing us how to survive and how to live.

MAP 1. Islands of the Northern Aegean showing the eastern boundary between Greece and Turkey. Created by Erin Greb Cartography.

Aegean
Sea

Skala
Sykaminias

Eftalou

Molyvos

Sykaminias

Petra

Stypsi

Mantamados

Kalloni

Eresos

Gulf of
Kalloni

Skala
Eresou

Moria

Kara Tepe

Agiasos

Mytilene

Gulf of
Yera

Mytilene Strait

Plomari

0   10 mi

0   10 km

MAP 2. Above: The island of Lesvos showing routes along the north coast and the principal route to Mytilene that passes through Petra and Kalloni. Created by Erin Greb Cartography.

MAP 3. Following page: Detail of the villages of Molyvos and Skala Sykaminias. Also shown are the high road and coastal road to Skala, and Oxy just to the south of Molyvos. Created by Erin Greb Cartography.

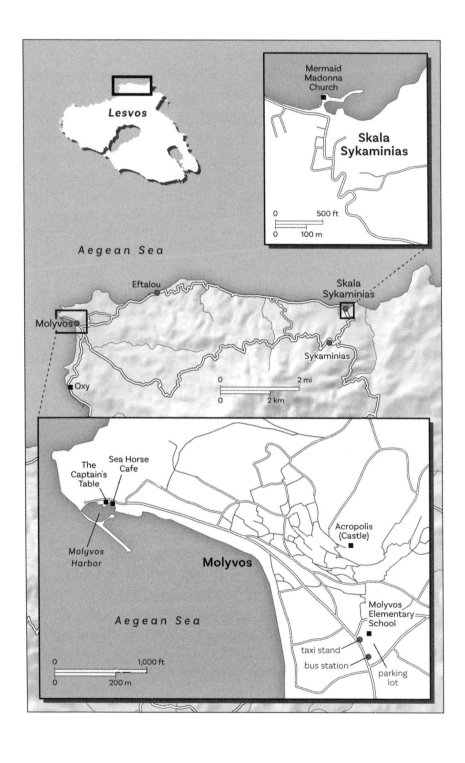

Lesvos

Mermaid
Madonna
Church

Skala
Sykaminias

0   500 ft
0   100 m

Aegean Sea

Eftalou

Skala
Sykaminias

Molyvos

Sykaminias

0   2 mi
0   2 km

Oxy

The
Captain's
Table

Sea Horse
Cafe

Acropolis
(Castle)

Molyvos
Harbor

Molyvos

Molyvos
Elementary
School

Aegean Sea

taxi stand

bus station

parking
lot

0   1,000 ft
0   200 m

1

Inescapable Memories and an Uncertain Future

April 2018

A glowing and delightfully warm afternoon sun bathed the small harbor of Molyvos as I sat near the edge of the water at one of the outdoor tables of the Sea Horse Café. The tourist season had not yet begun in earnest, so most of the restaurants in the harbor were still closed, except for the Sea Horse, where a few tables with their trademark yellow cloth covers and brown and yellow folding chairs were set up. I was spending two weeks in Molyvos meeting with the people who had been at the center of the refugee crisis in 2015. That afternoon, Melinda had arranged for me to meet Ute Vogt, the owner of a gift shop that looks directly out onto the harbor's stone-paved plaza where I was sitting.

Winter's chilly damp winds that often blow off the waters of the Aegean were a distant memory for everyone that afternoon as the balmy breezes wafted over the sun-filled plaza. A few tables away, an elderly couple sat, having their lunch and watching fish as they jumped out of the water to grab insects that flew close to the surface. The two were munching contentedly on their Greek salads laden with the season's first fresh tomatoes, green peppers, and red onions, topped with a large slice of feta cheese generously sprinkled with golden olive oil and dried oregano. Their comfort and familiarity with their surroundings suggested that they might be long-time seasonal residents who had chosen to return to Molyvos a bit early to enjoy the preseason tranquility that would soon disappear with the arrival of the summer crowds.

Fishing boats of many sizes were tied to the moorings of the concrete wharves that stretched around the harbor and out along the wall that protected it from the winds and waves of the open sea. The sun's bright light reflected off the muted gray bow of the Coast Guard boat as it pulled away from the pier with its crew on its way out to patrol the bay. The decks of the smaller boats were piled high with nets waiting to be cast by the fishermen once they were out at sea. The larger boats boasted big rollers that held the nets used to reel in the catch mechanically. Many of the boats, already back from their daytime fishing run, bobbed around in their moorings as lazily as the couple having lunch at the table, or even as lazily as the fish swimming about. Blissful in the middle of it all were the resident cats, either sleeping in the sun or licking their paws and washing their faces after having feasted on remnants of the morning's catch that had been thrown their way by generous fishermen. A few of the fishermen were preparing their nets and their boats in anticipation of setting out a little later to fish under the elegant mantle of the evening Aegean sun as it slowly descended behind the Turkish hills only four miles away across the Mytilene Strait. The tranquil scene was punctuated from time to time with the rattle of trucks on the cobblestones as electricians, air conditioning technicians, carpenters, plumbers, food purveyors, and other service providers came and went, busily preparing for the start of the new summer season only a few days away.

I hadn't been waiting long when Ute opened the door and appeared on the front step of her shop. When she did, I could see the shop's interior, flooded with the sun's bright rays as they reflected off the water. Nelson and I had been in Ute's shop on our first trip to Molyvos in 2013 and went home with a couple of unique and exquisitely handcrafted bowls, but this was my first time meeting Ute herself. A stylish and sophisticated woman whose kind, friendly eyes and gentle manner of speaking mirror her approach to life and her interactions with others, Ute had witnessed the evolution of Molyvos over her twenty-five years there. When she first came to Lesvos from her native Germany, the island had a population of approximately ninety thousand people, some thirty thousand fewer than in 2018, and Molyvos was a quiet seaside village of fishermen and shepherds who, during the summer months, lived side by side with the growing number of tourists and seasonal residents who were beginning to venture there from Greece's mainland.

In those early days, after taking the ferry or a flight from Athens to Mytilene, travelers had to make their way over the mountain range that separates Molyvos from the capital on a road that had not yet been fully paved. The trip required considerable time and perseverance. However, people were drawn to the village by its warm sun and beaches, delicious food, tranquility, and its almost medieval appearance that made visitors feel as if they were stepping back in time.

From the front windows of her shop, Ute witnessed the entire refugee saga unfold there in the harbor from its beginning in late 2014 and throughout 2015. As she began to tell me about what had happened in the harbor, it seemed, initially, as if she was grasping for the right words to adequately describe it, but then she simply said, "There were refugees everywhere. At first, you didn't know what to do, because there were so many of them; thousands and thousands came by day and by night." Many of them were picked up at sea and brought to the harbor by the Coast Guard boat when their vessels sank. The rest of them made their way to the harbor from the beach at Eftalou, just to the east of Molyvos where they had landed. The side windows and doors of Ute's shop look out onto the single corridor by which everyone enters and leaves the harbor. From there she watched the endless streams of refugees pass by on their way in from the beaches to the Coast Guard station where they had to register for entry to the EU. Then she saw them all once again as they left the harbor to go to the bus stop by the elementary school where police buses would pick them up for the trip to Mytilene. Through those side windows and doors, Ute could also see the medical transport vehicles as they carried the sick, the injured, and the dying to the nearest doctor in Kalloni or the nearest hospital in Mytilene. Many refugees succumbed to their injuries right there in the harbor, so the site of the black body bags being taken away became chillingly familiar to her. Neither she nor anyone she knew had ever experienced anything like this, but she decided that "it was better to do something than nothing at all." So she pitched in and did what she could, frightening as it was.

On that same April afternoon, Melinda McRostie and her husband, Theo Kosmetos, were at work in their restaurant, the Captain's Table, only a few hundred feet down the harbor from Ute's shop. They had just returned from a vacation abroad, one final escape before the start of the new season. In contrast to Ute, who was about ready to open her shop for business, Melinda and Theo were just beginning to contemplate their restaurant's upcoming opening night. Like the owners of the neighboring restaurants, Theo had put up the canopies that protect their outdoor dining area from both the intense afternoon summer sun and the occasional rain shower that drifts in off the Aegean. Inside the kitchen, everything had been cleaned and refreshed. The stoves and ovens, storage and work counter areas, sinks, cooking utensils, silverware, and plates all gleamed after being idle through the winter months.

The chairs and the tables, with their colorfully checkered pastel cloth covers, were still in storage, making the area in front of the restaurant somewhat barren compared to the summertime when it is alive with the hustle and bustle of servers coming and going with plates of food and the sounds of animated conversations as diners share the conviviality of a Molyvos evening. The only furniture in sight at the Captain's Table on that particular afternoon was the table and chairs on the porch just to the right of the kitchen door where I sat with Melinda and Theo. Those familiar with the Captain's Table know that at least one of them could be found at that table each evening, keeping watch over everything when they were not out among the diners taking food orders or in the kitchen dishing up their restaurant's fare. The food and the setting were always the draw, and once diners had tasted a meal or two, they wanted to return. Like Nelson and I on our two previous trips, many end up joining Melinda and Theo at that table on the porch to talk about their day's activities, reconnect, or catch up on their lives since their last trip to Molyvos. On many occasions, the rest of the family will also show up. Sometimes even the family cat makes an appearance.

Work on that season's menu had recently begun in the kitchen of their home across the passageway that runs behind the stores and restaurants on that side of the port. Theo and Melinda invited friends to taste a number of the new dishes that they were testing out, and Nelson and I were very happy to be included among the invitees. Of course, an invitation to one of the food tastings also meant tasting a few glasses of the trusty wine that bears their restaurant's label. This was not a task that either of them took lightly; the Captain's Table was one of Molyvos's most frequented restaurants, with a long-standing reputation for authentic Greek food and a long list of devoted regulars who returned night after night and season after season.

Melinda was born in Australia, but in the summer of 1968, when she was only three years old, her mother, Jennifer, left with her and her sister and headed for London, stopping in Molyvos to visit an aunt and uncle who were staying there at the time. One night during their stay, Jennifer went out dancing at a nearby taverna, where she met a local Greek sea captain named Giorgos, also a fine dancer, and it was love at first dance for both of them. After the visit with her aunt and uncle, Jennifer and her daughters went on to London, where she found work and Melinda and her sister enrolled in school. As it turned out, Giorgos followed them to London and convinced Jennifer to return with him to Molyvos. They were married in 1972.

In 1987 Melinda and her mother opened what turned out to be a very successful restaurant named "Melinda's" in Molyvos, and that same year, she met the man who was to become her husband, Theo, who joined the family business. Seven years later, the two opened their own restaurant in the harbor and named it the Captain's Table.[1] Even though Melinda was born in Australia, she considers Molyvos her true home. It's where she has spent almost her entire life. She knows its history, understands its character and its way of life, and she cares deeply about the village and the people in it. In addition to running a successful business and raising their children there, she and Theo became the ones to whom people have turned whenever the community is in need. Over the years this earned them the respect of the townspeople, much as if they both had been born there.

The harbor of Molyvos was not the only place where preparations for the approaching 2018 summer season were underway. It was equally evident the next day when I drove to neighboring Eftalou to meet Eric and Philippa Kempson. The road east to Eftalou leaves the village of Molyvos by the elementary school parking lot and adjoining bus stop and winds around the foot of the hill behind the castle before heading west in its gradual descent toward the sea. There, homes with their newly planted spring garden plots dotted the landscape, and work crews at the restaurants and seaside hotels that line the beach were busy sweeping walkways, tending flower beds, and setting their terraces with tables and colorful umbrellas in anticipation of their guests. A little farther down the beach, banners waved in the wind by the thermal bath, where a thick layer of fresh cedar wood shavings had been spread to make a soft bed for barefoot bathers making their way from the hot spring to the bracing Aegean waters.

Tourists are drawn to this unspoiled, uninterrupted expanse of beach that extends for eight kilometers west to east along Lesvos's rugged north coast from Eftalou to Skala Sykaminias. The seaside road offers a one-of-a-kind experience for drivers and hikers alike, hugging the coast so closely that waves wash over it at high tide. Once the road reaches the thermal springs just east of Eftalou, its smooth macadam is replaced by a rugged dirt surface littered with volcanic rocks. There, it curves to the right and heads up the steep incline into the hills high above the beach on its panoramic and breath-catching way to Skala Sykaminias. On all but the haziest of days, even the weakest binoculars reveal details of Turkey's coast, readily visible from almost every point along the road. Since tourists had not yet arrived, the beach was largely deserted and windswept when I stopped and walked over to the water. The waves that afternoon were buffeted by the accompanying wind, and when they crashed with some of their remaining winter strength and chill, the stones that covered the beach rattled like dry bones.

When I was midway between Eftalou and the thermal springs, I spotted the long driveway leading to the Kempsons' residential compound, which is not readily visible from the main road because it sits back behind a grove of olive trees. It wasn't until I reached the parking area near Eric's studio that I could finally see the main house. Though it is still partially hidden among the trees, its location offers a wide view of the beach and the Aegean.

Eric and Philippa had just returned home after spending the day working at the distribution warehouse they run as part of their family's Hope Project, an organization they created in 2017 to provide assistance for refugees. The Hope Project and the opening of the warehouse evolved from the massive and life-changing relief effort that they launched single-handedly early in 2015 to help the refugees on the beach directly in front of their home.[2] Their warehouse, located in a strip mall on the northern outskirts of Mytilene, had become an important destination for refugees staying in the two largest camps on the island of Lesvos: Kara Tepe, just across the road, and Moria, a few kilometers north of there. It was in those two camps where thousands of refugees were housed while they waited for their documents to be processed and their asylum cases heard.

Each day, approximately thirty refugees from both camps went to the warehouse to obtain most of the basic supplies they needed, including clothing, shoes, blankets, disposable diapers for the babies, and a wide variety of products for personal hygiene, all at no cost.[3] I learned that the Kempsons were almost single-handedly responsible for maintaining an adequate stockpile of supplies, and therefore, when they were not at the warehouse, a large part of their time was spent soliciting donations of all kinds from many sources worldwide to replenish their inventory. In order to keep the day-to-day operations running efficiently, they relied on a number of refugees who came from the camps each day to staff the warehouse. Their presence and their ability to speak the refugees' languages generated a sense of mutual respect and trust among those who came there each day. They were further assisted by additional volunteers, most of them women, who were either residents of Lesvos or who came from abroad for periods of time to work at the warehouse.

In 2000 Eric and Philippa and their daughter, Elleni, moved from Buckinghamshire in the United Kingdom to this spot along the beach on the outskirts of Eftalou. There, they set up an artist's studio and showroom where Eric, a woodworker and painter, carved unique sculptures from the wood of local olive trees and painted tableaux of the local landscape, which he exhibited and sold to islanders, tourists, and connoisseurs of his work from all over the world. Philippa had always been her husband's right-hand business partner, but once they opened the warehouse, she became its manager, along with overseeing the Hope Project's ongoing operations that are headquartered at their home. Elleni, also an artist in addition to being a singer, musician, and songwriter, had recently moved back to London to attend school after having spent much of her youth with her parents in Eftalou. That afternoon, their home setting was peaceful in spite of the comings and goings of a number of the volunteers who had just finished their day's tasks, either at the warehouse or there on the family compound. While we talked, Eric and Philippa paused to greet each volunteer warmly and enthusiastically, and everyone interacted with them as they would with family and friends all brought together by a common bond of commitment to an effort in which they believed fervently.

The scene in the harbor on that April afternoon was a familiar one for Ute, Melinda and Theo, and other business owners and Molyvos residents who had spent years living and working there. To some extent the same might be said for Eric and Philippa in their beachside home in Eftalou. Before the fall of 2014 and the start of the massive migration, nearly everyone lived according to the predictable rhythm of the tourist season that would begin slowly in late April, with its warmer weather and tranquil afternoons, reach its peak in the hot and sunny months of June, July, and August, and then gradually slow its pace from early September through October, when the days and evenings would cool down and the tourists would depart. Local business owners would always look forward to the arrival of fall when they would close their shops and restaurants for the winter and leave the port to the fishermen and the Greek Coast Guard.

However, on that April day in 2018, they could readily recall how, starting in the early months of 2015, that rhythm was jolted and all predictability or anything resembling normality in their lives vanished. That was when the lives of everyone in Molyvos and along the entire coast from Eftalou to Skala Sykaminias became intertwined with the desperate needs of the hundreds of thousands of refugees arriving from the coast of Turkey. It would be almost impossible for the couple enjoying their quiet afternoon lunch at the table of the Sea Horse Café, while I was waiting there to meet Ute, to begin to imagine the endless mayhem and wrenching human suffering that played out right there in the now peaceful harbor where they were sitting. For all of them, Ute, Melinda and Theo, Eric and Philippa, and anyone else who was in Molyvos at the time, there was no escaping the memories of what they had seen and done when the refugees came.

It all began as a trickle in November 2014 and then grew steadily and dramatically for the next sixteen months until March 2016, when an agreement was concluded between the EU and Turkey that altered the course of refugee arrivals in Greece. The first refugees were mostly from Syria, Afghanistan, and Iraq, but as time went on, Congolese, Iranians, Pakistanis, and Palestinians joined the ranks, all of them desperately trying to escape the violence and death of savage wars, civil strife, and brutal dictatorships in their homelands. The war in Iraq had dragged on for years, and brutal political repression was on the rise in the Republic of the Congo. The war in Afghanistan that dated back to the era of the Soviet Union had never really ended, and the fighting there only intensified when the United States moved to avenge the attacks on the World Trade Center and the Pentagon in September 2001.

Syria's ongoing civil war had a dramatic impact on the crisis in Lesvos because of the sheer number of refugees who fled that country after 2011, when Syrian President Bashar al-Assad launched a campaign of torture and destruction in response to pro-democracy demonstrations and uprisings against his rule that came on the heels of the Arab Spring. With the help of his Russian and Iranian allies, he gained control of the country by destroying entire cities and carrying out military operations that ravaged the countryside and caused widespread death and destruction. Millions, including tens of thousands of children, were either wounded, mutilated, or killed, and half of the country's population was displaced, all of which precipitated a mass exodus of people into Turkey, which shares its northern land borders with Greece and Bulgaria, two EU countries. Initially the refugees took the land route, crossing the border into Greece or Bulgaria. Once they had reached the anticipated safety of Europe, they headed primarily for Germany, Belgium, Holland, and Scandinavia, their most sought-after destinations, where they ultimately hoped to find safety and a new future for themselves and their families.[4] Greece and Bulgaria were seen as stopping points on their route north. Eventually, however, Bulgaria and other EU countries to the north began to close their borders, and as they did, the refugees were forced to change course and attempt to enter Europe via the sea route from Turkey's western coast to Greece's islands in the Aegean. The route from Turkey to Molyvos was the shortest.

Young and old, the refugees came from all walks of life. Among them were highly trained and educated professionals, as well as manual laborers. There were young men traveling alone. Many of them were strong and enterprising, while others were severely handicapped with limbs that had been mutilated irreparably by torture at the hands of dictators and armed strongmen. Among them were also soldiers bearing open gangrenous wounds from warfare. There were entire families journeying together, widowed mothers with children, children orphaned by war traveling alone, and elderly and infirm who had to rely on canes, crutches, and even wheelchairs. Many were bringing sick and dying family members, hoping to obtain essential medical treatment in Europe that was unavailable to them in their home countries. By the time they reached Molyvos, they were all hungry and utterly exhausted from not eating or sleeping for days, weeks, and even months on end as they made the perilous excursions from the terror of their far-flung homelands to the coast of Turkey, where they would face yet another terrifying and often deadly leg of their journey: the boat trip across the four miles of the Mytilene Strait to the north coast of Lesvos. When they arrived, the refugees were soaking wet, and many, particularly the children, were already showing signs of severe hypothermia. Some were consumed with grief after witnessing the drownings of spouses or children when their boats sank. Some were nearly comatose from the trauma, and some were in such critical physical condition that they needed immediate medical care, but none was available.

In the early months of 2015, most of the boats landing on the beach were met only by Eric, Philippa, and Elleni. Whenever they detected movement that turned out to be a refugee boat approaching the shore, they would head quickly to the beach with whatever supplies of water, food, and dry clothes they could muster. At times, small groups of local volunteers pitched in, but they were all inadequately equipped and untrained with few, if any, resources, medical or otherwise, apart from their own brawn strengthened by their human concern and goodwill.

European law required all refugees to register with the local Coast Guard immediately upon arrival, and since the Coast Guard office was located in the Molyvos harbor, the arriving refugees all ended up gathering there. With the Captain's Table only two doors away, Melinda and Theo found themselves at the center of what soon would become a massive undertaking as they tried to care in some way for the crowds of people assembled just outside their restaurant's door. Whenever a group of refugees appeared, the two of them would open the restaurant and put a large pot of water on to boil for tea. Melinda had always spearheaded clothing drives for needy families in the village and, therefore, had enough of a supply on hand, at least at the very beginning, to provide the refugees with something dry to wear. Eventually they began to prepare sandwiches so that the refugees, particularly the children who were suffering so visibly from the wet and cold, would have something to eat.

At first the number of arrivals, although steady, was fairly small, but during the first two months of 2015, the boats started to come in ever-increasing numbers. By the middle of March, Melinda and Theo realized that the situation in the harbor was becoming too large for them to handle all by themselves, as did Eric and Philippa who were working all alone out on the beaches. Growing somewhat desperate, Melinda began to contact people she knew and post messages on Facebook, asking for donations of clothing and groceries and help with food preparation. Equally concerned on his end, Eric carried his cell phone with him every time he and Philippa went to the beach and filmed hundreds of landings that he posted on the internet, appealing for help from governments and international aid organizations, or from anyone who might take heed. By midsummer of 2015 refugee boats were arriving day and night in a never-ending stream that grew to a mammoth fleet of unseaworthy rubber boats; it was September before the outside world woke up to the crisis and its magnitude. The resulting panic that set in was more than justified because there was no help whatsoever from any outside source. Frantic appeals to the Greek government, efforts to alert the EU to the unfolding crisis, and even attempts to involve the European press were all unsuccessful.

Greece was in the throes of a critical economic emergency that threatened the integrity of its physical and societal infrastructure, with one in four Greeks out of work.[5] Europe was plagued by an economic decline—triggered originally by the worldwide financial crisis of 2008–9—that forced governments to enact austerity measures, and this, in turn, fueled an already growing concern about immigration that was blamed for the fiscal crisis.

Many on the far right also used this as a pretext to further bolster growing nationalist sentiments and call for the "preservation of national culture" that they felt was undermined by the influx of refugees.[6] In the face of all this, tensions ran high in European capitals, where leaders found themselves conflicted as to what to do about the situation in Greece, with its sagging economy and the refugee invasion that took place all at the same time. Meanwhile similar economic conditions, accompanied by a widespread growing antagonism surrounding issues of immigration, mounted in the United States.

That summer, when news of the refugee influx in Lesvos started to become more widespread, tourism quickly began to fall off, and the summers of 2015, 2016, and 2017 saw a decline by as much as 80 percent, wreaking havoc on businesses throughout the village of Molyvos and the surrounding area.[7] Hoteliers, restaurant owners, merchants, their families, and all of their employees who were entirely dependent upon tourism for their livelihoods began to experience serious financial hardship, and an otherwise prosperous and seemingly harmonious community grew deeply divided as people scrambled desperately to identify causes and seek solutions. Onlookers who were quick to note all the refugee activity that took place at the Captain's Table and out on the beaches near Eftalou opined that the refugees chose to come to Molyvos because they were helped upon arrival. They concluded that if the help stopped, the tide of refugees would be stemmed, and the lives of everyone in Molyvos would go back to normal. Before long, people began to place blame for the crisis on Melinda, Theo, the Kempsons, and all of their local friends who joined in to help them, claiming that their efforts encouraged refugees to head for Molyvos.

It was clear when I spoke with Ute, Melinda and Theo, and with Eric and Philippa that the events of the previous four years were on their minds and, according to them, on the minds of every other business owner in the village. I thought to myself, *How could they not think about it?* There was every reason for them to be apprehensive and to worry, even amid the bustle of preparations for the new tourist season. While they all hoped the 2018 season that was about to begin would be better, their optimism was mixed with great concern. They all knew that, in spite of the EU-Turkey accord

INESCAPABLE MEMORIES

signed back in March 2016, refugee landings on Lesvos had continued, and the landings that had occurred on the beach at Eftalou within the previous month were no secret to anyone. In fact the morning before I visited their family compound, Eric and Philippa had gone to the beach to help bring a boat carrying twenty-four refugees to shore. Eric also knew that three other boats had landed on Lesvos in the previous two days and that there had been five boats the week before with three to four hundred people aboard. Neither was it at all comforting that more than eight thousand people were being held in the island's two refugee camps, Moria and Kara Tepe, with the number expected to increase to over ten thousand by the end of that month.[8]

Anyone making the drive on the upper road between Molyvos and Skala Sykaminias, as I did a few times, could not help but notice the activity at the Lighthouse Relief Project encampment at one of the highest points on the road. Lighthouse Relief is an NGO established in 2015 to help refugees arriving on the northern shores of Lesvos. When I stopped there to speak with the two people who were on duty, I learned that volunteers kept a round-the-clock vigil using high-powered binoculars, infrared telescopes for use at night, and cameras with telescopic lenses to monitor any refugee movement out on the water. They also had cell phones to contact the Coast Guard and their own headquarters in Skala so that teams could be sent to meet any arriving boats.[9] Their presence up on the high road and in the seaside village of Skala Sykaminias, where their volunteers were still stationed, along with teams from the United Nations High Commissioner for Refugees (UNHCR) and other NGOs, all served as stark reminders that the course of their lives remained very much intertwined with the refugees.

Melinda and Eric were both well aware that, consciously and subconsciously, their eyes were always trained on the shores of Turkey in an intense and fretful vigil, watching for any signs of movement that might suggest the launching of rafts filled with refugees. While I was interviewing the Kempsons, Eric would jump out of his seat every ten minutes or so and stare through his binoculars across his lawn to the sea. Melinda told me that her heart would start to race each time the Coast Guard boat looked as if it was rushing out of the harbor on what appeared to be something other than its normal schedule.[10]

The daily reports of landings and rescues left the gnawing thought in the back of everyone's mind that the coming warmer weather and calmer seas could prompt more refugees to attempt the crossing. Only two weeks before we left the United States to come to Molyvos, articles in international newspapers reported emerging refugee problems on Lesvos, including riots in protest of the deteriorating conditions at Moria and Kara Tepe, where refugees were forced into longer and longer stays while their documents were processed. One of the articles contained graphic pictures of two young Syrians and an Iraqi clinging to an electricity pylon and threatening to kill themselves unless they were allowed to leave the island to go to the mainland. Almost everyone I encountered, particularly business owners in the harbor, feared that tourists considering a vacation in Molyvos would be threatened by these reports and choose not to come.[11] Consequently people's attention was focused, almost obsessively, on the number of passengers holding reserved seats on flights into Mytilene and any fluctuations in the number of reservations in the local hotels.

Mixed with everyone's excitement and anticipation of the new season, therefore, was the anxiety about what would happen if the season turned out to be disappointing once again or if a new tide of refugees were to overwhelm them as it had in 2015. Melinda and Theo, Ute, the Kempsons, and their friends had been there to witness the "ocean of humanity" that came ashore.[12] They knew firsthand the extent to which the sheer force of their numbers overwhelmed Molyvos. It was as if floodgates had opened up somewhere and refugees just came pouring in, catching everyone utterly surprised by the magnitude of the influx as well as completely unprepared to deal with it. Unable to convince governments or aid agencies, national or international, of their desperate need for help at that time, they were left alone for months to face the colossal and catastrophic events that unfolded right in front of their eyes. It has been called "the worst refugee crisis since the Second World War," and its impact on the village of Molyvos and its people may always remain unmeasurable.[13] However, one thing they all knew was that the crisis had changed their lives forever.[14]

1. Top: Village of Molyvos taken from the coastal road to Petra. Courtesy of Nelson Mondaca.

2. Bottom: Molyvos Harbor taken from the village's main road where it runs along the edge of the cliffs. Courtesy of Nelson Mondaca.

3. The Captain's Table restaurant in the harbor on a quiet afternoon, September 2013. Courtesy of Nelson Mondaca.

2

The Tide of Refugees Began as a Trickle

November 2014

Erasmia Grigorelli—Eri—was awakened around five o'clock one rainy morning in September 2014 by an unexpected knock on the door of the Coast Guard office in the port of Molyvos. She was the only member of the Coast Guard crew in the office at the time.

Eri began her career with the Greek Coast Guard stationed in Athens, but she transferred to the Molyvos office, where she had worked for the past sixteen years. During that time she had come to know that when the cooler and damper weather of fall came, the tourists frequenting the port's restaurants and shops and the holiday boaters out on the bay would all depart. This meant that crew members could expect nighttime duty assignments to be quiet and uneventful enough to catch a few hours of sleep, as Eri had done that night. This particular September had turned chilly and rainy a bit earlier than usual, prompting business owners to close somewhat ahead of schedule, leaving the harbor mostly deserted after dark. Thus the sound of someone at the door was startling to Eri, but she made her way to the entrance of the outer office to find out who it was.

When she opened the door, Eri saw a small group of people, mostly young men but also a few women with children, standing there in the chilly downpour, wearing only lightweight clothing, all of them drenched and shaking uncontrollably. She concluded at first glance, based on stories she had heard from locals who lived along the north coast of Lesvos, that these people were most likely refugees who had just crossed from Turkey, fleeing their homelands to seek the safety of Europe. Eri had no idea whether they had landed right there in the harbor or whether they had come ashore

31

somewhere along the beaches to the east or west of Molyvos, but she figured that they had made their way to the Coast Guard office door because it was the only place in the dark harbor with light.

Eri had heard about refugees crossing from Turkey and landing along the beaches of Eftalou, but this was her first face-to-face encounter with them, and she was unsure of what she was supposed to do. Coast Guard regulations strictly forbade anyone from entering the office during the night unless more than one crew member was on duty. Although Eri was conflicted about leaving them standing outside, she also felt that she had no choice but to obey the rule. When morning came and the other crew members reported for work, she was able to invite them inside to warm up. As it turned out this was a first encounter for her colleagues as well, so they were all at a loss as to what their next steps should be. One thing was clear: the refugees all needed dry clothing. Eri rummaged through the boxes of clothing she had brought from home in Kalloni and stored in the office, just in case there was someone in need. She managed to find a few items for the children, but she did not have enough for everyone. She made a quick mental note to check around her house when she was off duty and replenish her supply.

Later that same morning, still deeply affected by what had occurred, Eri happened to spot Theo as he passed the Coast Guard office on his way to the restaurant. Eri was familiar with the popular Captain's Table that Theo and Melinda owned and ran in the harbor near the office, and she was accustomed to seeing Theo there every day during the tourist season. She liked him a lot because it seemed that "he was always smiling and helping everyone."[1] She had never actually met Melinda other than to say hello to her when she passed by, but she knew that Melinda was a respected member of the community whom everyone called upon whenever a family needed clothing. During the off-season, neither Theo nor Melinda came to the restaurant with any regularity, so Eri ran out, hoping to catch Theo so she could tell him about the refugees who had arrived during the night. He urged her to call him if it were to happen again and assured her that he and Melinda would come out to help.

It did happen again. By the last week of October, three more boatloads

THE TIDE BEGAN AS A TRICKLE

of cold, soaked, and weary refugee families had appeared in the harbor, and Eri had no clothing to give them. She ended up bringing to the office every piece of extra clothing that she had left in her house, including some of her husband's very good shoes, shirts, slacks, and everything that their son had outgrown, even some that he had not. When a fourth boat arrived one morning in early November, she knew it was time to call Theo and ask for the help that he had promised. Before long, he and Melinda appeared, carrying a big pot in which they were planning to boil water to make hot tea for the refugees.

Melinda vividly remembers that early November 2014 morning call that came from the Coast Guard office, telling her that they desperately needed coats for a group of about sixty refugees who had just arrived in the harbor. Melinda's stepfather was very ill and had just been admitted to the hospital in Mytilene. This sudden request for clothing for that many people all at once caught her off guard, and she began to rush around the house frantically looking for whatever she had stashed away. Realizing that this was going to take her far too long while sixty people were waiting out in the cold, she grabbed a big pot and set out for the restaurant with Theo, figuring they could at least make hot tea to warm the refugees.

When the two arrived at the front porch of their restaurant, they found Eri anxiously waiting for them. Melinda was immediately taken aback when she saw all of the refugees standing under one of the restaurant's white tents that had not yet been taken down and stored for the winter. They were all completely soaked and shivering. Melinda could "see their breath in the cold air and the puddles of water that were forming around their feet from their clothes that were dripping wet."[2]

For a moment Melinda froze as all sorts of thoughts and questions began to race through her mind: *Obviously they all need dry clothing, but there are children! What might they need most? Suppose some of the refugees are sick or injured and need a doctor.* But the nearest doctor was in Kalloni, twenty-five kilometers away on the other side of a mountain range, and would take too long to reach. She figured everyone had to be starving, but it was winter and there was nothing to eat in the restaurant's kitchen. Finally she took a deep breath and, together with Theo, opened the restaurant, filled the large pot with water, and set it to boil. They ladled hot tea into cups and served it to the shivering but grateful refugees. While everyone stood around drinking the tea, Melinda raced back home to start making calls that would soon bring friends and acquaintances from their homes to the harbor bearing dry clothes. They all laid their goods out on a table, and the refugees took what they needed. In the weeks and months ahead, the threesome of Melinda, Theo, and Eri found themselves recreating the same scene countless times.

That November morning marked the beginning of a direct, up-close, and all-consuming personal engagement for local people with what was to become a massive refugee crisis that would quickly engulf not only the village of Molyvos but the whole island of Lesvos. It would eventually catch the attention of the entire world and bring thousands of volunteers from across the globe to Molyvos to help with all of the refugees who would pass through their village. They might not have known it yet, but on that particular morning, Melinda, Theo, and Eri were about to become players in a new chapter in the long history of migration, which has been an indelible and intractable presence in Greece, particularly on the island of Lesvos.[3] Although the circumstances that would unfold were different this time around, they were not entirely new.

The history of the island of Lesvos is closely connected to people fleeing persecution. Those who call it home—natives and long-time residents alike—claim that refugees have always been a part of life there. Many can trace their own family's history back to ancestors who were refugees. A fisherman, whose family has always lived in Skala Sykaminias, recalls that history when he says, "People in Lesvos have experienced being refugees," and adds, "There was a time when we were leaving too."

One day, overhearing this particular fisherman's conversation about refugees with a tourist, a local woman standing nearby waved her hand and said, "We have lived it in our skin. Our grandparents went through this with the Asia Minor disaster. At that time, 60 percent of this island's population were from Asia Minor."[4] She was referring to what happened after the defeat of the Ottoman Empire in World War I, when Greece attempted to take over parts of Turkish Anatolia, leading to the Greco-Turkish War in which thousands of Greek Orthodox Christians were massacred or forcibly expelled from Turkey.[5] In 1916 the Greek Ministry of Welfare estimated that some 42,780 refugees fleeing the Greek genocide arrived on the island of Lesvos from Asia Minor.[6] Many people remember stories that were told to them by their parents, grandparents, and even neighbors about their own migration from Turkey, recalling how they were harbored and protected by Syrians as they made their way to Greece.

Stratis Kabanas, a strong-minded and proud native of Lesvos, can trace his roots to his grandfather who came as a refugee from Turkey in 1922. Stratis lives on a small property that he calls "Escape Land" on the outskirts of Molyvos, and he owns a boat that he keeps moored in the harbor. He gives tours of the bay during the tourist season and, over time, has gained a sort of fan club of admiring clients who follow him on Facebook. For the rest of the year, he is content to tend his acreage and take care of his dogs and farm animals. Looking at him with his skin and hair that have been burnished by the sun and sea air, one would be hard-pressed to think of him as anything other than a seasoned Molyvos fisherman. Regardless he never fails to point out that he grew up in a section of Mytilene surrounded by neighbors who, like his grandfather, fled Turkey and, in those days, built entire sections of the city. He claims that today's residents of Mytilene are almost all descendants of refugees, and he appears to find a great deal of satisfaction in being a part of that heritage.[7]

Eri Grigorelli also acknowledges that "Greeks know what it feels like to be in the refugees' place." As an example she tells the story of her husband's grandmother, whose family migrated to Turkey in 1921 because there was no work in Greece and people were starving. When the Greco-Turkish War broke out and Turks began to slaughter Greeks, the family turned to the Syrians, who opened their doors to them in their time of crisis. "So how can we say 'no' to Syrians who come here?" Eri says. "We owe it to them to help."[8] The Greeks refer to this as philoxenia, the expression of love and friendship to those who are far from home.[9] The group of refugees standing in front of the Captain's Table that morning served as a reminder, not only of the island's history of migration but of its current residents' personal connection to it.[10]

This was not the first encounter with refugees for Melinda or anyone living in Molyvos, for that matter. Kyriakos Papadopoulos, the Coast Guard boat captain in Molyvos whose efforts saved countless refugees from drowning in the sea during the height of the crisis in 2015, recalled in 2001 that when twenty Afghan refugees arrived on Lesvos, "it was that year's biggest news event."[11]

The Kempsons have spotted refugees landing on the beach in front of their home in Eftalou since as early as 2001, not long after they first moved there. Eric recalls that, at first, the majority of the refugees were young Afghan men, fleeing the military action that the United States launched there after the bombing of the World Trade Center and the Pentagon. A year or two later, Iraqis began to arrive after the U.S. invasion of Iraq in search of the weapons of mass destruction that the Americans incorrectly claimed Saddam Hussein was manufacturing. Many of the Iraqis would actually row over from Turkey, maybe ten in a boat, because the first boats did not have motors. Eric remembers that the men wore black life vests, covered their faces with dirt, and put black tape on the oars so as avoid detection by the Turkish Coast Guard. They usually arrived on the beach near Eftalou in the early hours of the morning, immediately made their way to Molyvos, and would already be there in the harbor when the townspeople woke up. This first wave of young men did not tarry long in Molyvos. So fiercely determined were they to get to their destination—wherever that was at the time—that they would land and start walking.

In 2007 Melinda and a group of her friends began actively helping refugees who were landing from time to time on the beach at Eftalou. One of those friends, Dina Adam, who at the time was working at one of the local hotels, recalls that her first involvement with refugees began when she joined that group. Dina is native Greek, born in Kamena Vourla, a city on a western gulf of the Aegean about 175 kilometers north of Athens, but she lived in both Kuwait and Great Britain for many years before moving from Thame in the United Kingdom to her home on the outskirts of Molyvos in the late 1990s. Once there, in addition to her full-time position at the hotel, she also spent a great deal of time volunteering, so when she learned about the group's work helping the refugees, she was eager to join in.

THE TIDE BEGAN AS A TRICKLE

Another friend, Dionisis Pavlou, now a high school mathematics teacher in Mytilene, remembers that his involvement with refugees first began when he joined the Greek navy in 1996 and was stationed in the small port of Sigri on the western coast of Lesvos. Whenever a boat of migrants was spotted crossing from Turkey to Lesvos, their assignment was to report it immediately to the Greek Coast Guard. Once out of the navy he moved to Molyvos and began his career as a mathematics teacher in the regional high school in nearby Petra. Dionisis was in charge of international exchange programs and other kinds of cross-cultural experiences for the students in the school where he worked, so he was inspired by what his contemporaries were doing to help the refugees and enthusiastically joined in.

Initially the group got together to hang out and enjoy each other's company, but little by little, most of their time together was spent handing out food, water, dry clothes, and blankets to refugees landing on the local beaches. They all exchanged phone numbers, and when any of them received word that a boat had landed, they notified their comrades, loaded their cars with supplies, and went directly to the beach together. Early on they noticed that the refugees were crossing in flimsy, overcrowded rafts made of rubber or plastic and that they arrived tired, wet, hungry, and frightened. Dina clearly remembers receiving a phone call from someone in the group at four o'clock one morning in 2007, informing her that seven Afghan refugees—five adults and two children—had reached the shore. The friends quickly assembled, loaded everything into their cars, and headed for the landing site. They had no sooner arrived at the beach when a second boatload landed only a short distance away. Once the refugees were all safely ashore and had been given water, blankets, dry clothing, and something to eat, Dina and her group gave them directions to the harbor in Molyvos. Then they called to notify the police that refugees had arrived and were on their way. At that time the Coast Guard crew managed registration at their station in the harbor, and the police coordinated bus transportation to Mytilene. As socially conscious young people, the group also became actively involved with other local issues that brought them into the public spotlight. By 2008 they had evolved into a kind of "team for public action."[12]

Ute Vogt has a very clear recollection of her first encounter with refugees.

It was during the summer of 2008. She had closed her shop that evening, and rather than going straight home, she drove to meet a friend over in Petra. While she was on her way back, around two in the morning, her friend called to make sure she had arrived safely. Ute pulled into a space along the shoulder of the road to talk, and all of a sudden, four young men approached her car from out of the darkness. One of the young men spoke English and called out to her, "Mother, mother, don't do anything. We are nice people." Ute remembers that they were in their twenties, all from Afghanistan, and all without shoes. A couple of them were without any clothes at all. They had just come from Turkey by boat and had landed on the shore that runs along the road between Molyvos and Petra. They did not know where they were, and as it was the middle of the night, Ute drove them to her house where she brought out dry clothes, towels, and blankets, gave them something to eat and drink, and let them sleep there for the night.

Like most Afghan refugees Ute had heard about, these young men were eager to move on and told her they wanted to take the first bus to Mytilene the next day. Much to her surprise, when she came out of her room that next morning, all five of them were sitting naked on the living room floor, waiting for their wet clothing that they had hung on the line in the courtyard to dry. At the time, Ute was recently divorced from her husband, but he still came to the property regularly to take care of the animals that he kept there. Whenever she tells this story, she laughs and says that she has always wondered what he would have thought had he come in to feed his chickens and found all those men sitting there naked. The refugees still wanted to catch the bus to Mytilene, but first they wanted to go to a bank to exchange the money they had brought with them for euros. Ute set about making sandwiches for them, and by the time she emerged from the kitchen, they were all fully dressed. However, they were all barefoot from losing their shoes in the sea. Ute knew that the only men's shoes in the house might be some that her husband had left behind, but he wore a size 45, and she only had to look at their feet to see that they were much smaller than her husband's. Nevertheless she went to the basement to see what she could find and came back with not one, but several pairs of new leather shoes that her husband had bought just before their divorce. Even though they were way too large, the young men put them on and declared them "perfect." She then drove them to the bank where she bade them goodbye and good luck.[13]

Over time, people in Molyvos and the surrounding area started to realize that what was once just an occasional boat carrying ten to fifteen refugees had become many boats arriving regularly each month. As the number of boats grew, a group of what Dionisis calls "clever locals" set up a business stealing the motors from the refugees' boats and selling them on the black market, where they could make as much as two hundred euros per motor. According to Greek law, it is illegal to take a motor once a boat has landed, but being "clever," as Dionisis claimed, they figured out that the motor was fair game if they managed to steal it while the boat was still in the water. From strategic lookout points along the beach, they watched for refugee boats, and when one neared the shore, they would rush in, force the refugees out of the boat, and make them wade to shore while they removed the motor before the boat could land.[14]

When some of the group's members learned about this, one of them—an avid photographer—positioned himself at the beach with his video camera and made numerous recordings of motors being stolen. From his videos he created a short film that was then screened in Molyvos and Skala Sykaminias, where it caught people by surprise and sparked serious controversy. Many were incensed by the film, claiming that its portrayal of locals—fishermen in particular—was unfair because it implied that everyone engaged in this sort of theft. Once the group realized how strongly people were reacting, they decided to call a public meeting and invite speakers to talk about the black market for stolen boat motors in an effort to highlight what was happening to refugees when they arrived on the area's beaches.[15]

Although locals were aware of refugee arrivals back in 2008, no one was as tuned into the situation as this group of young friends. As the months passed they gained more firsthand experience meeting refugee boats out at the beaches than anyone else, and before long it started to become increasingly evident to them that the tide of refugees was on the rise. They also noticed that there were more women and children among them and that many more people were suffering from war-related wounds. Not wanting to be caught unprepared as the numbers increased, the group decided to set up a system to streamline their efforts and make them more efficient. The outcome was an organization that they chose to name "First Stop" because it accurately reflected what they were doing. Theirs was the first place in Europe where the refugees were given food, water, dry clothes, and blankets—things they needed most—before they set out on the next leg of their journey.

With the war in Syria escalating and endangering the lives of thousands of its people, and with the number of casualties stemming from the armed conflict with the Taliban in Afghanistan also on the rise, refugee arrivals in Molyvos increased so steadily that those involved with First Stop knew that it had the potential to become problematic. By 2012, two years before Eri's early morning encounter at the Coast Guard office, the group's predictions proved to be accurate. That year the Greek Coast Guard reported that approximately 3,500 refugees had crossed the Aegean into Greece, and the numbers kept increasing: 33,000 made the crossing in 2013, and in 2014 the number rose to 44,000. Not all of the refugees landed on mainland Greece; many headed for other Greek islands off the coast of Turkey. Nevertheless with the north shore of Lesvos being the shortest sea route from Turkey, there is little doubt that what the people in the First Stop group saw reflected the refugee surge reported by the Greek Coast Guard.[16]

Thinking back on those early days and the group of friends who formed First Stop, Dina recalls, "We started first as friends, then friends of friends, then people from Molyvos who came together and embraced the whole thing. We were all very liberal. Maybe we were on automatic pilot. We said to each other, 'This is it,' and we just did it. In the years between 2008 and 2014, the system that our group of friends set up was pretty much adequate . . . until it wasn't."[17]

3

In the Harbor and on the Beach

Midwinter 2015

According to the law in the EU, all refugees are required to register in their first country of debarkation, and once they are registered, they have a legal status that allows them to travel, as well as obtain goods and services, within the member countries. Since they were coming into Lesvos via the sea, registration was assigned to the Coast Guard. However, in Lesvos, the law was much more restrictive. After the Coast Guard had completed the registration process, the refugees were only allowed to be transported to Mytilene on buses that were provided by the local government, with routes and schedules coordinated by the police. Those buses did not run frequently, but the law did not allow refugees to use regular public transportation of any kind—buses or taxis—even if they were registered and had the money to pay the fares. That same law also prohibited them from being transported by privately owned vehicles, and drivers who gave rides to refugees in their own cars risked being charged with human trafficking and were subject to arrest and even imprisonment.

Across Europe an economic downturn and a rising tide of nationalism had bolstered the hardline conservative point of view that refugees were the cause of the continent's fiscal problems and cultural conflicts. Those sentiments became further entrenched as the upsurge in the number of migrants seeking entry into Europe intensified, which, in turn, spawned the widespread belief that any effort to help refugees was tacit encouragement for more of them to come. What resulted was a policy of deterrence, a "refusal to provide humanitarian support," and its objective was to make everything so difficult for new arrivals that they would discourage others from migrating.[1] Nowhere was the law's impact felt more forcefully than in Lesvos, with its growing number of refugees. Locals and tourists alike shied away from offering them rides for fear of being charged with breaking the law. This left refugees with few options. Other than waiting long periods of time for the police buses with their unpredictable schedules, their only other recourse was to walk, even if it meant hiking long distances over difficult terrain.

The nearest Coast Guard office was the one in the harbor of Molyvos. The next closest office was twenty-five kilometers away in Kalloni, on the other side of the mountain range separating the north coast from the rest of the island. Beyond that, the only other registration point was the Coast Guard station in Mytilene, some forty kilometers beyond Kalloni. As a result all refugees ended up in the harbor only steps away from the Captain's Table. It was the start of winter, so the restaurant was closed and would not reopen until sometime in late April or early May 2015. However, Melinda and Theo went there every day to make tea in large pots of boiling water, which they then served to the ever-increasing flow of refugees.

By the beginning of December the need for dry clothing had already become critical, so in addition to making tea in the restaurant, Melinda had to keep calling friends and villagers to ask for donations of whatever clothing they could spare. At first the response was generous, but within a short time, people's closets grew bare, and the need far exceeded the supply. Melinda remembers being in the hospital with her ill stepfather, whose condition had worsened to the point where he was in intensive care, when a woman called her, looking for coats for babies who had just landed. When the phone call ended, it hit Melinda that she had run out of coats several days earlier and now had no more clothing at all. It was just before Christmas, with cold temperatures already spreading across northern Lesvos, and all of a sudden more and more families were making the crossing. Up to this point, Melinda could not remember there having been more than an occasional family with children among the arriving refugees. Most of them had been young men. Now not only was there a steady increase in the overall number of refugees, but there were also more women with small children and babies. As Melinda sat in the intensive care unit with her terminally ill stepfather, all she could think of was how she was going to get more dry clothing, especially for the little ones.[2]

The new year brought no relief. In fact from January to March, when the weather is normally at its coldest and stormiest, not only was there a spike in the number of refugees making the crossing but there were also more women and children, more elderly people, and a growing number of young men needing serious medical attention for debilitating wounds sustained in their countries' wars. Many had not eaten or slept for a very long time. The number of boats varied. On some days there were as few as three, while on other days there were as many as sixty. They were always overcrowded and rode so low in the water that they were easily inundated by waves, even when the sea was calm. When the sea was rough, the waves caused countless boats to capsize. Refugees were always at risk for hypothermia, even those making the crossing later on during the warmer months. However, the water temperatures in the Aegean in winter and early spring are so cold that the majority of the refugees suffered from severe hypothermia, particularly the children. Many died from it.[3]

Neither Melinda, Eri, nor anyone else—not even the people in First Stop a few years before—had ever encountered anything like this, and none of them had ever been trained in any kind of first aid. Nevertheless they soon came to recognize the uncontrollable shaking and the change in skin color that were the distinct signs of hypothermia. Children would actually be "numb in response to stimuli and have totally blank expressions on their faces."[4] They also learned very quickly, and sadly, from experience that if those symptoms were not addressed immediately, they could lead to loss of consciousness and death. As time went on they learned about emergency blankets made of silver-colored material, resembling large pieces of aluminum foil, which could be wrapped around the wet refugees to help warm them up. As it turned out, the Coast Guard kept a supply of them in their office, but since neither Melinda nor Eri had any experience or training with them, their instinctual and immediate reaction was to wrap the blankets right over the refugees' clothing in a frantic attempt to get them warm as quickly as possible. Eventually emergency medical workers who occasionally appeared on the scene taught them that the blankets were most effective when they were placed directly on the skin, and they showed them how to put the blankets on over the refugees' heads and necks and then continue wrapping them the rest of the way down their bodies to maximize contact with their bare skin.[5]

Melinda refers to those first months of 2015 as "a period of unbelievable chaos and hardship for which no one involved was in any way prepared." It all began so quickly back in November that there was little time or opportunity for much thoughtful planning. Melinda and Theo, along with their children when they were home after school and on weekends, jumped in to do whatever they thought needed to be done, and they were eventually joined by a small group of Melinda's closest friends when they were available. Looking back on that time, she recalls, "Molyvos has a long tradition of assisting neighbors in need, so a group of us were used to pitching in at short notice, and with the restaurant sitting so close to the Coast Guard office, it became, by simple default, the central meeting place for refugees and anyone else who showed up to help. This also meant that coordinating the basic refugee relief ended up falling to me very early on."[6] Once the refugees had registered at the Coast Guard office, they would congregate at the Captain's Table, where they were served tea and received dry clothing. After that, they often lingered in the harbor before walking to the other end of the village and waiting at the bus stop for transportation to Mytilene, where they would take the ferry to Athens and continue their journey to the countries of northern Europe.

Meanwhile, over on the beach at Eftalou where their home was located, Eric and Philippa Kempson also began to realize that the number of arrivals had been growing steadily since the beginning of the year. They, too, found that there were more and more women and children, along with an increasing number of refugees with infections from bullet wounds, shrapnel burns, and gangrene that all needed medical attention. They also knew that the Aegean in winter was extremely cold, with very rough waves buffeted by strong winds that made navigation challenging, if not outright dangerous, even for the most seasoned fishermen. They had seen how dangerously overcrowded the rubber dinghies were and how they were thrown about at the mercy of the sea, with screaming passengers unable to save themselves from being tossed overboard.

In February 2015 the Kempsons "decided as a family to start their own relief efforts to help refugees as best they could because there was way too much suffering on the beaches." At that time they were the only ones going out to the beach to help the landing refugees, just Eric and Philippa, along with their daughter Elleni on weekends when she was out of school. For several weeks no one knew they were doing this, not even Melinda; she did not find out until May, when Philippa's mother was having lunch at the Captain's Table. Eric says, "We were down on the beach all the time because the boats kept arriving. We watched twenty-four hours a day to try to spot the boats as soon as possible so we could get out there to help." They always kept their car loaded with bottles of water, dry clothing, towels, some food from their own cupboards, and disposable diapers for the babies so that whenever they saw movement on the beach or on the water that turned out to be a refugee boat, they were prepared to leave their house and head for the beach. As Philippa says, "You just couldn't go down to the beach and ignore what was happening there."[7]

4

The Refugees

Their Origins and Their Perilous Journeys to Molyvos

The beaches on the north coast of Lesvos that stretched from Molyvos in the west to Skala Sykaminias in the east were the principal landing site for the vast multitude of refugees crossing the four miles of open water from Turkey. Their starkly rugged beauty on any given day would have concealed the monumental human saga that played out there between 2014 and 2016 were it not for the wind and the waves that shift the stones and sand, like archeologists' brooms, exposing bits and pieces of debris, fragments of clothing and life vests, and any other evidence that revealed the story. On some days anyone standing on the beach can hear the faint murmur of the wind and the sound of the waves, which grow louder as they travel the length of the beach and then fade off into the distance. At high tide it is a captivating rhythmic cycle that repeats itself over and over again, with each successive wave spreading a layer of stones as it comes in and then scatters them as it recedes.

Toward the middle of that stretch of beach—roughly halfway between Molyvos and Skala Sykaminias—lie the hulls of metal and wooden boats that capsized or crashed against the rocks and broke apart, killing many, if not most, of the people on board. One of them, a large deteriorating hulk with upper and lower decks, lies partially submerged in the surf after finally being washed ashore. Dozens of refugees were swept to their deaths when the hulk sank on October 28, 2015, at the height of the crisis, in a monumental disaster that still haunts everyone who witnessed it or was part of the desperate rescue effort. At almost any spot along the beach, it is not uncommon to come upon such objects as babies' shoes—frayed and bleached from exposure to the elements—that summon discomforting thoughts and questions about the fate of those who last wore them. Here and there, exposed pieces of black rubber or plastic serve as chilling reminders of the thousands of unseaworthy dinghies in which the refugees made their crossings.

These remnants and the memories they invoke are familiar to Eric and Philippa. In the first weeks of 2015, when there were no tourists or seasonal residents around and few people ventured to the beaches, they were the first and often only responders facing the initial onslaught of refugee boats. They had little or no training and limited personal financial resources to deal with such emergencies, and there was no one else to help them except for a local resident or two who might happen to show up.

Little by little, as they dealt with boatload after boatload of arriving refugees, Eric and Philippa came to know who the refugees were. Philippa says they quickly discovered that most of them were neither helpless nor poor.[1] Among them was a cross-section of their countries' professionals and intelligentsia, such as neurosurgeons, engineers, dentists, professors, and soldiers. Some were desperate to find medical treatment that was available only in Europe. Others were fleeing in the hope of sparing their children from the bombs, torture, and death in the violence of wars that had been racking and destroying their countries for years. Some fathers had to make the gut-wrenching choice to leave some family members behind because they could not afford to travel together. Women and many unaccompanied children ended up traveling alone after losing their entire families to either war or famine. Some refugees had even been employed as translators, secretaries, or general service personnel in the United States' embassies and consulates in their home countries, and they now had to flee because that former affiliation only meant death. They had witnessed gruesome murders of fellow countrymen, including family members and loved ones. Certain that time was critical if they wanted to escape a similar fate, they set out on foot, in trucks or cars, on worn-out bicycles, or by any means possible or available to them in their desperation to get away. Out there on the beaches, Eric and Philippa witnessed their resourcefulness and determination, and it inspired them and all the volunteers who would eventually join them in the months ahead.

The refugees' grueling, almost inhumane treks started in far-flung countries, such as the Republic of Congo, 6,000 miles away; Afghanistan and Pakistan, from which they traveled between 2,500 and 3,000 miles; and Syria and Iraq, at distances between 900 and 2,100 miles. Their common destination was Turkey's westernmost coast near the city of Izmir. Entire countries, deserts, and mountain ranges lay in front of them as they pressed forward for days, months, and sometimes years, in searing heat, savage cold, and merciless storms. A reporter who was on the Eftalou beach wrote about a young refugee whom he witnessed helping an elderly man get out of one of the boats. While he was carrying him to land, the young man slipped on the wet rocks in the heavy surf and nearly fell. He quickly managed to regain his footing, but in the process he discovered that the elderly man's legs were so weak that he couldn't stand on his own. Cradling the man's frail body securely in both arms, he carried him safely to the dry rocks. Impressed by the young refugee's tenacity and thoughtfulness, the reporter approached him and asked how long he had been traveling. The young man quietly replied, "Three years."[2]

Severe hunger and dehydration were commonplace, and countless refugees were in extreme physical pain, suffering from wounds or other debilitating conditions. Their routes were made all the more perilous by bands of ambushers that were bent on robbing or killing them. When family or fellow travelers succumbed to the overwhelming obstacles of their journey, they had no choice but to leave their remains behind; the trails were often dotted with the haunting skeletons of refugees who had met a similar end.

Like the majority of the estimated twenty-six million refugees displaced globally due to conflict and persecution in their homelands, these refugees shared the common goals of finding safety, freedom, and an opportunity to live normal and productive lives, and thus they had no choice but to embark on this treacherous migration.[3] News spread that alternative land routes out of Turkey that passed through border countries, Hungary and Serbia in particular, were quickly being blocked in the race to stop the flow of refugees into Europe. Razor wire fences were installed, and there were reports of police threatening refugees with tear gas if they did not move away from border-crossing points.[4] Fearing that they would be trapped and killed or forced to return to their home countries if they took one of those land routes, they chose instead to take the sea route across the four-mile stretch of Aegean from the west coast of Turkey to the island of Lesvos.[5] It was the shortest route, and although they were well aware of the extreme risks associated with the crossing and knew that many had perished, they saw it as their only hope, their last chance to escape certain death in their home countries. One Syrian refugee explained, "We die in Syria. We die here. We die everywhere. So we have to risk it. To take this chance. We want some life."[6]

Once on the coast of Turkey the refugees found themselves at the mercy of smugglers who had total control of all transportation across the short stretch of the Aegean to the north coast of Lesvos. Working in "smuggling gangs," each with its own code number, the smugglers advertised crossings on Facebook and hustled refugees on street corners and in any other commonly frequented gathering place.[7] Refugees couldn't arrange for their crossings without dealing with one or more smugglers, and this left them with no choice but to pay the smugglers' fees and follow their orders. Some smugglers offered reduced rates for children and babies, but otherwise their fees were in excess of $1,200 per person for passage, with some documented cases of refugees paying as much as $2,800 per person. Most of the refugee families had financial resources that they managed to bring with them, but in many cases they ended up having to spend everything they had on the fees.[8] Since they did not really know where they were going when they left the Turkish coast, they had little choice but to believe the smugglers who told them that when they landed on the opposite shore they would be in mainland Europe—a place from which they could readily reach their final destinations.

Smuggling became a widespread and lucrative business in Turkey, particularly in places like Izmir, where refugees' long overland journeys often ended; an entire economy developed around the smuggling of refugees into Europe. If hundreds of thousands of them all paid the standard minimum rate of $1,200 per person for the crossing alone, that would generate huge sums of money for the smugglers. However, the smugglers were not the only ones to profit. Merchants sold the material used to make the boats. The smugglers did not buy the boats. They had them made from material that they bought in bulk because it was cheaper; it was also less seaworthy.[9] Real estate brokers collected rental fees for apartments where refugees who could afford to pay were housed while they made the arrangements for their crossings. Families with no money left to pay for lodging were forced to remain outdoors under nothing but branches of trees to shelter them from the rain or the hot sun. As a result cafés were packed with patrons, and life vests were for sale everywhere, including those cafés, stores, and newspaper and tobacco kiosks.[10] Then there were the payoffs to the Turkish Coast Guard. Smuggling was presumed to be an undercover operation, but it was hardly clandestine because it was further fueled by the involvement of organized crime, and it operated largely out in the open, with the full knowledge of Turkish officials.[11]

Refugees could not choose the date or the time of their departure from the Turkish coast, and announcements of boats leaving were often made without much notice. Alex Crawford, a reporter for Sky News out of the United Kingdom, secretly accompanied a group of refugees on their voyage from the Turkish city of Izmir to Lesvos, where they landed at the hot springs near Eftalou. The smugglers, with whom this particular group of approximately seventy refugees had booked their crossing, met them at night in a designated grove of olive trees in the center of Izmir. There they were loaded into cattle trucks for the four-hour trip to the Aegean coast—directly across from Eftalou—where they were dropped off the next morning amid other groups of refugees from other smuggling gangs who were also waiting for their boats to leave. A tractor pulling a trailer loaded with boxes of rubber boats arrived, and once they had been dropped in the water and inflated, the refugees were lined up according to the codes of their various smuggling gangs. Then the boarding began. When the boat was finally loaded, Ms. Crawford noted that it was weighed down so heavily with people that its edge was barely above water. Since smugglers did not make the crossings with the refugees, they always designated a passenger as the "skipper." Rarely did any of the appointed skippers have any boating experience whatsoever, as everyone in the boat that the reporter was on discovered one particular morning when the raft started rotating shortly after it left the shore.[12]

Profit was the smugglers' principal motive, so they always loaded as many refugees as they could into each boat without any concern for safety or weather conditions. On days when the weather was good and the sea calm, the smugglers might even decide to increase the fares, forcing those carrying less money to take boats that left when the weather conditions were not as favorable. Boats were always loaded as quickly as possible, and smugglers never hesitated to use brutal intimidation to scare the refugees and force them to follow their directives. If refugees faltered or showed any fear of boarding an overcrowded boat, they might be kicked and beaten and told that they would have to pay again to make the crossing. Oftentimes the smugglers pointed guns at refugees' heads and threatened to kill them if they hesitated to get on board. In the chaos of such boardings, every family's greatest fear was being separated and ending up on different boats that might take them to completely different destinations on the other side.[13]

The vast majority of the refugees did not come from countries that adjoined bodies of water, so few of them knew how to swim, much less maneuver or even have the courage to ride in a boat. In actuality the boats were nothing but dinghies, ranging in length from twenty to thirty feet, all made from rubber or cheap plastic held together with adhesive material that, in many cases, did not withstand exposure to the cold, rough water or the strain from the weight of the refugees and their belongings. Their maximum capacity was twenty-five to thirty passengers, but the smugglers routinely crammed as many as sixty or seventy people on board. Many of the dinghies did not inflate properly, and motors were often in such bad shape that they gave out in the middle of the sea. All the more distressing for the Kempsons and those working with them on Eftalou beach was the discovery, early on, that most of the life vests actually contained no flotation material at all. They were instead filled with something akin to pillow stuffing that, rather than keeping the refugees afloat, weighed them down and sometimes pulled them below the surface of the water, nearly condemning their chances for survival. Under those circumstances crossings were almost invariably traumatizing, even when the weather was good. In bad weather there could be high winds and a churning sea. Sometimes the dinghies were shrouded in fog or deluged with rain. Nighttime crossings were even worse.[14]

Before launching the boats, the smugglers issued a number of strict instructions about what the refugees should and should not do between the time they left Turkey and their arrival in Lesvos. Some even distributed leaflets containing all of the instructions to the refugees as they were boarding the boats. It was their final act of intimidation, but this time it was not just to keep the refugees cowed and compliant. The smugglers also wanted to ensure that the refugees could not and did not return to Turkey. They feared that if they returned, they would seek reprisals for having been swindled and thereby disrupt the lucrative commerce that was in place.[15] First the refugees were warned to leave any passengers who fell overboard behind and to avoid helping any stranded boats along the way because stopping to make any kind of rescue could be fatal for everyone. The smugglers further warned them to avoid being apprehended by the Greek Coast Guard, who they falsely claimed would immediately send them back to Turkey. The truth was that once refugee boats reached Greek waters, the Greek Coast Guard routinely monitored their movements until they had landed safely or, if necessary, came to their aid, in which case passengers were transferred immediately to a Greek port.[16] At that time, back in 2015, the real danger came from the Turkish Coast Guard, which was known to harass the refugees' boats and cause them to capsize.

In her Sky News video, Alex Crawford captured those very actions by a Turkish Coast Guard vessel. Before the refugee boat in which she was a passenger had reached Greek waters, a large, high-speed Turkish boat approached the rubber dinghy with its siren blaring and crew members firing guns into the air. One of the men on deck, presumably the captain, ordered the refugee boat to stop. Surprisingly undaunted by what was happening, many of the refugees waived their fists in the air and shouted angrily for the Coast Guard boat to go away. The refugee who had been made skipper did not stop the boat—an act of heroism for which he would be applauded when they finally reached the other side. Having failed to force the refugee boat to stop, the Turkish Coast Guard boat increased its speed and began to circle them, coming closer and closer and creating larger and larger waves with each turn. Rifles were pointed directly at the refugees and more guns were fired into the air. Children crouched, shielding their heads in terror as the boat rose and fell on the crest of the waves. If the goal of the Turkish Coast Guard crew had been to sink the boat, this time they failed and were forced to withdraw when the refugee boat sailed into Greek waters.[17]

At that time Syrians had a special status as "refugees" under the Geneva Conventions because they were fleeing a civil war in their homeland. This meant that Greece was required to provide protection for Syrians as "refugees," while the other arrivals, even though their countries were ravaged by violent political unrest, were deemed to be "migrants" and did not have that same guarantee. Knowing this, the smugglers told non-Syrian passengers to throw their passports and other documents overboard to be able to claim that they were Syrian. Otherwise if they were caught they could be sent back to Turkey. As a result the beach at Eftalou eventually became strewn with refugees' documents that washed up with the waves, along with copies of the instruction sheets that the smugglers had given them.[18]

One final order from the smugglers was to slash the boats and sink them once they had reached Greek waters. They told the unsuspecting refugees that this would force the Greek Coast Guard to come to their rescue, but it was only so the boats would be destroyed and couldn't turn back. The boat slashing posed a serious problem of its own because refugees had no way of knowing when they were actually in Greek waters or how far from shore they really were. Often they slashed the boats prematurely, leaving their groups stranded in deep water where few survived.[19]

Franck Genauzeau, a reporter for France 2, shot and narrated an extended video of his trip hidden aboard a boat transporting a large group of Syrian and Iraqi refugees from the Turkish coast to Lesvos. As the boat they were to travel on pulled close to shore, they could all be seen emerging from the bushes where they had been waiting for some twenty-four hours for their boat to be ready. A smuggler can be heard telling the refugees that it is safe to board. Genauzeau states, "All are extremely nervous. Many can't swim. Children, all wearing life jackets that are much too big for them, are crying and looking terrified. The youngest passenger on board is a baby barely two months old. His parents are holding him."

One of the smugglers shoved people and waved a gun to frighten them into moving faster. While he did, the refugees went about helping each other get into the boat. One refugee told Genauzeau that he was happy to start the journey, but the smugglers had forced everyone onto the boat so brutally that he had become separated from his family, a refugee's worst fear. At that point, he did not know whether they had been able to board or whether they might still be on the shore. Once the boat was loaded, that same smuggler directed one of the refugees to steer the boat—the skipper. The smuggler then jumped off, gave the boat a final push, and turned to the rest of the smugglers in his gang, who were already hugging and kissing each other as they danced happily in the water. Genauzeau says, "They have their money, and whatever happens to the refugees is no longer their business." At the very last moment, one migrant who had apparently been left behind began to swim toward the boat in a fierce attempt to join his wife and children, who had been able to board. After what must have been an agonizing several minutes, he managed to reach the boat and climb in. Everyone squeezed together to make room for him, and he lay there wet and exhausted.

Unlike the majority of the boats that were made from rubber or plastic, this one was an old wooden craft, and its motor did not work well; the sound of its sputtering could be heard above the commotion of the terrified refugees. Before long it started spewing a thick black smoke, causing all of the passengers to cover their faces to keep from coughing and their eyes from burning. As the boat reached the open water, passengers began to pray. One young man stood at the edge of the boat and wept visibly as he prayed. When night fell they had no lights and were forced to navigate in total darkness, hoping not to collide with the cargo ships that move through the Mytilene Strait between Turkey and Lesvos. All of a sudden, after they had traveled only a couple of kilometers from the Turkish coast, the engine quit, and they were left to float in the pitch black of the moonless night. They yelled and waved their yellow life vests in the air, hoping to alert any nearby boats or cargo ships so they would either be able to steer clear of them or come to their rescue. In the reporter's video, someone's voice is heard in the background pleading with everyone to stop moving, for fear that the boat might capsize.

After they had been drifting for some time, one of the French reporters accompanying Genauzeau used his cell phone to call for help, and soon a small fishing boat approached on what had now become extremely choppy water. The fisherman, one who was often seen on his boat moored in the harbor of Molyvos near the Captain's Table, threw a rope, but both boats were pitching so badly in the rough sea that he had to throw it several times before anyone was able to catch it and tie it securely enough for him to tow them to Molyvos. The whole voyage took a total of four hours. Once safely in the harbor, the refugees, weeping with relief, thanked the reporters, whose intervention saved them on their difficult crossing. Even the man who feared that his family had been left behind happily discovered that they had managed to get on board. Everyone arrived unharmed, contrary to a majority of the refugees' journeys across the Aegean.[20]

Most refugees were all too aware as they boarded the boats that the crossing was dangerous and that there was no guarantee they would make it to the other shore alive. However, once their boat was underway, they very soon discovered just how perilous the trek across this short stretch of the Aegean could be.[21] When motors failed—as they frequently did—the refugees were left stranded in the middle of the channel at the mercy of the elements, while other refugee boats sailed past them without stopping, as the smugglers had ordered. If there were storms, the high waves would easily wash over the flimsy, overcrowded, low-riding boats, causing them to either capsize or split completely apart at their seams, sending the passengers plunging into the icy water. When that happened, if they were wearing one of the defective life vests, they could only flail about desperately in the frigid, choppy waters and strong currents. Mothers and fathers—most of them not knowing how to swim—would frantically try to keep their children's heads above water, but all too often they sank to their own deaths, leaving their children to often meet the same tragic end.

One refugee, a former mechanic for the U.S. Army in Afghanistan who managed to flee after the Taliban threatened him for working with foreigners, told Patrick Kinsley, a reporter for *The Guardian*, how giant waves washed over his boat when it was halfway between Turkey and the Eftalou beach. He said that everyone shouted and screamed for help as they desperately threw their bags into the water, but they were unsuccessful in lightening the load to keep the boat from sinking.[22] In those horrifying times, chaos, mayhem, and death were everywhere out in those waters unless the Coast Guard or nearby fishermen and boat owners were able to make an immediate and almost miraculous rescue. No one knows for sure how many died this way.[23]

5

The Kempsons Are Still Alone on the Beach

Spring and Summer 2015

In February 2015 the Kempson family decided to start a rescue effort in Eftalou on their own. They created it with the full understanding that, once they had begun, there would be no going back. And indeed, from then on there was no stopping them; work with refugees took over their lives. With Eric's binoculars trained almost continually on the beach in front of their home, Eric was quick to spot any movement, and whenever it appeared to be a refugee boat, he, Philippa, and Elleni—when she was at home—jumped in their car and headed out.

When the Kempsons arrived at the beach, their first task was always to help as best they could to bring the boats to shore. They learned, over time, that there were fewer problems with a landing when the bow of a boat pointed directly toward the beach so that it could approach at a perpendicular angle. They also tried to guide the landing so that the boat would come aground in an area with fewer rocks, where the water was the shallowest, with no unexpected deep pools. When a boat's approach to the shore went as planned, the task of bringing it in became fairly routine. On the other hand, if a boat started to turn sideways, it was always a struggle to maneuver it into a position that was stable enough for the passengers to get out safely. A worst-case scenario was for a boat to come in sideways in a rough sea because the waves could crash along the side of the boat and move under its hull, causing it to capsize. When this happened the passengers were thrown into the water one on top of the other, and since most of them were unable to swim, some would drown before they could make it to the beach, even if it was only a short distance.

Knowing that none of the refugees on board were skilled at maneuvering a boat, the Kempsons would stand at the water's edge, waving their arms to attract the passengers' attention. Then, much like ground crew personnel that guide arriving planes as they approach a jet bridge, they would motion in a way that signaled the passenger whom the smugglers designated as the skipper to direct the bow of the boat straight toward the beach. Landings were further complicated when, following the smugglers' instructions, a passenger would stab the side of the boat, causing a sudden and startling explosion that created panic on board. The boat would then start to deflate, making it all the more difficult to steer. In spite of everything, Eric and Philippa eventually became quite adept at bringing boats in safely, even in turbulent waters. They must have passed on their skills to future volunteers, who can be seen in videos taken along the beach in which they are waving their arms and lanterns, guiding boats to shore.

Under normal circumstances, when a boat was about to come aground, Eric and Philippa waded into the water and, with the help of a few of the younger men who had jumped out first, grabbed the sides of the boat, pulling it forward until it rested solidly in the sand. The remaining men then climbed out of the boat and formed a line all the way to the shore. As the women handed the children to them, they were passed along that line until every child was placed in a dry spot on the beach. Then they would proceed to help the women, taking them by the arms and steadying them as they ambled out of the boat and waded through the water. Finally they would return one last time to help any elderly passengers or people with canes, walkers, or wheelchairs; some of them had to be lifted from the boat and carried to dry land. Although many stumbled and fell in the process, they almost always managed to get everyone onto the shore safely.

As soon as Eric and Philippa were sure that all of the refugees were on land, they went around to check on everyone's medical and physical conditions, children and women first, then the men. After that, they distributed water, fruit or some other food, dry clothing and blankets, diapers, baby formula, and whatever else they had brought from home. Just like the first round of check-ups, water and food were always given to the children and women first and then to the men, if there was anything left. This was the rule, but the men did not always react favorably. For them, culturally and historically, it had always been the other way around, but Eric and Philippa stood firm. Even when they did not have much to offer, they found that simply being kind and letting the children put on some dry clothes, have a little something to drink or eat, and sit calmly on the beach helped everyone relax. On only one occasion that the Kempsons can remember, a group of refugees, whose trip across had been particularly harrowing, arrived so desperately hungry and thirsty that they became alarmingly aggressive when food was being distributed. Otherwise, the Kempsons were awed by the graceful and respectful politeness of the refugees in spite of the traumas that they had endured.[1]

They also learned early on that many of the refugees did not know where they had landed. The smugglers had led them to believe that they would arrive in mainland Europe, or at least in some location that was readily accessible to Germany, Belgium, or Scandinavia—the most sought-after destinations. Many of those who knew they were in Greece assumed that they were near Athens, and occasionally some would even ask where they could hail a taxi to get there. No one planned to remain in Greece; it was not viewed as a country that offered opportunity or stability. Even if the refugees knew they were in Greece, it certainly had not occurred to them that they would end up on a Greek island somewhere off the coast, far removed from the Europe they hoped to reach. Maps did little to soothe their frustration and disappointment, but they nevertheless provided a visual orientation for where they had landed. Most immediately and critically, the refugees could use the maps to help them find their way to Molyvos and eventually to Mytilene. Eric and Philippa always carried a supply of maps with them, and they taped a larger version with the routes to Molyvos and Mytilene clearly marked on the back window of their car. Refugees with smartphones took pictures of that map to keep with them.

Landings did not always go smoothly, and to make matters even more complicated, fishermen used aggressive tactics to steal the motors from the refugees' boats before they had landed. Witnesses reported that fishermen repeatedly stalked the refugee boats closely from behind as they approached the shore, checking to see whether the motors were viable. If they were, the fishermen would jump into the water and physically push refugees off their boats in order to steal the motor. In videos taken on the beach, men can often be seen running out from the shore to intercept the refugee boats and remove the motors before the boats landed. This created a very hazardous situation, as the refugees, unable to swim, could drown in the deep water or break their arms and legs if they fell onto the rocks. Equally frightening was the risk of someone getting caught in a propeller that was still in motion. Once, a child died when he was mangled by the propeller after being pushed off the boat by someone intent upon stealing the motor.

Refugee arrivals began to spike dramatically in June 2015, and with the increased number of boats coming in, dangerous and traumatic landings with innumerable injuries and deaths were far from uncommon. On one particular day, somewhat weary from having already guided four boats onto the beach, one right after the other, Eric and Philippa found themselves unable to keep the skipper steering the fifth and final boat from coming in sideways on a treacherous stretch of beach, where there were deep pools of water and boulder-sized rocks. The boat flipped over in the waves, and everyone on board was dumped into the water with all their belongings. The refugees were thrown against the rocks, breaking their arms and legs, and some of the children drowned from inhaling too much water. Those who survived had to lie on the beach for some time to recover.[2]

On another day soon thereafter, the Kempsons were out on a remote part of the beach several miles from both Skala Sykaminias and Molyvos when four boats came in, almost at the same time. The weather all along the coast was clear with little wind, and many boats had already crossed that day. When the last of the four boats was still well over five hundred feet from shore, one of the men, apparently in a moment of joy over having reached Europe and thinking that he was in the shallows, jumped into water that was nearly fifteen feet deep. In the meantime the boat he was on continued toward the shore. Eric knew that he didn't have the strength to swim that far, so his only option was to get the boat unloaded as quickly as possible and take it back out to rescue the man. First he had to stop the passengers from stabbing the boat and sinking it, then he had to push away a man who was already trying to steal the motor. Finally, once the boat was empty and the passengers were safely on shore, Eric grabbed the tiller, turned the boat around, and sped out into the open water along with two other refugees who had chosen to accompany him. When they got to the man, he was struggling desperately to keep his head above water, but together, Eric and the two men managed to pull him onto the boat.

When they got him to shore, he was breathing but with great difficulty. That day Eric and Philippa were on the beach by themselves, dealing with over one hundred refugees from all the boats and the man who had nearly drowned. Philippa had taken some first-aid classes years ago and attempted to apply what she remembered having been taught when, all of a sudden, the man started vomiting. She thought, almost helplessly, "This has to be a good thing." She and Eric brought him back to their house for a warm shower because he was shaking so badly. After he had eaten an apple and finally calmed down a bit, he told them that, unlike the water in Afghanistan's rivers that tends to be murky, the water along the Eftalou shore was so crystal clear that he could see the pebbles on the bottom, and he thought they were in shallow water.

The Kempsons both agree that this particular event shone a spotlight on their vulnerabilities on the beach, particularly in the first six months before outside aid organizations began to appear. There were many injuries during those months, and many refugees came off the boats already in need of medical assistance, but neither Molyvos nor Skala Sykaminias had a doctor. The nearest medical facility was in Kalloni—well over half an hour away—leaving them far from anyone trained to deal with medical emergencies. Situations like this were deeply unsettling, but as Philippa said, "We just patched things up as best we could."[3]

On yet another day that June, Eric noticed a rubber boat approaching the shore, carrying about seventy people. Like so many of the overcrowded refugee boats, it was riding so dangerously low in the water that it had caught the attention of the Coast Guard crew while they were out on their routine patrol. They followed it, but they also stayed far enough away to keep their boat's wake from interfering with the landing or, worse yet, causing it to capsize. Eric was standing on the shore motioning, as usual, to bring the boat straight in to a spot on the beach that appeared safe for a landing. Suddenly the boat turned sharply, and the waves pushed it side-ways toward the shore. When it got close to the beach, many of the men jumped into the water in their excitement. One of them slipped onto the rocks and gashed his leg. The grisly cut was large and deep, and the man bled so profusely he left a trail of red in the water as he dragged himself toward land. Eric called for help to a local volunteer who happened to be out on the beach that day and was carrying a few medical supplies in her bag. Together they tried to bind the wound with gauze and bandages to stop the bleeding, but their efforts were futile.

Fortunately one of the refugees on that particular boat was an Afghan American interpreter who knew a little first aid from the training he had received while working for the U.S. military in Afghanistan. He placed a tourniquet on the man's leg, and the bleeding finally slowed to a stop. Then a BBC reporter who had arrived at the scene shortly before the boat landed agreed to transport the injured man to the medical office in Kalloni. The two men helped Eric load the injured refugee into the reporter's car and followed Eric to Kalloni so they would not get lost. Upon arrival at the facility's emergency entrance, the reporter ran to grab a stretcher, and he and Eric rolled the injured refugee inside. Once he was in proper care, the interpreter stayed with him while Eric and the reporter rushed back to the beach to help the remaining passengers and any others that might have arrived.[4]

Eric and Philippa found, over time, that a good number of the Afghan and Iraqi refugees—like the interpreter who stepped in to apply the tourniquet to the injured man's leg—had received medical aid training in their home countries while working for either the Americans or the British. There were also formal doctors among the refugees, and many of them ended up providing help on the beaches. Philippa tells a story about a landing in which a little boy's leg was slashed open when the man carrying him to shore slipped and fell on the rocks. The boy's leg was completely marred from the wound and bled profusely. Not knowing what else to do to help the pain and slow the bleeding, Philippa circulated among the refugees, begging for anyone with medical training. One man offered to help but warned her that he was a dentist in his home country. With a sigh of relief,

Philippa replied, "You'll do," and the man patched up the little boy's leg. In most instances the refugees turned out to be highly resourceful, helping one another and working with whatever they could in any emergency.[5]

The weather in June tends to be pleasantly warm, with milder winds that create relatively favorable conditions for boats to cross. However, strong storms can also arise, making navigation dangerous, particularly for the refugees' rubber boats. Very early one morning, Eric was scanning the sea through his binoculars from a vantage point where the road between Molyvos and Skala Sykaminias runs high atop the cliffs, affording him a panoramic view of the beach below. He could see huge white-capped waves all across the stretch of sea between Turkey and Lesvos, and he could hear the roar of the waves as they crashed against the rocks along the shore below him. No fishing boats were out that morning, confirming his suspicion that the sea was far too turbulent for even the most seasoned navigators. He and Philippa had come to realize that smugglers still launched boats on days such as this and that those boats usually carried refugees who could not afford to pay the going price. Sure enough, he spotted a refugee boat emerging from the Turkish shore, just before seven o'clock. When the boat was a little more than halfway across, with still nearly two miles yet to go, Eric, from his vantage point high above the water, could see that a high, fast-moving wave was rapidly propelling it toward the shore. As he watched, the boat was hurled against the rocks on the shore below, where it burst apart and threw all of the passengers into the water. Pieces of rubber flew into the air and then fell among the foamy waves. To his horror Eric saw a second boat coming in close behind the first one. It, too, rocked violently back and forth on the crest of another huge wave. When the front end of that boat hit the rocks, the impact was so forceful that the boat shot backward almost seventy feet, just as another monstrous wave thrust it forward one more time against the rocks, where it capsized, pitching all of its passengers overboard.

Eric stared in disbelief at what had just happened, but his gaze was interrupted by the sight of three more boats heading toward this same expanse of beach. He could tell from their location on the water that one of the boats had departed from a section of the Turkish coast used primarily by Syrian refugees, while the other two boats came from a departure point normally used by Afghans and Pakistanis. Eric found himself almost involuntarily focusing on what he believed to be the Syrian boat because, at that point in time, most Syrians traveling together were families, while a majority of the Afghan and Pakistani refugees were men. This meant that the Syrian boat was more likely carrying women and children. As Eric watched that particular boat, he spotted a towering wall of water swiftly approaching it from behind. It lifted the stern so high that it appeared as if the entire boat was hanging perpendicular to the surface of the sea. When the wave crested and broke, cascades of water swallowed it whole. He stood there transfixed, watching for about fifteen minutes, but nothing and no one surfaced.

The thought of easing some of the refugees' suffering is what drew the Kempsons to the beach in the first place, and now to watch such a tragedy unfold while Eric stood alone and helpless on the high cliffs was incredibly unnerving. Trembling and weeping, he headed for his car and rushed home to get Philippa and Elleni, and together they drove as quickly as they could to the beach to help any refugees that had managed to land. Eric is always emotional whenever he talks about that morning. His sadness over the tragic loss of life in such a horrifying way is heavily tinged with anger because it was June and there was still no help from the Greek or European governments or any international aid organizations. The first humanitarian aid did not come until late August 2015, and until then, he and his family had to confront everything alone, with little volunteer help other than tourists and the occasional journalists and cameramen, who had begun to learn about the crisis and started to show up in Molyvos.[6]

Once on land, refugees often danced for joy, kissed the ground, and shared hugs, even though they had no idea where they were or where they were going. Many knelt facing Mecca, to offer emotional prayers of thanksgiving. Those who came with cell phones kept them tightly sealed in waterproof bags usually hanging around their necks. Once on shore, they unwrapped them and took smiling selfies to send to people back home, letting them know they had arrived, as if the trauma they had just endured was momentarily forgotten. Depending on the stretch of beach where they happened to land, some of them faced a long, steep, and difficult climb up to the road, where they would start their walk to Molyvos. Eric and other volunteers carried children, elderly men and women, and people with wounds of all kinds on their backs up the steep and what, at times, felt like vertical paths to reach the road. To everyone's amazement children often found the fortitude to run and pick flowers among the nearby grasses to give to the volunteers who had helped them and their parents safely come ashore. Philippa always has difficulty holding back tears when she recalls feeling the small hand of a child tugging on her arm and looking down to find happy eyes staring into hers, an arm outstretched offering her a small bouquet of flowers.[7]

During those first six months of 2015, thousands of refugees landed on the ten miles of coast between Molyvos and Skala Sykaminias, and in the coming months there would be hundreds of thousands more. Eric, Philippa, and Elleni in Eftalou and Melinda, Theo, and their children in Molyvos all endeavored to provide the basics such as water, dry clothing, shoes, baby formula, emergency blankets, and medical supplies to the refugees. Lacking administrative structure or special bank accounts, they posted appeals for assistance on social media. They received donations of money and supplies, but they also ended up paying many of the expenses out of their own pockets. Apart from a handful of volunteers made up largely of friends, local residents, tourists, and the occasional reporter, no one else was there to help them with their rescue and relief efforts.[8] They were truly alone.

6

Enduring the Screams of Desperation

The Coast Guard at Sea and Melinda in the Harbor

In January and February of 2015, sometimes as few as three boats might land on the beach on any given day, carrying between one hundred and two hundred passengers who would then make their way on foot to Molyvos. However, by the end of May, that number had steadily increased to an average in the thousands, with as many as sixty boats arriving each day.[1] The refugees formed an almost endless procession, trudging together along the steep coastal road leading from the beaches to Molyvos. Even if their crossings from Turkey went without incident, most of them had not actually slept or eaten much of anything for days or, in some cases, weeks. They were hungry, thirsty, wet, and often shoeless. Parents carried children who were too exhausted or too small to walk. Many struggled with canes, walkers, and even wheelchairs. Observers reported seeing more and more refugees covered with shrapnel wounds from the wars at home.[2] When summer arrived, they faced a hot, sun-drenched trek, surrounded by clouds of dust that were stirred up either by the winds or by vehicles passing by.

Now and then, tourists or local residents stopped to offer rides, mostly to women and children or the elderly and infirm, but they did so at their own peril because of the aforementioned law that forbade the transportation of refugees in anything other than the police buses to Mytilene, of which there were usually no more than two a day.[3] Fearing legal reprisals, motorists tended to pass the refugees by, and thus the vast majority ended up walking the roughly fifteen kilometers to their destination: the front door of the small Coast Guard office in the harbor, where they were required to register. Refugees who were rescued by the Coast Guard when their boats stalled or capsized out at sea were brought directly to the harbor. Many of them were very near death from exhaustion or hypothermia, and some had been driven to hysteria from watching their spouses or their children drown, or from their rubber dinghies breaking apart and sinking into the cold, dark waters.

The Coast Guard's primary job was to conduct routine border patrol operations, not search and rescue missions. At the time, there were only four Greek Coast Guard boats on the whole island of Lesvos, each with a crew of four or five members, none of whom had ever been trained to administer basic cardiopulmonary resuscitation (CPR), much less deal with people who were drowning. Suddenly their routine border patrol responsibility had escalated into a monumental search and rescue operation to "keep the small bit of water they patrolled from becoming a mass grave."[4] Their efforts were further exacerbated by the absence of outside governmental agencies and NGOs to provide either assistance or guidance as they faced this huge influx of refugees. When writing about her award-winning short documentary *4.1 Miles*—which focuses on the Coast Guard in Molyvos and boat captain Kyriakos Papadopoulos—Daphne Matziaraki states, "The scale of the emergency was so big, but there was no help, and the Coast Guard felt alone and abandoned, as if the entire world was turning their backs to the crisis."[5]

Eri Grigorelli remembers that by the summer of 2015, as many as thirty boats might cross in a single hour, all carrying at least sixty or seventy refugees. She and her fellow Coast Guard crew members had to work in continually rotating twelve-hour shifts, day after day and night after night. They would leave the harbor immediately whenever calls came in, alerting them of refugee boats in trouble or refugees adrift in the sea. Oftentimes they would also spot people in the water while they were on one of their regular patrol assignments.

Whenever the crew moved in for a rescue, they would first move their boat as close as they could to the sinking rubber dinghy or any refugees in the water and then throw ropes down so that refugees could be pulled aboard Frightened, unable to swim, and often holding tightly to a child or another family member, the refugees were like dead weight clinging to the rope, while the crew, having to work in teams of two or more, struggled to pull them up onto the deck. When refugees lost their grip on the rope, they tumbled back into the sea, creating as much panic for those on board as those in the water. Still the crew worked tenaciously as a team, with some pulling the ropes while others lay flat on the deck, holding their arms out to grab refugees and help them up. The refugees in the sea were "half drowned, half naked, all in really bad condition."[6] Children were often near death. Yet despite the crews' lack of training, they immediately began to either administer mouth-to-mouth resuscitation and pump the children's chests or hold them in the air by their feet while they slapped their backs— anything to drain the water from their lungs. If the crew members had not already learned to do this from previous experience, they followed fellow crew members who had done it before or they simply acted on instinct. Many children's lives were saved during those rescue operations, but not all.

The deck of the Coast Guard boat in Molyvos could only hold forty to fifty people, which was too small to accommodate all of the refugees being rescued from one boat at the same time. As a result, once the Coast Guard boat had reached capacity, the crew had no other choice but to leave the remaining refugees behind while they went to the harbor, discharged the passengers, and returned. If it was night or if the waves were too high, the crew called for backup boats—local fishermen from Molyvos and Skala Sykaminias or independent boaters like Stratis Kabanas. In keeping with the requirement of international maritime law, whenever fishermen or independent boaters were out on the water and spotted a boat in trouble or someone drowning—or if they received a call from the Coast Guard— they would either tow the boat to the harbor or pull the passengers on board their own boats. With the large number of refugee boats making the crossing, this happened with increasing frequency until finally, in the fall of 2015, once NGOs began to arrive and there was remuneration for the fishermen, they carried out rescue operations, even after they had finished their day's fishing run.

Recalling her daily rescue missions during that spring and summer, Eri says, "The first screams you hear from a person who is drowning are something you never forget." Long before joining the Coast Guard, she had been taught to jump into the water and rescue people as part of a lifeguard training seminar, so knowing that most of the refugees could not swim and that many of them were wearing faulty life vests, her first instinct was always to dive into the sea right away to try to save them. However, she resisted the temptation, remembering her lifeguard instructor's admonition that people who are drowning could grab their rescuers in desperation and take them down. This kept her standing on the deck rather than immediately jumping into the sea, but it was almost unbearable for her because there were times when all she could hear was the dreadful sounds of refugees drowning while she stood there helpless to do anything about it. Finally she and the crew devised a plan wherein one of them would lie flat on the deck and grab her feet when she jumped. Once in the water, she would grasp the arms of the drowning person and then the crew member holding her feet would pull both of them back onto the boat. They did this over and over again and saved many people. Eri always says, "The worst part of every one of [our] rescue missions was picking the dead from the sea, especially the kids, and I've done it many times."[7]

Amid all of the chaotic and agonizing search and rescue missions, the small Coast Guard crew in Molyvos still had to follow EU regulations and register everyone who landed. It was not a simple process. They were required to fingerprint every refugee, verify their identity and country of origin, note all requests for asylum, review passports, and deal with those who had tossed their documents overboard so they could claim to be Syrian and receive the treatment to which all Syrians were entitled under the Geneva Convention. The crew also had to prepare the official registration papers that the refugees needed to take with them, and they did everything without the benefit of proficiency in any of the refugees' native languages. The result was a kind of cultural, bureaucratic, linguistic, and emotional pandemonium that the beleaguered crew was left to deal with on their own, despite continual pleas for additional support from the higher authorities in Mytilene and Athens. Eventually it became so hard to manage the registration process, in addition to their grueling shifts on the water, that they turned to Melinda for help and then started recruiting locals to take care of registration. Stratis Kabanas, who spent a lot of time in the harbor with his boat, found that "if you were there showing a willingness to help in any way, the Coast Guard would deputize you for the task," and indeed, in no time at all, he became one of those deputized along with Melinda and many others.[8]

Meanwhile, as the early months of 2015 passed, oversight for all that was happening in the harbor fell more and more to Melinda, who by this time already devoted almost every waking hour to providing for the refugees, both those arriving on foot from the beaches and those brought to the harbor in the Coast Guard boats. During the coldest weeks of that winter, it became apparent that the refugees, particularly the children, needed more than a warm beverage when they landed ashore. Most of them had not eaten in so long that, in addition to being cold and wet, they are also desperately hungry. Thus Melinda began to prepare sandwiches and whatever else she could assemble for the refugees to eat. Her first sandwiches were large, with turkey, lettuce, tomato, and butter, until the number of refugees began to exceed one hundred or more every day and she was forced to cut back to nothing more than turkey and cheese.

Melinda explains, "That's why I became involved so intensely. All of the refugees ended up here in the harbor, and with my restaurant being so close to the Coast Guard office, almost everything landed in my lap. My phone would ring at any time of the day or night with messages that boats had arrived. More often than not, it was still dark, but I would get up and head down to the restaurant where I set about making sure that the people were fed and cared for. My life became an endless ringing of phones, with me dashing around making sandwiches and looking for dry clothes—shoes in particular because so many refugees lost them during the crossing. There were nights when I hardly slept for more than two hours," to which she adds, "and I'm a serious sleeper who likes to sleep! Theo couldn't believe it. I would get four or five phone calls a night telling me that another group of refugees had landed, and I would head to the restaurant to do whatever I could."

It reached a point where Melinda's permanent daily routine began before dawn and ended sometimes well after midnight, but it was one that she felt she could not control. Once she started to help the refugees, there was no turning back. She says, "How could I do otherwise? I simply couldn't let them go without something dry to wear and something to eat, especially the children. There was no other choice."[9] No doubt, Eric and Philippa as well as Eri and her fellow Coast Guard crew members all felt the same.

It was clear to everyone who went to the harbor that Melinda was the person in charge. Even amid the pandemonium, it was impossible to miss seeing her as she darted about, doing almost anything she could to help, always with the utmost compassion. In times when the Coast Guard boat came in, carrying passengers who had been thrown into the sea, and it seemed that the harbor could not be more chaotic, Melinda would spring into action, yelling instructions for those on the pier to wrap the freezing women and children in the silver-colored emergency blankets, get them warm, and calm those who had nearly drowned or been injured. The bodies of the dead—refugees who had drowned at sea or those who hadn't made it before the Coast Guard boat reached the harbor—were there on the harbor pavement. Melinda saw that their remains were tended to; the Coast Guard, the police, or medical personnel loaded them into body bags and arranged for them to be taken away.

Perhaps most gut-wrenching of all was the need to comfort grieving survivors who had watched their family members drown and disappear into the sea or die in the harbor. On one such occasion, Eri worked next to Melinda, desperately trying to administer mouth-to-mouth resuscitation to save a little boy, while his mother—who had already lost her other two children in the sea—stood by, wringing her hands and screaming entreaties to God to save her last remaining child. Ute distinctly remembers watching as the Coast Guard carried three young children off the boat and laid their lifeless bodies on the pavement. Their mother had fled Syria with them following her husband's murder, but their boat had capsized in the waves, and the sea swallowed her children right before her eyes. When the Coast Guard pulled her drowned children out of the water, they laid them next to her on the deck of the boat as they made their way to the harbor. Ute said that the sight and sound of this mother weeping over her three dead children is something she will never be able to forget. In fact everyone who was in the harbor that day—Melinda, Eri, local volunteers, the Coast Guard crew members—know it is impossible for them to forget the bone-chilling cries of the survivors that echoed from the stone walls of the buildings surrounding the harbor.

Eri remembers that, in times of emergency, the Coast Guard could always rely on Melinda to come immediately, either by herself or with her team of helpers. "They would pull themselves together and head for the port, no matter what, because being there for the refugees was what was needed most at those moments, and that's what they were there to do. Melinda was always there to hold my hand and reassure me that we would be able to get through this."[10]

At the same time, as busy or as crazy as things were, it was not uncommon for observers to also see Melinda pause to admire a child. The gesture was thoughtful and brought warm smiles to the faces of the parents who were grateful for this brief expression of kindness after their harrowing experiences crossing the sea. And whenever any new volunteers showed up, as hundreds eventually did in the ensuing months, they would start by asking the simple question, "Where do I go to . . . ?" Before they had even finished the question, people would interrupt them to answer "Melinda" or give a nod in the direction of the Captain's Table. Once the volunteers met her they immediately sensed her level of devotion by the sincerity of her welcome . . . and by how quickly she would set them to work.

4. Philippa and Eric Kempson tend to a baby whose family has just landed, May 2015. © Nikolas Georgiou.

5. A typically crowded refugee boat about to land on the beach near Eftalou. Courtesy of Michael S. Honegger.

6. Refugees struggle to disembark after their boat turns sideways in the surf. Courtesy of Michael S. Honegger.

7. Soaking wet passengers make their way to shore. Courtesy of Michael S. Honegger.

8. Deflated rubber dinghies that were slashed by the refugees and remnants of useless life vests line the shore of this rocky inlet where refugees face a hard climb up the cliffs to reach the road. Courtesy of Michael S. Honegger.

9. A mother and her young son embrace upon landing safely. Courtesy of Michael S. Honegger.

10. Two brothers' emotional embrace after their boat lands at Eftalou. Courtesy of Michael S. Honegger.

11. Eric Kempson and other refugees carry a wheelchair-bound passenger across the rocky beach. Courtesy of Eric Kempson.

7

The Situation in the Harbor Worsens

May 2015

The arrival of more and more refugees created a serious backlog in the Coast Guard's registration process, despite having enlisted local volunteers to help them, and refugees were forced to wait for longer periods of time in the harbor. Moreover, once they had finally managed to register, there was yet another long wait for transportation to Mytilene. Since they were not permitted to ride in private cars or taxis or public buses, their only legal means of leaving Molyvos was in the police buses that departed from the school parking lot at the other end of the village. The bus schedules were erratic and undependable, causing the wait to gradually increase from several hours to several days. At first, rather than journeying to the parking lot, the refugees remained in the harbor where there was at least something to eat and drink, and as a result the harbor grew dangerously congested.

With the number of refugees escalating and the wait growing longer, the need for food, dry clothing, and shoes also grew to the point where Melinda started to run out of everything. She canvassed the community repeatedly and posted on social media asking for donations, not just of food, clothing, and shoes, but emergency blankets, baby formula, diapers, medical supplies such as bandages and disinfectants, and any other essentials she could think of. At first, people donated generously. Villagers came to the restaurant bringing as many items as they could carry—milk, bread, jam, peanut butter, and whatever else they had in their cupboards. Many of them even stayed to help make sandwiches and serve tea. Eventually, however, donations began to dry up because by that time everyone upon whom Melinda relied had emptied both their cupboards and their closets.

Initially she saw no recourse other than to replenish supplies using money from her own pocket, but with the tide of refugees showing no signs of abating, it soon became obvious that she and Theo could no longer afford to pay for everything on their own. Despite her strong resolve, Melinda knew that the influx of refugees had already exceeded their restaurant's capacity to provide food, and Theo started to grow concerned about her stamina. They both also understood that when the restaurant reopened for the 2015 tourist season, it could no longer be the center of operations for the refugees, nor could Melinda continue to keep up such a mad pace day and night in addition to running the restaurant.

Another and perhaps even larger concern loomed ominously in the minds of everyone involved in the growing crisis. They all knew that if significant amounts of additional resources were not forthcoming in the near future, the situation in Molyvos would inevitably disintegrate into a major human catastrophe, and there would be nothing they or any of the locals could do to prevent it. This grim realization was made all the more urgent and terrifying by the complete absence of any form of outside help. Local government officials were aware of what was happening in Molyvos but had confined their efforts to Mytilene, the island's capital, where there was also a very large refugee presence, not only because it, too, was a landing spot but because refugees congregated there to wait for the ferry to Athens. Time passed, yet neither the Greek government nor the European Union had stepped in, let alone any international aid organizations. It was as if Molyvos was being abandoned and the responders were left totally on their own. They could only imagine what the ultimate impact of this overwhelming wave of refugees might have on their village, their economy, and their lives, and it terrified them.

In April Melinda put out another call for help, this time on two fronts. First she set up a Facebook page called "Help for Refugees in Molyvos."[1] It caught on quickly, and even people abroad began to donate money. This enabled Melinda to start buying the kinds of essential items she needed—clothing, water, meat and bread for sandwiches, toys, baby items, and sanitary supplies for the women—without having to exhaust her own resources. When tourists started to arrive for the season, many were so bewildered by what they saw that they, too, became generous with their money and offers to help.[2] Realizing that it would be both unwise and illegal for her to accept money directly from anyone and then spend it on supplies, even if her purchases were legitimate, Melinda requested that all monetary donations be placed in open accounts earmarked for the refugees that she had set up in the village's stores and supermarkets. This enabled her to order food and other supplies directly from them, and they, in turn, delivered everything without her personally handling any of the money. She believed that this procedure would be doubly effective because she was supporting local merchants by buying what she needed from them rather than ordering from outside suppliers. She was also aware that village busybodies were starting to spread rumors that she was pocketing donations, and while she was never able to fully quell such gossip, she believed that at least those who worked with her would know she dealt with the money in a forthright and honest fashion. Her second call for help was an urgent personal appeal to her friends from their days working together with First Stop, some ten years earlier.

One of those friends, Ilektra Pasxouli, had recently returned to Molyvos after spending the winter in Athens. Ilektra's mother, Ismini, owned and operated a shop located on the main road leading into the village, and Ilektra would return each year in late March to help her mother during the busy season. Neither of them was a native of Molyvos, but they had lived there for quite a long time. Ismini was part of the original First Stop team, and Ilektra could recall the many stories her mother used to tell her about those days. Therefore the presence of refugees in Molyvos was nothing new to them, although they had noticed groups of them passing by the windows of the shop from time to time. One day, shortly after Ilektra had returned from Athens, a friend came by the shop to tell her and her mother that there were serious problems with refugees in the harbor. In retrospect, when Ilektra talks about that particular day, she says, "We understood about refugees from my mother's early days working with First Stop, but if you don't really see what's going on with your own eyes, you don't think it's a big deal, and you don't necessarily pay attention to it . . . or maybe, to some extent, you don't really want to know."[3] Just a few days later she received a phone call from Melinda, asking if she would come to the Captain's Table to help.

Melinda made the same call to her friends Dina Adam and Dionisis Pavlou, who were also among the originators of First Stop. Since that time, they, like Ismini, had become involved with their own pursuits: Dionisis in his position as a math teacher and coordinator of international programs in the public high school in Petra, and Dina in the hotel industry working at a resort on the beach at Eftalou. However, they responded immediately to Melinda's call. They all admit that when they arrived in the harbor, they were jolted by the extent of the chaos and the life-threatening situations their longtime friend was struggling with. Refugees were everywhere—hundreds of them. Most were congregated in front of the Captain's Table, where Melinda, Theo, and their children, along with a handful of people who either lived or worked in the harbor, were frantically making sandwiches, handing out dry clothes, and trying to take care of everyone. It was almost impossible to fathom the number of injured people who had nearly drowned before being rescued from their sinking boats, either by the Coast Guard or by fishermen and boat owners. Nothing from those earlier days of helping with refugee landings on the beach was even remotely akin to the humanitarian crisis they witnessed as they came into the harbor that day.

The stone pavement was strewn with blankets where everyone slept. Clothes covered every inch of the seawall where they had been hung to dry while the refugees waited for their turn to register. Then there were the dead and dying. Sanitation had become a major problem. Melinda arranged to have the port's two already-dilapidated public toilets opened and cleaned in an effort to cut down on the number of people relieving themselves in the public areas, but they proved to be completely inadequate and next to impossible to maintain under the existing circumstances. The seats on the European-style toilets were easily and frequently broken because most of the refugees, accustomed to toilettes turques, ended up standing rather than sitting on them. Furthermore Afghan refugees came from rural areas where there were no such toilet facilities. Despite everyone's efforts to instruct them in their use, they reverted to what was familiar and dug a hole somewhere nearby, relieved themselves—even threw in their dirty garments—and covered it all up before they moved on.

Melinda believed that her friends, like her, rarely cowered in the face of challenges, even ones as monumental as this. Operating under the assumption that there would be no help from the outside, at least not for the foreseeable future, Ilektra, Dina, and Dionisis immediately joined Melinda to devise a plan of action that they hoped would bring some order to the chaos. They had little experience and even less training to deal with the problems at hand, but everyone involved pitched in and did what they felt they had to do, even if it was all largely improvised.

They began by convening a meeting of everyone who was still around from their original First Stop group. Around twenty people—including Ute Vogt, Stratis Kabanas, Eri Grigorelli, and several others who had been working with Melinda more recently—showed up at the Captain's Table one evening. They all knew that First Stop had been a success, primarily because they had set up a workable system to provide what the incoming refugees needed most: food, water, dry clothing, and directions onward. With that experience in mind that evening, they went about developing an organizational structure that they hoped would consolidate everyone's efforts and thereby alleviate some of the frenzy and confusion. First they set up lines of communication, just as they had back then, so they could all be in direct contact with each other quickly and reliably. Next they listed all of the tasks that needed to be performed on a daily basis, and everyone in the group was allotted at least one specific task. They created work schedules, assigning each person to one or more shifts during a given period of time to ensure that all tasks would be completed as needed. Finally they each pledged an initial contribution of fifty euros to help Melinda cover the expenses she was paying personally. Knowing that Melinda did not want to handle money herself, they followed her instructions to purchase supplies themselves or deposit the money in the open accounts that she had already set up at the supermarkets.[4]

Everyone attending the meeting at the Captain's Table that night agreed that a record-keeping system must be set up to account for all donations and expenditures, and a woman named Rena, another member of the original group, agreed to assume that responsibility. Lacking any formal accounting training, Rena created a system using white paper napkins from the restaurant. Whenever anyone donated money, she wrote the person's name on the napkin with the amount given. She then took a picture of the money, folded it inside the napkin, and asked the donor to sign it. When the money was spent, she put a copy of the receipt inside the napkin and filed it in a box. Because the box contained a complete record of all transactions, Rena could produce hard evidence of how much money had been given, by whom, and how it had been spent if there was ever an audit or an accusation of fiscal malfeasance. As the official treasurer and bookkeeper, she stored the box in her house for safekeeping, but as the amount began to grow larger she became fearful that someone might break in and steal everything. She asked Eri where she should hide it, and together they decided that the safest place was in her refrigerator, where it remained throughout the summer and into the fall.[5]

Shortly after the group's first meeting, they managed to locate an unused space where they could store food, water, blankets, clothing, and other supplies. This step was paramount to establishing a successful organization. They already had been forced to store supplies in people's offices and homes because there was no longer enough room in the restaurant, and when the tourist season began in just a few weeks, they would not be able to use the restaurant at all. Their new location was dust-ridden, but once they cleaned it, they happily set about installing a large refrigerator and lots of shelves, along with several large worktables. They even hung bulletin boards where they could post schedules and announcements. As mentioned, sandwich-making was a central part of Melinda's efforts, but now it became a large-scale operation that required several shifts of workers each day just to keep up with demand. An elderly lady from the village who was always helping out, became the self-appointed supervisor, overseeing the entire sandwich-making operation. She wanted an assembly line operation with one person each to prepare the bread, the turkey, and the cheese, and a fourth person to place the sandwiches on the trays. Someone also needed to make tea. Everyone went along with her, and soon the space became known to all of the volunteers as the "Sandwich Factory."[6]

Dina recalls that there were some funny moments at the Sandwich Factory. May was the start of the busy season in the hotel where she worked, and she was often there for twelve-hour shifts before going to the Sandwich Factory for several more hours. One day when there were only two of them making sandwiches, they decided to make fifty more and store them in the refrigerator. Just as they began, Melinda called to say that over one hundred refugees had just arrived and that they would need to make at least one hundred forty sandwiches. Things became even more of a frenzy when they ran out of bread and had to run to the store to get more. Before that day's shift was over, the two of them ended up making 350 sandwiches, and even those were not enough. The next day they had to make 800 sandwiches, then 1,000 the day after that. Eventually bread had to be delivered by the truckload to keep up with the demand, and volunteers set up their sandwich-making operations out on the beach where refugees were landing.

With their much-needed space and their newly created systems of task management in place, they were able to populate their work shifts, maintain their supply inventories, track income and expenditures, and concentrate more methodically and effectively on the needs of the growing number of refugees. The Captain's Table was also freed up for the start of the new season. There was no way to completely avoid confusion and mayhem, but everything started to function in a much more organized and professional manner, and that enabled the volunteers to sustain the scope of their relief efforts through the challenging months of May, June, and July 2015. Dina describes it as putting themselves on "automatic pilot" and doing what had to be done "like an army." In one conversation about that period of time, she says, "It was so in our face. The need was so acute. If we had stopped to think about it . . ." Then her voice trails off as if to suggest that she did not know what might have happened if they thought about it too much.[7]

8

Locals and Tourists

How They Felt about the Refugees and What They Did . . . at First

Initially many locals and long-time seasonal residents reacted favorably, even compassionately, toward the refugees and wanted to help in some way. Right from the start in November 2014, when Eri first called Theo about the group of refugees standing in front of the Coast Guard office, the villagers became Melinda's supply line for clothing, which they brought to the harbor and placed on tables that she had set up outside the restaurant. As time went on, when refugees passed in front of homes or businesses, many townspeople opened their doors to offer whatever they had available, some bread, water, or maybe fruit. One gentleman even appeared at the Captain's Table carrying a small paper bag containing figs that he had picked from the tree in his yard.[1]

Speaking of the spring and summer of 2015, Stratis Kabanas says, "It was impossible not to meet refugee boats out on the water; there were so many of them."[2] Whenever he was in his boat, either alone or giving tours, if he spotted a refugee boat, he would call the Coast Guard to alert them and to report the boat's general condition. If a boat did not have a working motor or was in any kind of trouble and the Coast Guard was unable to make a rescue, Stratis would tow it to the harbor. Even when the Coast Guard informed him that they were on the way to a beleaguered refugee boat, he would wait for them to arrive, knowing that the vessel and its passengers remained at risk in the meantime. In those early months before any outside help had arrived, Stratis became the go-to person for the Coast Guard crew, for they knew that he would offer help, even if he had tourists on his boat. Once, his own boat's motor broke down and had to be replaced, causing him to lose a lot of tourist business. Nevertheless people who know him say that he did what he did because there were people in trouble. When asked how many boats he rescued, instead of attempting an answer, he turned and stared off into the distance, leaving one to wonder whether there were too many to count or if the memories were too unsettling. Perhaps both.

Whenever Ute reflects on her early involvement with the refugees, her first thought is always about how many there were and how hard it was to know what to do for them: "At the time, I had the shop, so my availability was limited, but at first, when so many refugees started arriving, the one thing I could do was to give people whatever they needed. I would bring things from my home, or I would buy them things with my own money. If the children wanted an ice cream or women needed new clothes or lady things, if the family needed food or medicine such as aspirin, or if they needed to replace batteries or things like that, I would provide them. Every person and every family had different needs. I talked with others in the village about helping, and I worked to collect money to buy food and water, or toys for the children. We helped by trying to provide whatever they needed at the moment."[3]

One of Ute's most vivid memories from that period is of a family—two parents and their five small children—whom she saw late one night as she closed up her shop. "It was after midnight, and there they were, these very nice parents with their beautiful children, all sleeping in each other's arms. I fell in love with them from the moment I first saw them. It made me cry to see them lying there on the ground." Ute has two bedrooms in her house, so she walked over and invited them to come spend the night in her home, promising that she would bring them back to the harbor the next morning. As it turned out, they told her they could not go with her because they feared missing the others when they left Molyvos at daybreak. When she went to her shop the next morning, they were gone.[4]

Robert and Robin Jones have been coming to Molyvos so regularly for over forty years that they consider it their second home.[5] Molyvos was actually one of the first places they visited after meeting in Greece in 1974, and in the intervening years while they both worked in the corporate world, they regularly returned with their three sons. Finally, in 2007, they purchased a house, which is located toward the western section of the village, just up the hill from the elementary school, and they come back each spring from their home in Santa Barbara, California, to spend at least three or four months. When they arrived in the spring of 2015, they found themselves face to face with the tide of refugees inundating the village. They had no sooner settled in for the summer than they began to help and found themselves drawn to the beach, where they became deeply involved in helping refugees as they landed.

While working on the beach, Robin observed families lying on the stones, numb with exhaustion. She was particularly struck by the vacant look in the children's eyes, and the more she saw of that, the more she contemplated the effect that this migration would have on their well-being. There was no doubt in her mind that an experience of this magnitude was so powerful and so self-defining that it would shape their future and the people they would become. With that in mind while their parents were "doing the survival thing," she wanted to find "at least some small way to make it a positive experience for the children, even though they had left everything behind." At home she had a supply of watercolors that she used herself. One day she decided to bring them with her to the beach and start painting with the children. She saw it as "a way of offering a moment of relief . . . a way for them to step outside the harsh reality of their current situation." Working with paper and paint on the beach proved challenging with the wind, the water, and the children somewhat unsettled from having just landed. Nevertheless, she persisted and soon discovered that "the simple act of drawing concentrated the children's thoughts on a quieter world where they could express what they were experiencing or, for a moment, just have a little fun." From then on she brought her painting supplies every time she went to the beach, and she encouraged the children to sit near her and paint. Some were more hesitant, but most of them quickly settled in together, seated on the dry sand and rocks, away from the surf, and they created paintings that offered an awe-inspiring glimpse into their private reality, while their parents looked on from just a short distance away.[6]

The Joneses also gave refugee families rides from the beach to the school parking lot in their small Fiat. Even though it was illegal, the heat of summer was already upon them, and they found it unbearable to watch the refugees struggle as they made the trek to Molyvos on foot, especially after their harrowing experiences crossing from Turkey. The refugees were always completely drenched when they landed, and since there were never enough dry clothes available at the beach, the seats of their Fiat were perpetually wet. Robin also ended up soaked most of the time because she would hold at least one of the children on her lap and place another on the gearshift box next to her.

Local residents of the village of Skala Sykaminias responded similarly when it, too, became overrun with refugees. Three elderly women who were lifelong residents of this unique and picturesque little village went to the harbor and adjoining beach every day to pick up refugees' wet clothes, take them home to wash and iron them, and bring them back the next morning. One of the women says, "We're poor so we didn't have much, but we gave whatever we could," to which a second woman adds, "It wasn't just us who helped. It was the whole village." The third woman says, "It's satisfying when you do a good deed for people who have suffered so much. It feels good."[7]

Eric Kempson would later grow bitter as the locals' attitudes toward the refugees and those who chose to help them became more negative, but in those early months he and Philippa often found bags of groceries marked for the refugees that villagers had left hanging on the gate at the entrance to the driveway leading up to their house in Eftalou. Most of these donations were given anonymously because some locals did not want others to know of their help. A storeowner in Molyvos, after learning that Eric needed bread, used to give him leftovers from the day before. Eric says wryly, "It was a bit stale, but it was edible." Whenever he bought a crate of water, the same store owner gave him an additional crate for free.

Eric also posted videos in which he spoke highly of people's willingness to reach out, attributing it to philoxenia, the Greek devotion to hospitality. In one of his videos he described how a local Greek man, upon learning that a boat carrying many women and children was in trouble some distance from shore, swam out and helped bring it in without casualties. Eric also spoke about how tavern owners let refugees sleep in their establishments after they had closed for the night and how local people brought food to the refugees who were congregated in the parking lot by the bus stop; they even invited them to come home with them. In the same video, he went on to state, "Even though authorities higher up are saying that you can't help the refugees, people are just stepping forth to help and defying the government to arrest them."[8]

At first, owners of dozens of hotels in the area also helped by giving out food and dry clothes or blankets. Dina remembers being at one of the hotels out at the Eftalou beach area when a refugee boat landed. She was there in response to a call from the hotel owner asking for baby clothes for children who had come in on a boat that morning. When the hotel guests sunbathing by the pool saw the boat approaching, they all ran to the edge of the water, where they lined up and waved their colored beach towels to guide it away from the rocks and straight in to the shore. Then they helped everyone get out of the boat safely. The owners of the Afrodite Hotel in Eftalou "practically turned over their hotel to the refugees at times. They laundered their clothing and put them up in some of the guest rooms, all at great cost to them personally because their clientele diminished after that."[9] The Kempsons recall how, when a boat landed on the beach close to one of the hotels, the guests and hotel staff came out to feed the children and give the refugees water. Eric and Philippa were in Molyvos that day, and by the time they heard the news and were able to get back to the hotel to help, the refugees had all been taken care of.

As time went on, however, hotel owners found themselves in a dilemma. At first, they and their guests showed compassion, particularly for the families with children who appeared on the beaches in front of their hotels, and did whatever they could to help them. However, when the number of refugees began to increase so dramatically, they lacked the capacity to offer clothing, food, or shelter to everyone, and many of their paying guests whose vacations were disrupted grew impatient and started to check out. Eventually they felt they had no choice but to keep the refugees moving along and clean up after them as quickly as possible; guests were starting to check out early and people holding future reservations were calling to cancel them. The hotel owners were afraid that their entire businesses were in jeopardy.

When tourists started to arrive at the beginning of the 2015 season, many of them also lent a hand, as did the first reporters who appeared after receiving word of the refugee crisis. Tourists were actually the first volunteers from the outside, and they played an "indispensable role" before any other help arrived.[10] Instead of spending their time on the beach or by the pools sunbathing, many tourists staying in hotels in Eftalou helped Eric and Philippa by bringing bags of food and cases of water to distribute to the refugees. As far as Eric Kempson is concerned, "all of the volunteer work helping refugees early on was done primarily by tourists," and many became quite caught up physically and emotionally with the relief effort.[11] Some even extended their stays, and some returned to Molyvos to help later in the season or the following year.

In the village, tourists' involvement predominantly started with those who frequented the Captain's Table. As soon as they saw and heard about what was going on, they pitched in—almost without hesitation—to assist Melinda with all kinds of tasks. They used their credit cards to leave money at the supermarkets for food and supplies, or they purchased what was needed at local shops and brought it to the restaurant themselves.[12] When the refrigerator in the Sandwich Factory broke down, a tourist went out and bought a new one. One couple from England, who had heard about the refugee problem before they left on vacation, brought extra suitcases full of clothing and other supplies. Another couple from Holland, who had come to Lesvos for a twelve-day vacation, stayed for another five days so they could continue working with the refugees. When they left, they pledged to raise money upon their return home to buy a car to transport refugees across the island.[13]

Michael Honegger and his partner, Timothy Smith, are what one might call "regular tourists" because they have spent every May and September in Molyvos for the past fifteen years. Many regular tourists like them come to Molyvos year after year, but Michael and Tim have developed many friendships over the years, which have deepened their connection to the area. When they arrived in Molyvos that May, the first thing they did—as has always been their custom—was to go to the Captain's Table for dinner. Melinda explained what had been going on, but they only had to look around to see that the refugee situation had already reached a fever pitch.

Michael and Tim both offered to help her at the restaurant and ended up making sandwiches every morning at dawn and taking them to the refugees who waited in the parking lot for the bus.

Recognizing Melinda's need for financial assistance to buy food and other supplies, Tim sent out appeals of his own to their friends and acquaintances, a task that he continued to perform even after they had left Molyvos at the end of May and one that he continued to work on when they returned in September. The response was so generous that he was able to pay for "tons of food and other products needed by the refugees such as hats— sixteen thousand of them—for protection from the brutally hot sun, some eight thousand rain ponchos in anticipation of fall weather, thousands of sweatpants, and a couple thousand pairs of shoes."[14] For his part, Michael went to the beach every morning after sandwich making to help guide the rubber rafts to safe landings whether it was in calm waters or pounding surf. He also handed out water, food, and blankets and tended—as best he could—to the immediate needs of the masses of arriving refugees. An avid photographer, Michael also documented the scenes in pictures that captured harrowing landings, emotional and physical suffering, as well as the spirit of triumph among many refugees for surviving the journey to Lesvos.

Tourists also were among the first to start picking up the mounds of trash accumulating on the beaches and in the roadways. Some who had rental cars brought them to the beach, specifically to drive women and children to Molyvos in defiance of the ban. Stories of tourists being stopped by the police for illegally transporting refugees circulated frequently enough to be extremely intimidating. One tourist who was working with Eric told him that she had been pulled over just as she rounded the bend near the school parking lot with her car loaded with wet refugees. The officer warned her that she would be arrested if she were caught a second time. She heeded his warning, but shortly thereafter, she received a call from her rental car agency demanding that she return the car immediately because they possessed the police report. From then on she was unable to rent another car anywhere on Lesvos. Michael was stopped while driving eight Afghan refugees to Mytilene in a van that two German women had rented for him. He was able to resist arrest by pretending that he was a tourist who spoke no Greek and could not understand what the officers wanted. However, when the proprietor of the rental car agency—a good friend of Melinda and someone whom she always recommended to many of her customers—learned that he used the van to transport refugees, he was furious, and according to Michael, it all "got quite ugly."[15] In spite of such stories, tourists remained stalwart volunteers, and in the end Eric affirmed none of them were actually arrested or jailed.[16]

Not all tourists responded favorably or helpfully. Ute described them as being "Fifty-fifty on the issue." Some tourists came to the harbor with bags of items to give to the refugees. Others did not return to the harbor after they saw what was happening. Many did not want to come at all because they found it impossible to sit and relax over their coffee or a meal with soaking wet refugees in all kinds of physical conditions all around them. Ute observed that "some tourists came to the harbor because of the situation, and some did not come because of the situation." The business in her store reflected the events in the harbor, and she believes that the same was true for all the other businesses there as well.[17]

9

The Situation in Molyvos Goes Out of Control

Summer 2015

Everything escalated in May and June to the point where the crisis became so huge that every effort seemed inadequate. The organization that Melinda and her core group had put in place functioned as envisioned, but the number of refugees continued to increase until it was beyond anything they ever could have imagined. Five hundred a day turned into six hundred. When the number approached one thousand a day, everyone thought the wave would finally crest, but it only continued to rise. The need for sandwiches skyrocketed, requiring more and more volunteers to work longer and longer hours, and even then it was a struggle to keep up with the demand. At the same time, the crew in the understaffed and ill-equipped Coast Guard office was called out on rescue missions around the clock, while the backlog of refugees waiting to be registered at their office increased. Even after locals had been enlisted to take care of registration, refugees still had to wait as long as four days, with only the water and food that Melinda and her helpers provided. Since there was nowhere else to go while they waited, the harbor overflowed with refugees, sitting and sleeping wherever they could find a space on the pavement or on the seawalls.

Meanwhile the area's roads and beaches were becoming strewn with trash as well as human waste. "Mountains of abandoned life vests and fraying black rubber dinghies began to blanket the shoreline and drift to areas of the beach that were largely inaccessible by land. Each time the tide changed, more mountains were added."[1] The beaches turned red, pink, and orange—the colors of the thousands of abandoned life vests—and the deflated dinghies took on water, making them impossible to move without a monumental effort. Boat motors not worth stealing lay every-where, leaking oil onto the sand and rocks. Big plastic bags containing the refugees' belongings that they had cast overboard to keep the boats from sinking floated in with the tides, adding to what was already on the beach and riding in the surf.[2] Mounds of rubbish accumulated everywhere so fast that all the village workers and local volunteers couldn't keep up.

In May Melinda knew that she absolutely had to do something to relieve the congestion in the harbor; it had reached the point where tourists were forced to step over refugees just to get to the stores and restaurants.[3] Human urine and feces became a serious problem. Despite efforts to refurbish the existing public toilet facilities, they were completely insufficient and refugees were left with no other choice but to relieve themselves in public areas, right in front of tourists while they were shopping and eating.[4]

Up in back of the Captain's Table, there is a small field with grass and trees, like a small plateau in the rock ledge that borders the harbor. Melinda determined that it would be large enough to set up a makeshift holding area for as many as 180 refugees.[5] Its location was far enough from the tourists that they could eat and shop more freely, and she felt it would at least allow the refugees some dignity and a little privacy to get some rest and food while waiting to be registered. Melinda approached the owner of the property and asked if she could rent it for the time being.[6] Once the owner consented, volunteers built a short flight of stairs to provide easier access to the area, hung tarpaulins, and erected tents to provide additional shade and protection from rain and the sun. They also set up tables where refugees could eat and where parents could change their children's clothes.[7] Tourists offered to donate money to pay for rent and electricity for the space, and at one point, their donations were so generous that everything was paid for six months in advance.[8]

The holding area filled completely as soon as it opened, and that sent shock waves through the village. Many people saw it as a full-fledged refugee camp right in their midst, and its presence became a sudden and graphic warning signal for the impact that the staggering number of refugees had on their lives. It revealed to everyone a situation that was already spiraling beyond control, leaving them confused, alarmed, frightened, and incensed.

They only had to look at what was taking place at the Captain's Table—the making of sandwiches and tea, the storing of supplies, the feeding of the refugees, and now what they perceived to be an actual refugee camp—to conclude that this was all largely Melinda's fault.

In their minds it seemed clear that the refugees were only there because Melinda had taken it upon herself to organize and lead efforts to welcome them. Rumors began to spread that refugees, once on shore, called their friends and families still in Turkey and told them to look for a woman named Melinda as soon as they landed. As a result the locals began to blame her for the situation and for what it would do to tourism, their economic lifeblood. Before long, the blame erupted into open hostility. Initial resistance to the holding area in back of the Captain's Table came from certain business owners in the harbor who did not share Melinda's point of view that it would help alleviate the immediate crowding that disrupted their businesses. They were furious about its location near their shops and restaurants, and they grew frightened that it would become a permanent installation. One local restaurateur, in a fit of rage over the holding area, stood in front of the Captain's Table, pointed viciously in its direction, and screamed, "Get them away from here!"[9] As the number of refugees mounted, local frustration turned into anger that quickly spread throughout the village, so much so that, after the holding area had been set up and was in full operation for some time, the pressure on the owner who had rented the land to Melinda became so intense that he finally told her to evacuate it right away.[10] It seemed that her caution in the handling of money, her efforts to buy locally, and her attempt to reduce the congestion in the harbor were all forgotten as the whole village turned against her.

Melinda was not alone in feeling people's wrath. She was the target in the village, but Eric and Philippa also endured anger, resentment, and even threats to their personal safety. Eric was frequently accosted on the beach by angry business owners screaming at him to stop helping the refugees, threatening him aggressively, and warning him of horrible consequences if he did not cease and desist. Eric, already hardened by the extent of the human suffering that he had witnessed on the beach, had little patience for their complaints and made it clear that he would not be intimidated.

Nevertheless he acknowledged the need for caution because he had captured videos of the altercations and genuinely feared that, if his assailants on the beach, all influential local businessmen, called the police and put pressure on them, they might decide that such recordings were illegal, confiscate his cell phone, and delete everything.[11]

Public ire extended to almost anyone seen helping refugees. Stratis remembers bringing in a refugee boat that the Coast Guard had called on him to rescue. That day, the Coast Guard instructed him to tow the boat to the beach near the parking lot at the other end of the village rather than the already overcrowded harbor. There were resorts along that stretch of beach, and the spot where he landed was close to the main road, so people came from all around to watch them come in. "You cannot imagine the negativity I received from everybody for bringing the boat to that beach," he says. Their reactions had a huge and lasting effect on him, and looking back on that period, he says, "I tried to help as much as I could, but there were so many refugees—thousands of them—that it got to be too much for everyone, and the village got divided."[12]

When Robin and Robert Jones returned to Molyvos that spring, they quickly caught on to the division of the village, but they always had a feeling that there was a degree of tolerance, both for the refugees and the people who helped them, at least in the early weeks and months of the crisis. The Joneses were well aware that locals on both sides of the divide, for the most part, tended to treat refugees with civility and actually did some things to help. They also sensed, at least in their part of the village, that everyone "knew who was going to the beaches to help or sneaking down to make sandwiches at six in the morning," but none of the neighbors said anything to them about it. Therefore, during that summer when they were there, each time they came back into the village from the beaches, the two of them chose to remove the yellow vests that they wore to avoid flaunting their involvement in their neighbors' faces. Even though everyone knew that they were going to the beach, they still "didn't want to advertise it."[13]

Personal, social, and economic stress and exhaustion began to set in as the summer wore on, and locals grew overwhelmed by the throngs of refugees in the harbor and exasperated by the uncontrollable accumulation of refuse, both in the streets and on the beaches. To make matters worse, they also felt that their government had abandoned them and left them to grapple with the situation on their own. Eventually their patience reached the boiling point, with verbal conflicts erupting almost daily. People paraded through the streets proclaiming, "Our city does not belong to us anymore." Vasileia Digidiki from the Center for Health and Human Rights at Harvard University posits that these altercations, most of them verbal, were rooted in "emotional" rather than "rational beliefs," and it was not uncommon for someone to be "one day seen arguing against providing assistance to the migrants and then be found helping to rescue them in times of peril."[14] Time would reveal just how deeply the emotional and rational beliefs were ingrained and the extent to which the differences would end up impacting life in the community. In the meantime many locals outside of Melinda's core group stepped forward to lend a hand, finding it simply impossible to just do nothing, while others railed angrily against them.[15]

The diverging viewpoints and the growing antagonism against the refugees and those helping them were not confined to Molyvos or Lesvos as a whole. They reflected a split along liberal and conservative lines that swept over all of Europe and had a particularly powerful impact on Greece because of the severe economic crisis that rattled the country. On the liberal side the refugee issues were viewed from a humanitarian perspective, one shared by Melinda, her family and friends, the Kempsons, and the tourists who pitched in to help. Those who held that point of view focused on the conditions in the countries that forced people to flee their homes; the brutally long and difficult treks, including the water crossings that refugees had to make; and the recognition that they desperately sought safety and a better life for their families. Their position was further bolstered by their confidence that the economy of the EU was strong enough to accommodate the current migration. In Greece the liberal perspective was also connected to the basic sense of Greek philoxenia, the sensitivity to the needs of strangers—in this particular case, refugees—that dated from the time of Greek migration during the Greco-Turkish War.

The conservative stance emerged prior to 2012 with the beginning of the economic downturn and resulting austerity that swept across Europe and led to the rise of far-right extremist groups that either viewed immigration as a political opportunity or a primary cause for the continent's economic and social malaise. Among those groups were factions that went as far as to claim that immigration was gradually leading to the loss of national identity. In defense of their position, the factions cited the difficulties that the authorities had to face when dealing with all the migrants: the possibility of infectious diseases that refugees might spread; the unsanitary conditions that having so many people in one place created, particularly in urban centers and at border crossings; and the "downgrading" of residential areas that was caused by the construction of temporary housing needed to accommodate the influx of refugees.

In Greece these ideological differences were further magnified by its own economic crisis and the harsh austerity imposed on the country by its European creditors, particularly Germany. The refugee crisis could not have come at a worse time with the country "teetering on the verge of total economic collapse," threatening its ability to maintain its national infrastructure or take care of its own people, many of whom lived in poverty and could not even afford housing. Deep cuts had been made in government services and benefits that placed serious hardships on its citizens and provoked intense anger and opposition that threatened to derail Greece's relationship with the rest of the EU. In Molyvos there was the additional and ultimate concern about the negative impact that refugees had on tourism and people's livelihoods.[16] An ultranationalist group, Golden Dawn, gained a foothold in Greek politics with its slogan: "Get the stench out of Greece," referring to the growing immigrant presence, specifically targeting the 1.5 million refugees and migrants coming from the Middle East, South Asia, and Africa. Golden Dawn members—operating largely on Greece's mainland but with an increasing presence throughout the islands as well—promoted the concept of "Greece for Greeks" and allegedly with the help of the police, vented their anger at immigrants by carrying out vicious personal attacks, smashing market stalls, and breaking the windows of immigrant-owned shops.[17]

Vasileia Digidiki asserts that the policies of "open borders" and the "absence of maritime borders" announced by the new Greek government when it came to power in January 2015 gave the green light for migration across this four-mile stretch of sea between Turkey and Lesvos. While these policies adhered to the Geneva Convention and seemed admirable from a humanitarian perspective, Digidiki also claims that they were fundamentally flawed in that no provisions were set forth to deal with the massive flow of refugees that they generated. Under these circumstances, it was inevitable that the consequences would ultimately fall on "the shoulders of the native populations who were forced to assume the burden of caring for hundreds of thousands of migrants without proper preparation or infrastructure."[18]

Molyvos might not have succumbed to these national sentiments and turned against itself so intensely were it not for what seemed like an isolated struggle for survival with no outside help. Everyone found themselves in a state of utter disbelief that the immensity of the crisis had not brought the world to their doorstep. In news reports they had seen of disasters elsewhere—domestic and international—resources were always rushed to aid the victims and those who helped, but in Molyvos there was nothing, not even from their own country or the EU. In fact there was not even any media coverage. From their perspective it was clearly an international humanitarian crisis, spawned by a political and military conflict that should have at least summoned the United Nations and international aid organizations like the Red Cross, but there was nothing.

Their plight was not due to a lack of effort in trying to spread the word. Michael and Tim posted hundreds of pictures and narratives on Facebook in an attempt to alert the world to the unfolding crisis. They also sent out appeals for help to media organizations and their vast network of friends and acquaintances. In fact their postings informed people of the crisis long before there was any mention of it whatsoever in newspapers, on television, or even in online publications. Had it not been for Michael's steadfast and meticulous photographic documentation, it is safe to say that it would have taken far longer for people beyond Lesvos to grasp the enormity of what was happening. Eric Kempson used his cell phone to film and narrate hundreds of landings on Eftalou in real time, and he posted well over four hundred videos on the internet in which he pleaded for someone to take notice and come to their aid.[19] In addition he made repeated personal appeals to everyone he could think of, including such organizations as Save the Children and the Red Cross, among others.[20]

As a German citizen, Ute sent emails to German television stations describing the crisis and asking that someone come to Molyvos to report on developments firsthand. Given her perception of Germany's sensitivity to refugee matters, particularly those supported by Chancellor Angela Merkel, she felt that her requests were not only reasonable but that they would be heeded and bring reporters right away. To her surprise and dismay, the answers she received—probably a reflection of the political instability gripping Germany—essentially stated that "so much was happening in the world that they could not respond to every situation."[21] Everyone's appeals for help were made in the hope of communicating to the outside world the magnitude of what was happening in Molyvos and in the belief that, once the word had spread beyond Lesvos, the help that was so desperately needed would come. In the end they were all bewildered and disappointed by the lack of response.

In June, after receiving reports of the growing refugee presence on the Greek islands, representatives of the United Nations High Commissioner for Refugees (UNHCR) came to Mytilene, the capital, and then made a trip north to Molyvos. During their brief visit Melinda was able to show them everything firsthand and stress the urgent need for help. They informed her that the UNHCR's applications to work in Greece were denied on the grounds that this was a European matter and, as such, was not deemed an emergency. Apparently the same was true for other international aid organizations attempting to come to Greece.[22] They also told Melinda that their help would have come immediately if the crisis had occurred in a third world country.[23] And so the days and weeks passed with still no help from the outside. Robert and Robin Jones talk of how, when they were sitting on the balcony of their house, they would jump at the sound of a helicopter and frantically search the sky, hoping that someone was finally arriving with help. But for months there was no one.[24]

By the beginning of June the situation in Molyvos was out of control. Dionisis describes the scene as follows: "There were so many refugees crowded into the small area of the harbor where they had to register that there was simply not enough room, not enough square feet, in which to fit all of them. There was not enough space for them to sit or stand or walk. There were no toilets, no washstands, and no sanitary facilities available to handle this number of people. Every resource—human, physical, and financial—was being strained to the breaking point. The throng of refugees began to spill out of the harbor and extend all the way up the road along the cliff and out to the entrance to the village by the bus stop and the elementary school. It was akin to a tsunami of people so overwhelming in size that it left everyone feeling helpless in its wake."[25] Locals were too frightened to even imagine what might happen to their village, or even to the whole of Lesvos, if it were to continue. Eri Grigorelli said that, at one point, she looked up the population of Syria to see how many more could be expected to arrive because "it seemed as if all of Syria was landing in Molyvos."[26]

Adding to their nightmare were the rumors of an estimated four million refugees in Lebanon and Turkey waiting to make the crossing to Lesvos's north shore.[27] Looking back Robert Jones says that it was "an invasion as far as everyone was concerned, and it was way too long before any help came." He believes that "everyone could have handled it for a week or a month or two, but it continued to crescendo relentlessly to the point where it all grew truly terrifying."[28]

In a desperate attempt to reduce the unmanageable congestion that overran the harbor, the Coast Guard began bringing only the worst cases there: refugees who were sick, drowning, or who had already died. All others were taken by boat directly to the port of Mytilene, which also struggled with its own huge refugee flow. Ultimately Greek Coast Guard ensign Chrisafis Theofilos concluded that, with refugees numbering in the tens of thousands, the situation had reached a crisis level that his crew could no longer handle. In spite of his repeated pleas to the authorities, no additional help or aid had been forthcoming, and they were left without equipment or supplies that were essential to their search and rescue operations. In May he requested and was granted permission for the Molyvos office to stop registering the refugees arriving from the beaches.[29] From then on, only refugees rescued at sea and brought in directly by the Coast Guard after their boats capsized could be registered in the harbor.

Unable to register, the refugees on the beaches no longer had access to any form of transportation, not even the buses that had been provided by the police to take them to Mytilene—those were stopped altogether. This, coupled with the law banning refugees from all public and private transportation, left them with no other option but to make the extraordinarily long and difficult sixty-kilometer journey all the way from Molyvos to Mytilene on foot in the brutal heat of the beating summer sun. Eric Kempson called it a veritable "death march." Melinda said that, from that moment on, "everything changed." When she uttered those words, it was with a solemnity and a finality that signaled this was a turning point in the crisis that consumed their village and their lives.[30]

12. Clothes and shoes laid out everywhere to dry in the Molyvos harbor. The lone public toilet can be seen in the background. Courtesy of Michael S. Honegger.

13. Refugees wait in line just across the street from the school parking lot to board a bus to Camp Moria. Molyvos Castle is in the background. Courtesy of Michael S. Honegger.

14. Melinda and Theo deliver trays of sandwiches and boxes containing fruit and water to the parking lot in Molyvos. Courtesy of Michael S. Honegger.

15. The empty school parking lot on the morning after the fence was erected to prevent refugees from entering. Courtesy of Michael S. Honegger.

16. The blue tourist train from Petra passes through as refugees congregate by the school parking lot after the fence was erected. Courtesy of Michael S. Honegger.

17. Philippa Kempson at the Hope Project warehouse, where refugees go to receive clothing and supplies. © Nikolas Georgiou.

18. Eric Kempson carries a package of donated supplies that has just arrived at the warehouse from the United Kingdom. © Nikolas Georgiou.

19. Refugees' artwork hangs everywhere on the walls of the studio that the Kempsons have set up at the Hope Project warehouse. © Nikolas Georgiou.

10

A Long, Hot Summer

The Death March and the Caravan

The route from Molyvos to Mytilene—sixty kilometers south across two mountain ranges—begins at the elementary school parking lot on the eastern end of the village and is joined by the coastal road leading in from Eftalou and the upper road from Skala Sykaminias. From there it makes its winding way west past a number of commercial buildings—including a tiny strip mall, an auto rental, and a tourist agency—a couple of gas stations, and car repair shops, all located just on the outskirts of Molyvos. There are a few turn-offs onto unpaved local lanes that lead to hotels along the beach. Then the road rises several hundred feet above the sea, where it begins to hug the panoramic six miles of coastline to neighboring Petra, a small naval port and amiable, sun-drenched, beachside resort village, whose streets are lined with restaurants, enticing shops, small hotels, and rooming houses, all catering to the summer tourists. During the season a funky, multi-carriage sightseeing trolley called the Blue Train carries tourists back and forth between the two villages.

Shortly after entering Petra, the road makes a left turn and heads due south away from the shore. Within a few kilometers it begins a tortuous ascent with sharp hairpin turns leading up into the mountain range that separates the north shore from the rest of the island. It is a two-lane highway that requires drivers to exercise extreme caution because the terrain leaves little room for a shoulder and barely enough clearance in each lane for two cars to pass when they meet, much less two freight trucks, especially on the turns with limited visibility. Near the top of its ascent the road passes the left turn to Stypsi—the location of one of Lesvos's olive presses—and continues on past sheep and cattle farms and dense olive groves. There are places where the winding roadway descends abruptly into steep-banked ravines and then suddenly rises once again to rolling fields and pastures scattered with black volcanic rocks that look as if they have been strewn by a recent eruption. When the road reaches the southern side of the mountain range, it starts its equally steep and panoramic descent to a vast plain and the small city of Kalloni, which sits on the shore of the Gulf of Kalloni. This is a large but shallow bay that emerges from the Aegean and forms the vast salt flats that are filled with Lesvos's storied flocks of pink flamingos. At this point, it is still another thirty-five kilometers by car to Mytilene but on a wider and more modern road that skirts the salt flats and then ascends majestically into yet another mountain range before it drops down to the Geras Gulf for its final approach into Mytilene.

Drivers who dare to take their eyes off the road during the ninety-minute trip are treated to breathtaking vistas. It is hard to imagine that this one island of Lesvos could possibly be large enough to contain such vast expanses of territory. The thin layer of topsoil on the fields along the road yields lush greenery in the spring when the new leaves and fresh grasses emerge after the dampness and chill of winter. In the middle of summer the sun scorches the vegetation almost to oblivion, leaving the landscape barren and dusty against the hazy blue sky. Yet there are sheep and cattle grazing. Spread out across the mountainsides and valleys are thousands of hectares of olive trees that extend all the way to the top of slopes so steep and rocky that only donkeys can navigate them to transport the fall harvest, which produces some of the world's finest olive oil.

Small villages are perched precariously on the mountainsides, with commanding views of the valleys below. They evoke halcyon visions of fairytales, complete with castles, stone houses, vegetable gardens, flowers, and barns with haylofts and stables. Travelers who take detours to explore some of these villages discover that there is actually a real touch of the idyll in their shaded village squares, with shops and cafes where the older generation of men gather on hot summer afternoons to chat and drink ouzo for which Lesvos is well known. This is also where everyone in the village comes together on evenings and weekends for conversation, music, and good food.

This road from Molyvos to Mytilene is one that residents of Molyvos know well. It is the principal artery for all traffic heading toward the southern part of the island, and as such, it is their connection to the outside world. Nearly everyone with a car makes the trip regularly, and drivers of taxis, buses, emergency vehicles, and delivery trucks often make the run more than once a day. In May 2015, when the Coast Guard office in the harbor began to register only refugees rescued at sea, all other new arrivals landing on the beaches—then numbering in the thousands—were forced to walk that route to get to Mytilene, the only place on the entire island where they could register. For them it was another cruelly painful obstacle in their already harrowing migration. The Lesvos summer and its long days of hot sun and temperatures hovering around one hundred degrees Fahrenheit had already begun. With police buses no longer running and all other forms of transportation legally forbidden, the thousands of refugees—already exhausted from their long, death-defying journeys from their homelands— were left with no other option but to make the long and extremely difficult journey to Mytilene on foot, a trek that usually took at least forty-eight hours for those who were able-bodied enough to walk at a steady pace.[1]

Day and night the refugees lined the entire length of the route. Count- less adults as well as children who had lost their shoes in the sea struggled along wearing ill-fitting footwear, if they had any at all. One young girl, whose shoes had fallen off during the crossing and who had sliced the bottoms of her feet on the rocks while landing on the beach, faced having to walk shoeless until a volunteer gave her a pair of socks.[2] Parents carried their babies and small children when they were unable to walk any farther. Added to their already impossible burden were the bags containing any belongings that had not been tossed overboard in some futile attempt to save their boats from sinking. Those suffering from wounds or other medical conditions—the elderly and people with crutches or canes or those in wheelchairs—had to muster the strength to navigate the steep hills and sharp bends with only occasional help from fellow refugees who were struggling themselves.

During the night, when there was a respite from the intense daytime heat, the refugees still inched forward through the unknown terrain in total darkness, fearful that they would either wander off the road and lose their way or become separated from family members. Occasionally refugees carried lanterns that had been given to them by passing motorists, but they were more effective as warnings to approaching cars than they were as beacons to light the way. During the day there was little hope of finding shaded areas where they could rest from the relentless sun. At every turn in the road—from Molyvos to Mytilene—locals and tourists alike encountered refugees by the thousands, all making their miserable way without water or food, unless they took the juice and sandwiches that Melinda and her helpers distributed back in Molyvos. Even then those were minimal rations and would not have sustained anyone for very long under such conditions. Drivers reported seeing refugees huddling in small patches of woods along the way, trying to stay cool, while others pled for water or desperately tried to stop cars, hoping that they might be given a ride.[3]

Their destination—still known to them only by name—was Moria, a refugee transit camp located just outside of a small village by the same name, a short distance north of Mytilene. Originally registration was done by the Coast Guard at their offices in the harbor of Mytilene next to the docks from which the ferries to Athens depart. In 2014, with joint funding from the EU and the Greek government, Camp Moria—once a military base— was converted to a short-term holding center for asylum seekers waiting to be transferred to the Greek mainland, and the registration process was moved from the harbor to the camp.[4] At first, like the refugees registered by the Coast Guard in Molyvos, the refugees registering at Moria were then transported in police buses to the port where they would buy their ferry tickets to Athens. However, come May 2015—as the numbers grew and the Coast Guard stopped registering migrants in Molyvos—Moria became the only registration point on the whole island of Lesvos. This created a bottleneck in the process, resulting in refugees being detained for longer and longer periods of time in Moria while they waited to be registered one by one.

A large, imposing gate looms over the entrance to Moria, and the solid brick walls and mesh wire fence that surround the original compound give it the appearance not only of the military installation that it once was but of a prison. When the camp opened in 2014, it was initially designed to accommodate a maximum of seven hundred people, but eventually, by the summer and fall of 2015, with refugees pouring in by the thousands every day, it quickly became so densely crowded that tents had to be pitched on the inhospitably rough, hilly, and dry terrain outside of the main fenced-off area.

In that area outside of Moria's walls, refugees traveling alone were housed in large tents that, in order to accommodate their huge numbers, were filled with two-tiered bunk beds the width of camping cots. Each one was separated from its neighbor by a tarp and placed closely together in rows, running from one end of the long tent to the other. Their cots were the only personal space they had, and that is where they not only slept but where they also stored their belongings. While the lower bunks were less exposed and therefore offered greater privacy, they had little air circulation, which made them stifling in the summer. The upper bunks, on the other hand, had somewhat better ventilation, but they were completely exposed with little in the way of either privacy or security. However, refugees claimed that theft was not a problem inside the tents.

Families traveling with children and older family members were housed in domed, cabin-style tents, usually with several families in each one. There was no electricity in that outlying area, and there was no place to cook except for designated spots where they could have an open fire. Refugees had to pass through the front gate or crawl through holes in the fences to get food in the main facility. None of the tents had water or lavatories, so everyone had to use the toilet facilities that were sparsely scattered outside. Some were a considerable distance from the tents, which made them difficult to reach, especially at night without any lighting. As a result there were reports of refugees, women in particular, regularly developing urinary tract infections because they feared venturing out alone at night to use the toilets.[5]

Watching the parade of human misery that wound its way from Molyvos over those hills to Moria in the sweltering heat soon became unbearable for locals and tourists alike. People began to load their vehicles with bottles of water and drive along the road, handing them out to all of the refugees. When they ran out, they replenished their supply and headed back out onto the road once again. Recalling that period of time, Robert and Robin Jones say, "We did not go anywhere without filling our car with bottles of water, bananas, and cases of fruit to hand out along the road. And once our supplies were exhausted, we'd go back to get more."⁶ Michael and Tim did the same, as did Eric and Philippa, Dionisis, Dina, Ilektra on her motorcycle, and anyone else closely connected to Melinda's small group of helpers. Before long this effort became widespread, as locals and tourists, as well as taxi drivers and truckers, began filling every inch of available space in their vehicles with bottles of water to distribute. Many people reported that they kept this up day and night, hoping to reduce the hardship of the refugees' trek. There is no doubt that their efforts ended up saving many lives, but everyone involved refers to this period as one of the worst experiences of the entire crisis.⁷

Meanwhile a priest in Kalloni, Father Efstratios Dimou, also known as "Papa Stratis," set up the one and only oasis along the route. Although he was dying of cancer at the time, Papa Stratis created an NGO called Agkalia, meaning "hug" in Greek, and collected money and resources that enabled him and his team of volunteers to hand out food and water, provide basic medical aid, and pray with all of the refugees coming through. In a time of very mixed viewpoints regarding the refugees, Papa Stratis proclaimed, "We have to recognize that these people have the same problems; they are thirsty and starving and ill. They also have their own God, their own ethics, and their own traditions. We have to respect them and give them strength to carry on in their lives." That year Papa Stratis worked right up until the day he died, and Agkalia fed and clothed over six thousand refugees.⁸

The main street out of Molyvos and the road leading in from Eftalou both meet near the elementary school and the bus stop. It was the main intersection that all refugees passed through when they came in from the beaches after landing and from the harbor after registering with the Coast Guard. The parking lot at that intersection became a central meeting point for refugees coming and going. Then when refugees coming in from the beaches could no longer be registered in the harbor and there were no police buses, the school parking lot remained the place where large numbers of them congregated before starting their long walk to Moria. It was an open space bordered by some shade trees where they could rest, and the presence of the bus stop may have suggested the possibility, though remote, that someone might come along and offer them a ride.

Once Melinda and the people working with her learned that the parking lot had become the refugees' primary gathering place, they went there to hang tarpaulins from the trees to give added shade from the intensely hot summer sun and hand out water and sandwiches. Volunteers—mostly tourists—chose to spend time in the parking lot helping with the distribution of food and water. They also hung maps on the trees and gave directions for the walk to Mytilene. When the refugees learned that there was some kind of help available, even more of them began to stop there before continuing toward Moria. For a brief time at least, this lessened the congestion in the harbor just enough to bring some relief to the tourists as well as the restaurant and shop owners.[9] However, as more and more refugees began to congregate in the parking lot, the lack of toilet facilities eventually led to the same kind of overcrowding and unsanitary conditions there as had existed in the harbor. Melinda knew that, ultimately, the only remedy for the situation in both the harbor and the parking lot was to find a place for the refugees that removed them from the village entirely.

There came a point where Dionisis could no longer tolerate the misery that the law prohibiting the transportation of refugees was inflicting on the thousands forced to make the long journey on foot. Seeing their inhumane struggle became too much for him to endure. As a forceful individual with a talent for organization that dated as far back as 2008, when the local group of friends that he was a part of first began to help refugees, he took it upon himself to mobilize a convoy of cars to drive refugees from Molyvos to Mytilene. Dionisis envisioned it as a large, "symbolic procession" of forty to fifty vehicles, all filled with refugees being transported in open defiance of the law. He figured that if the cars traveled together in one long procession, the police would have a difficult time stopping them all and that this overt "power move" involving so many people would bring widespread public attention to the law's depravity and hopefully lead to its eventual repeal. He only had to mention it once to Melinda and his group of long-time friends to gain their overwhelming encouragement and support.[10]

Dionisis put out a call asking drivers who were willing to be involved to gather on Friday, May 22, on one of the shady side streets where refugees could be loaded into the waiting cars without blocking commercial traffic. That morning, cars driven by locals, long-time residents, and tourists began to pull up along the curb, and the loading process began. Some tourists even rented cars just so they could participate in the convoy—bringing the estimated total to forty-one drivers.[11] Loading priority was assigned much like the distribution of water on the beach: pregnant women and women with children first, followed by the infirm, and finally men, as space allowed. Some forty men, all of them young and fit, insisted on walking.[12]

Eric Kempson was there that day with his trusty camera, and in the film that he posted on YouTube, Dionisis can be seen overseeing the loading of the cars, going back and forth, making sure that all women and children had a ride, and telling the passengers to fasten their seat belts. For his part, Eric's voice can be heard extolling the virtues of Greek philoxenia, praising the volunteer drivers, and proclaiming that this is how good people should act in the face of injustice.[13] Once the cars were loaded, the convoy slowly pulled away from the curb, forming a steady line to prevent any drivers unfamiliar with the road from getting separated from the group. All together and uninterrupted, they made their way out of Molyvos and along the coastal road to Petra. There they made the left turn and began the steep and tortuous climb south over the mountains and down into Kalloni, passing by Papa Stratis's outpost and crossing the salt flats. The procession continued up and over the next mountain range, and ninety minutes and thirty miles from its start, it slowly and intently made its way to the front gate of Camp Moria.

The convoy succeeded in sending a powerful message to the government that the despised transportation law was untenable, but its real impact would not be felt until some two and a half weeks later. In the meantime reports circulated of people being arrested for transporting refugees and refugees being "herded" out of town with pickup trucks, all suggesting that nothing had changed.[14] If anything the existing law still appeared to be very much in effect and strongly enforced, despite the convoy. However, on June 8, 2015, the Greek government announced a lift on the transportation ban effective immediately.[15] From that point on, refugees were permitted to board buses and travel in taxis and privately owned vehicles. In addition, to help ensure the law's implementation, the police also issued a statement asking drivers who planned to transport refugees to supply them with their cars' license numbers, which were then placed on an approved list to prevent any unwarranted interference.[16]

Once the transportation law was repealed, people could give rides to refugees without fear of legal reprisal, but huge numbers still had to walk, and people continued to supply them with water and food along the route just as they had before. Like many others, Robin and Robert Jones had always given rides to refugees, but now they could comfortably and openly drive them to wherever they were going. However, it was all but impossible to accommodate many people in their small Fiat at one time. This meant that when they stopped to pick up a group of refugees on the road, they often had to choose who would ride with them. Robin says that she "would never want to go through that again" because it was utterly excruciating to separate families with fathers and mothers carrying their small children, or family members with canes, crutches, or wheelchairs. They gave women and children priority, but in an effort to avoid splitting families up, they always promised to come back for the others. Yet by the time they had driven part of the family to their destination and returned to pick up the rest, it was extremely difficult to locate them among the crowds along the road. On one occasion a little girl volunteered to ride back with them to help find her family. That trip was fraught with anxiety as they drove, searching for the faces of the girl's family among the masses of people along the route. Almost miraculously they located them and the family was reunited, but few were willing to take that risk, for fear of becoming permanently separated from their loved ones.[17]

Unfortunately not all of the drivers offering rides were motivated by good intentions. There were reports of scamming incidents in which drivers charged refugees hundreds of euros for a trip to Mytilene but would drop them off on some side road and steal all their belongings. Eric and Philippa Kempson claim that this practice was largely restricted to islanders, but rumor had it that the malicious practice was more widespread.[18]

Then came the unexpected! On June 25, 2015—eleven days after the Greek government ordered an end to the transportation ban—Amnesty International issued a press release that began with the following headline: "Greece: Humanitarian Crisis Mounts as Refugee Support System Pushed to Breaking Point." The press release went on to state, "Tens of thousands of vulnerable people making the perilous sea journeys to escape war or poverty arrive on the islands only to be met by a support system on its knees." Also included was a call for Europe's leaders to address the growing "global refugee crisis" at an EU summit that was to convene the very next day, June 26.[19] The release of Amnesty International's statement was likely due, in no small part, to the photographs and narratives that Michael and Tim had shared so widely online, but it was momentous in that it was the first official statement by an international organization, the long-awaited and hoped-for clarion call, drawing attention to the burgeoning refugee crisis on Lesvos and neighboring Greek islands.[20]

For the locals, particularly those working closely with the refugees, the convoy's success was a source of real encouragement. Up to this point, despite their repeated pleas for help and their unrelenting efforts to spread the word about the crisis in Molyvos, they had always felt ignored by the media, their government, and aid organizations. Now for the first time their actions had captured public attention and caused the Greek government to address the conditions that were devastating the region. Not only that but right on the heels of the government's action came Amnesty International's announcement to the world. At last, the word was out, and those on the island had reason to hope that the desperately needed help would finally arrive.

Help did come. Within only a few weeks, volunteers from other countries—after hearing word of the crisis—began to appear in Lesvos and make their way to Molyvos, where they looked for Melinda and Eric and Philippa, having learned about them from website postings or through inquiries with UNHCR. Finally toward the end of July, a month after Amnesty International's call to action, Doctors Without Borders/Médecins Sans Frontières (MSF) became the first international aid organization to arrive in Molyvos, with the UNHCR following shortly thereafter.[21] Their first act was providing funds for buses to transport refugees to Moria. That was met with a huge sigh of relief, but by then the volume of people needing transportation had grown so great that the number of buses was inadequate right from the start, and large numbers of refugees still ended up either making the trek on foot or congregating in long lines in the parking lot, waiting for buses to show up.

11

Skala Sykaminias

The Crisis Spreads

Refugee boats from Turkey had always headed in the direction of Molyvos and the beach near Eftalou, but starting that May, when the Coast Guard stopped registering refugees in the harbor, it was no longer necessary for them to go there, and more and more boats began to either land on the eastern end of the beach or come directly into the small harbor of Skala Sykaminias. Prior to that time, Skala Sykaminias had been spared much of the impact of the refugee migration. In fact when large numbers of refugees started to appear there, the residents assumed that the entire drama was unfolding in their village, unaware that boats of refugees had been arriving in Molyvos since the previous November.[1] When Melinda learned that refugees were going to Skala Sykaminias, she sent some of her volunteers there to help.

The addition of the word "skala" to the name of a place generally means that it is a small harbor located at the base of a steep escarpment. In this case, Skala Sykaminias—referred to by many in the area simply as Skala—is a picture-perfect fishing village, much smaller than Molyvos, that sits quietly at the edge of the Aegean about eight kilometers to the east. There are two roads that people use to travel between Molyvos and Skala: the road that follows the coast and the high road that winds through the mountains a few kilometers to the south. The coastal road goes through Eftalou past the hotels, and just a short distance beyond the turn-off to the Kempsons' compound, it veers sharply upward into the hills, where it changes abruptly into a rough, gravelly dirt road with a washboard surface, hairpin turns, and unnerving inclines. From there it inches eastward, sometimes at sea level and sometimes at dizzying heights along the edges of cliffs that plunge down to the beaches below. Eventually the road makes a steep descent and levels out as it nears the shore passing olive groves surrounded by stone walls on the land side. On the other side, the sea is so close that waves often wash up onto the pavement. The final kilometer into Skala is a narrow but pleasant, tree-lined roadway leading to the village square.

The second route is a much easier drive, though equally dramatic as it reaches even higher elevations, offering still broader panoramas of the sea and Turkey. It is from one of those lofty vantage points that Lighthouse Relief—one of the emergency response and refugee relief organizations stationed in Skala Sykaminias—has maintained a lookout, where trained volunteers keep their binoculars and infrared cameras focused on the sea in a twenty-four-hour-a-day vigil, monitoring any refugee boats moving off the Turkish coast. Like the lower road, it, too, rises and falls in the mountainous terrain. It also has plenty of sharp turns but is graded, paved, and wide enough to allow standard passenger vehicles as well as trucks and buses to navigate comfortably and safely. A short distance beyond the mountain village of Sykaminias, travelers to the seaside village of Skala Sykaminias leave the highway and begin a precipitous descent along a treacherously steep and winding narrow road that ends abruptly in the village square.

Whichever route one takes to get to Skala Sykaminias, once under the trees of the square, one cannot help but feel enchanted by its inviting restaurants, enticing gift shops, and the small fishing boats that bob gently at their moorings in the rippling waters of its little harbor. In the morning when the fishermen are about to set sail, there is always a bustle of activity as they load bait and other provisions onto their boats and check the nets before making their way out to the open water. Later in the day, after they have returned to the harbor, they stand on the decks of their vessels in the late afternoon sun, removing their catch from the nets, and occasionally tossing a fish to the eager harbor cats, or they sit quietly on the pavement holding one strand of netting tightly with their bare toes while they repair the broken threading with their hands.

Perched on top of a high rock that forms a natural barrier, protecting the harbor from the wind and waves coming in from the sea, sits the Mermaid

Madonna Church. This small but prominent white structure is visible from every vantage point, whether one is approaching Skala on the coastal road or the high road, gazing at it from the shade of the trees in the village square, or standing on the piers where the boats are moored. A modest stairway carved into the rock leads up to the flat open area on which the church is built. From there one can look down into the deep azure blue of the Aegean Sea. The church's elegant but simple hand-carved wood interior and the colorful icons adorning its walls are lit only by a few candles on a small altar and the rays of sun streaming through the yellow-hued stained-glass windows. It might be said that the church symbolizes how close this part of Europe is to its Byzantine neighbors, spiritually and culturally, as well as geographically, and its location overlooking the harbor and the sea made it a prominent backdrop in Skala's own refugee crisis. Before long, boatloads of refugees inundated the little village and, just as in Molyvos, turned its calm normality into chaos despite the valiant and compassionate efforts of its townspeople.

The Coast Guard crew in Molyvos was already being called out at every hour of the day and night, but now—with refugee boats coming in along the entire length of the island's northernmost shoreline, stretching from Molyvos to Skala—the scope of their rescue operations doubled. This forced them to rely more and more on fishermen and civilian boat owners from both ports for help. Fishermen from Molyvos had already grown accustomed to making rescues, either on their own when they encountered beleaguered dinghies on the sea or when they were summoned by the Coast Guard. The fishermen of Skala had certainly seen their share of refugees over the years, but it was June 2015 before they were officially called upon to make rescues on a regular basis. That was when they first came face to face with the level of distress experienced by the refugees out on the open water.

A fisherman from Skala named Thanassis remembers how calls from the Coast Guard often came at night, when conditions were most dangerous and the need for help was the greatest. He describes how motors would break down, leaving the passengers stranded at sea with waves falling over the sides of the boats while people started to drown. "It was mind-boggling," he says. "We were fishing for people instead of fish." Another fisherman—Pinteris, also from Skala—recalls how he would hear refugees calling or whistling to him for help from the water. Desperate to save themselves, they jumped in and tried to swim to the shore, but the waves and the cold water overcame them, and many were nearly drowning when he pulled them onto his boat. "Madness" he calls it.[2]

Pinteris remembers one night, when fishing for calamari, he found a man trying to swim to shore wearing one of the defective life jackets. When he pulled him out of the water, the man's arms were bleeding, probably from his long struggle with the life jacket. On yet another night, another fisherman by the name of Kostas came to the aid of a boat that was stranded after its motor fell off. It was riding dangerously low in the water, and the passengers were panic-stricken. Other fishing boats joined in the rescue effort, and together they loaded all of the refugees onto their boats and brought them to shore. As the passengers were getting out, one of them handed Kostas a small child to hold while he made his way to the safety of the beach. When Kostas went to hand the child back to the refugee, he refused to take it, claiming that he did not know to whom it belonged. Stunned, Kostas couldn't help but wonder whether the family, hoping that their child could escape from torture and death at home, had actually sent it ahead all alone or whether the man really was the child's father and he was trying to save it from the agony of migration by giving it a better life right away. Whatever the true story might have been, Kostas called what the man did "a serious act of despair."[3]

As the summer wore on, dozens and dozens of boats could be seen leaving the Turkish coast at any one time, especially during daylight hours, but the volunteers working along the beach knew that the pace did not lessen after dark either. Eventually there were so many boats crossing at the same time that it looked like a flotilla that needed the full expanse of coastline to land. Photographs taken that summer and fall show boats lining the beach as far as the eye could see.[4] The refugee crisis engulfed the entire north coast of Lesvos.

The same dramatic events that had been playing out for months on the Molyvos end of the beach were now repeated at the other end, in Skala Sykaminias: dangerously overcrowded and unseaworthy rubber dinghies with unreliable motors, defective life vests, and perilous and terrifying crossings that often ended in injury or death. Local volunteers guided boats ashore, distributed water, food, and dry clothing, and tried to attend to the refugees' emotional and physical needs. Even the Kempsons and their volunteers worked at that end of the beach. Once the refugees landed, people would direct them to take the shore road east to Skala. They had to make their way on foot along the coastal road that—like the road on the western end leading to Molyvos—was hot and almost unbearably dusty in the summer and turned chilly and slippery in the winter months. The refuges heading to Skala were also completely drenched, and many were shoeless; they were traumatized by the boat crossing, and unsure of where they had arrived. The story was much the same, just with a different landing spot.

Once in Skala, refugees faced the long, hard climb on foot up to the intersection of the main highway where they had to wait for one of the buses provided by the MSF and the UNHCR to take them to Moria. The bus drivers refused to take their buses down the steep road into the village, but sympathetic tourists and locals, including farmers in their trucks, drove many refugees up to the intersection. There they were met by Melinda's volunteers, who gave them food and beverages and oversaw the boarding of the buses once they arrived.[5]

Melinda's volunteers drove over from Molyvos in teams of two or three, their cars loaded with sandwiches, water, fruit, milk, juice, cups, diapers, biscuits, Band-Aids, and baby food—many things the refugees needed, even medication for any children with a fever or a sore throat. They usually took the upper road rather than the rough shore road from Molyvos because it was faster, and it also brought them directly to the intersection at the top of the hill where the refuges were waiting in a small pull-off area. "Chaotic" is the word that Kira, one of the volunteers, uses to describe the scene that she and her companions encountered each time they arrived from Molyvos. There was so little room in the pull-off area that everyone—even families with small children—was "camped out all along the road, sitting on pieces of cardboard or on what remained of their life vests." People clustered around a small roadside fountain to bathe or brush their teeth—if they had the means to do so; no toilets or showers were available to them down in Skala.[6]

Meanwhile the situation in the Molyvos harbor continued to worsen. The Coast Guard's standard practice had been to transport all refugees who were rescued at sea, dead or alive, back to their headquarters in the harbor, but those rescues became so frequent that the Coast Guard was forced to abandon that procedure. Instead only those refugees who were seriously injured, incapacitated, or dead were taken back to the harbor; the rest of the survivors were transferred to boats that took them directly to Mytilene. In spite of this change, the harbor remained overrun with the number of refugees coming into Molyvos, and Melinda and her volunteers no longer had the resources or the capacity to divide their time between the two places. She continued to provide food for the refugees and oversee the loading of buses in Skala Sykaminias, but only until she was able to train people from there to take over.

12

The Parking Lot by the School

August and September 2015

The repeal of the transportation ban did nothing to stem the tide of refugee arrivals, nor did it in any way alter the Coast Guard's decision to stop registering refugees in Molyvos; they still had to make the long walk to Moria to be registered. It was now early August, and the steady stream of refugees landing on the beaches had already surpassed a thousand each day and was still growing. The roads leading from the beaches to the village and over the mountains to Mytilene overflowed with refugees on foot. Although MSF and the UNHCR had provided buses, there were too few of them, and waits of several hours were not uncommon. Sometimes none came at all for a day or more, leaving masses of refugees in limbo and on edge as they were all forced to wait for the uncertain arrival of the next bus.[1] As a result the harbor of Molyvos was awash in people, as was the school parking lot, and there was no plan in place to relieve the congestion. In turn, all of this further stoked local fears that the worst might still be yet to come, and many villagers—particularly business owners—became increasingly alarmed and vocally antagonistic.

Discontent among the locals had been brewing for a long time, even before the Coast Guard stopped registering the refugees who landed on the beaches. In fact it began early that spring as people became more aware of the refugees' presence; yet everything came to a head in May when Melinda opened the temporary holding area in the empty field up in back of her restaurant.[2] That was when the locals' frustrations boiled over and Melinda was forced to close the shelter down. While its closing may have assuaged some of the anger, it was only temporary; the grim reality started to set in that tourism, their economic mainstay, was in serious decline. It was the height of that year's tourist season, and the number of visitors was already well below the average of previous years. Business owners were forced to admit that any improvement was unlikely with the end of the season only two months away and the refugee situation worsening.[3] It was also becoming frighteningly evident to them that there was no end in sight and that they had no clue as to what the future might hold. To make matters even worse, no one had a plan for moving forward. Unfortunately for the businesspeople, there was no simple solution to the refugee problem, and they appeared to be unable, or unwilling, to agree on any plan at all. They knew Melinda was right when she insisted that finding a place for the refugees to stay while they waited for the buses had to be a universally agreed-upon imperative, but they ended up opposing every idea that was presented.[4] Furthermore when the landowner forced Melinda to close the shelter that she had set up in the field, the challenge of finding a solution became all the more problematic.

At first they thought the military base in Petra would be a good site for a holding center. It was already a government installation with ample and immediately usable facilities, and it had an ideal location on the main road between Molyvos and Petra, far from any tourist center. As soon as the word got out, however, there was vehement opposition. Crowds of local demonstrators from the area in and around Petra and Molyvos—decidedly opposed to any refugee presence whatsoever and fearful that this would become a permanent refugee camp—closed the road for several weeks. The reaction was so intense that plans for the use of the military base were abandoned.[5]

For some time, Borderline-Europe, a German-based NGO refugee support organization with a branch office in Lesvos, had advocated the use of an abandoned site that the Lesvos government had acquired and developed several years earlier as a campground, complete with toilets, showers, sinks, cooking facilities, and offices. Located at a wide bend in the road just before a gradual descent into Eftalou, the camping area seemed like a good spot because it was well outside of the village, yet all refugees had to pass by it on their way from the beaches. It had an open space where the refugees could assemble to eat and drink while they waited for buses to arrive, and there was also enough room to bring the buses in and load them. Most importantly the refugees would not have to go into the village, thus avoiding any direct encounters with tourists. When a petition to turn the camping ground into a temporary refugee holding area was presented, the mayor of Lesvos approved it. Although it was a municipal site and clearly within the mayor's jurisdiction, his approval provoked a serious fight among the villagers of Molyvos.

A meeting of the village council was convened to discuss the issue, but it quickly deteriorated into an uproar of opposition led largely by local business people, all of whom claimed that its location so close to the beach hotels would completely wipe out the area's tourist trade. Again they voiced fears that this location would become a permanent refugee camp. Ilektra Pasxouli, a council member and one of Melinda's longtime friends who helped in the harbor, tried to explain to everyone present that, on an average day, at least two thousand refugees were staying in the parking lot by the school with no sanitary facilities. She stressed to everyone that the situation was so untenable that using the campground until the peak of the crisis had passed was absolutely critical. She repeatedly tried to point out that the campground's location on the outskirts of Molyvos would keep everything out of view from the tourists and that there were toilets, sinks, and running water that the refugees could use. Her appeal not only fell on deaf ears but was actually met with a great deal of hostility directed at her personally.[6] In fact the tenor of that meeting became so bitter that Dina Adam, who was in attendance to support the proposal, says, "I wish I had not been there because I really saw some awful behavior. They almost ate us alive with anger."[7]

All negotiations involving the campground came to a halt when public sentiment overrode the mayor's initial approval of its use for refugees. Ilektra concedes that "the locals simply did not want the refugees anywhere near Molyvos and did not even have the presence of mind to realize that this plan to use the campground could actually save the village."[8] Eric Kempson, also a target of people's ire, goes a bit further and suggests that the locals were so angry that they would not even entertain any solutions—as sound as they might be—if they were proposed by anyone helping the refugees.[9] Dionisis, who was one of the proponents of the campground, came from that tumultuous meeting saying that the only alternative left was the parking lot, even though everyone was opposed to that as well. Its location by the entrance to the village had already been a primary gathering place for some time. In the end, even though the number of refugees was far too great for its size, and despite the large-scale disapproval, the parking lot became the unofficial place where refugees waited for buses until the beginning of September.[10]

The shortage of buses to transport the never-ending stream of refugees from Molyvos to Moria meant that by the time a bus did arrive in the parking lot, hundreds of people were already lined up, waiting impatiently to board. Each time a bus pulled in, a surge of people pushed toward the door. Rarely was anyone from either MSF or the UNHCR there to help with the boarding, and many bus drivers—all alone with a disorderly crush of refugees—simply closed the door and left. Little prior thought had been given to the boarding process, probably because no one thought it would be much of a problem. It turned out to be a very big issue, and Melinda and her volunteers had to step in and figure out how to get crowds of anxious refugees onto each bus.

At first Melinda took charge of loading the buses with the help of a couple of Arabic-speaking volunteers who translated her instructions and helped her maintain order. She put families with children and people who had difficulty walking at the front of the line.[11] After loading a few buses she learned that a system was needed to get the line itself organized in advance to avoid last-minute confusion when a bus arrived. Melinda started out by writing a number on the arm of each refugee with a colored marker and then lining them up according to those numbers. That worked until refugees started getting their own markers and writing numbers on their own arms. Next she made lottery tickets of five or six different colors but soon found herself having to use more than twenty different colors, and she was unable to keep track of which colors were boarding and in what order. Finally she came up with a system using tickets of various colors and symbols. This worked so well that, from then on, there was minimal pushing and shoving, and everyone worked together peacefully and cooperatively. Melinda eventually taught all of the volunteers how to load a bus using this system, including those in Skala, staff members from MSF and UNHCR, and the legions of helpers who would provide aid in the weeks and months to come when the tide of refugees would grow even more intense.[12]

Everyone passing by the parking lot that summer—locals, tourists, and volunteers who came to help—witnessed a scene that was, in some ways, reminiscent of the crowded harbor. Clothes were hung to dry in any spot that might be available: on fences and walls, on the cross beams of the bus stop shelter, even suspended from tree branches or spread out in the sun on pieces of cardboard. In a video taken one August afternoon, two Dutch tourists, a young man and his girlfriend who had volunteered for parking lot duty that day, can be seen standing by a map showing the route to Moria that they had posted on one of the trees near the bus stop shelter. Pointing to the long line of refugees waiting for a bus that had not yet arrived, they urged a group of able-bodied young men to walk to Mytilene rather than wait there in the heat, particularly since women with children, the elderly, and the infirm would be given priority in boarding. They told the men that there might be drivers along the road who would pick them up and give them a ride at least part of the way. Speaking to the videographer, the young volunteer expressed disappointment that there had been no direct government intervention and no outside organizations coming to help. He said it was all very unfair because the "Greeks have their own problems at this time," and yet the entire responsibility for the refugees was left to locals and tourist volunteers who struggled to keep things as organized as they could and made sure that everyone at least had some food and water.[13]

Untenable though it was, and despite the growing tension in the community, this is how the situation remained until early September. By default, because nothing had been agreed upon, the parking lot became and remained the location where all refugees gathered to wait for the buses and where Melinda and her volunteers delivered food that they prepared. The place where the sandwiches were made began to live up to its nickname, "Sandwich Factory," as it was now operating twenty-four hours a day. Even then they could not keep up with demand, as refugees flooded in from the beach area. In fact one day they ran out of sandwich bread and couldn't find any on the entire island.[14] Crowds of refugees, numbering between the hundreds and thousands, milled around the parking lot aimlessly with nothing to do. Others sat or slept on mats under the trees or in the shade of the canopies that had been strung from tree branches to protect them from the hot summer sun. Despite the trauma of their migration and their miserable surroundings, some of the children happily played ball as if they were unaware of the troubled state of their lives. Still, hundreds of other refugees were lined up waiting for a bus to come. The sidewalks bordering the parking lot overflowed with people, and they often spilled out into the roadway, blocking traffic moving through the village.[15] Water wasn't available anywhere near the parking lot. Piles of rubbish and human waste accumulated at the end of the lot opposite the main road where thousands of people relieved themselves day after day.

While he was in Molyvos that spring, Timothy Smith purchased two chemical toilets using money that had been donated through his appeals to friends and acquaintances on Facebook and other social media apps, and the village council passed a resolution that gave the deputy mayor the authority to have these toilets installed behind the bus stop.[16] Once again, the deeply entrenched animosity toward the refugees and their presence in the village had become so intense that, when news of the resolution spread, the school's parents' association threatened to file a formal legal complaint to have the toilets removed as soon as they were in place. Sensing the extreme need for the toilets, yet wishing to be responsive to the opposition, the deputy mayor and the village council called a meeting of all the civic organizations in the village, hoping to find an acceptable solution to what was becoming yet another intractable problem.[17] Nevertheless the opposition remained so extreme that the village council rescinded the resolution, and the two toilets laid in the parking lot on their sides, uninstalled, until the end of August.

The village council constantly received complaints about the parking lot, but this particular meeting turned into a public free-for-all where hostilities became unrestrained. Tim left the meeting shaking with anger over the attitudes of the villagers.[18] Ilektra had already been a target of their outrage, but this time she felt that the villagers ganged up on her largely because they viewed her as a supporter of the refugees. Speaking about the meeting later she says, "Being a local, one who truly cared about the village and who was also involved with the refugees, presented a whole set of challenges, and I lost almost all my friends because of this."[19]

Toward the very end of August, with the beginning of the new school year approaching, Melinda received a call asking her to meet with the school committee. When she arrived she saw that the committee members were joined by the school's administrators and a number of teachers. She distinctly recalls what happened at that meeting: "The committee members asked me personally to remove these people from the parking lot because the children could not go through this mess to get into the school. They said they were afraid that the refugees had communicable diseases that the children would catch if they got near them. I responded, saying, 'Excuse me, but who am I to remove these people? They are not coming to the parking lot because of me. They are coming there on their own. We help them to move on.' It was as if the school felt that I was in charge of keeping the refugees there."[20]

Only a few days later an announcement came over the village loudspeaker asking people to bring food, clothing, water, and similar items to the school for distribution to the refugees. It was the voice of a representative from the Greek Red Cross who had apparently come from Mytilene to Molyvos specially to make the announcement. It all came as a surprise to Melinda and everyone who had been working with her—first, because so many of the people on the school committee harbored such strong feelings about the presence of the refugees and second, because, only a few days earlier, they had asked Melinda to remove them from the parking lot. Response to the announcement was generous, and townspeople brought bread and all kinds of food and clothing items to the school. Melinda received none of the donations collected from this drive, even though everyone knew she was largely responsible for feeding and clothing the refugees.[21]

As it turned out, the school's effort may have foreshadowed what was to come. On September 1, the village awoke to find that the parking lot was completely empty and that a fence topped with coils of barbed wire had been erected around its perimeter. The school committee had held a meeting, without informing anyone, and decided to close the parking lot and install the fence to prevent the refugees from being there when the school opened. Michael Honneger, who was there that morning with his camera and took photographs of the empty parking lot with its newly installed fence, says, "It was an extremely dramatic turning point because, after that, all hell broke loose."[22] From that time on, the refugees were all forced to stay on the streets and nearby roads leading into and out of the village, as they had no other place to go. Thousands continued to land on the beaches every day, and the number of available buses was still altogether insufficient to move them out of the area. It was total chaos with children running all over and rubbish and human waste accumulating everywhere. The parents' association's decision to put up the fence had made everything far worse than it had ever been.[23]

Ute, whose compassion and indignation were always aroused by the refugee families and their children having to face such hardships, was "infuriated" by the fence. One day after she closed the shop, she went over to the parking lot with a pair of wire cutters and asked the refugees gathered in the road if they would like her to cut the wires so they could use the parking lot once again. After some discussion she finally said, "I'll do it," and she went around to the back of the parking lot and cut the fence open. Some of the refugees wanted to go in, but most of them were afraid of what the local police might do. Unfortunately the parking lot remained closed, but Ute still seemed to find mischievous delight in having cut the fence.[24]

On September 2, 2015, when Molyvos was reeling from the previous day's incident, newspapers and television channels around the globe were flashing a picture of a three-year-old Syrian boy, Alan Kurdi, wearing a bright red shirt and blue shorts lying face down in the sand.[25] His body had washed up dead on a Turkish beach that morning. There was another picture of a Turkish soldier cradling the boy's lifeless body in his arms. That evening in the United States, NBC *Nightly News* anchor Lester Holt opened the broadcast with a warning to viewers that the upsetting photos they were about to see had "quickly resonated across the world as a heartbreaking symbol of a human catastrophe that we cannot close our eyes to."[26] The night before, young Alan, his older brother, Ghalib, and their parents, Abdullah and Rehanna, were crossing from Turkey to the Greek island of Kos when their boat capsized. Only the father survived.

Abdullah Kurdi, a Kurdish barber from Kobani, Syria, attempted the journey to Kos with his family in order to live with his sister, Tima, in Vancouver, British Columbia, where she had emigrated in 1992. Tima had applied to Canada's Department of Citizenship and Immigration for refugee sponsorship for another brother. The application was found to be incomplete, though, because it did not contain any documentation of that brother's refugee status, something that was virtually impossible for Syrians who were already in Turkey to obtain. It was, therefore, rejected. Tima then applied for sponsorship for Abdullah and his family, but Canada's Department of Citizenship and Immigration had no record of receiving the application.[27]

Like so many refugee families, the Kurdis did not want to leave Syria, but by June 2015 the situation had become increasingly violent. One day while playing in the street, the children witnessed a suicide bomber blow himself up, and it was then that the family knew the time had come for them to leave the country.[28] Abdullah had attempted to flee Syria via a land route twice before but was caught and forced to turn back. This time around he chose to take the sea route, even though he knew the risks. His sister gave him $4,450 to pay smugglers for the family's crossing from Turkey to Kos, considerably more than average, but it enabled them to travel in a wooden boat, which was deemed far safer than the rubber dinghies. It turned out to be a small vessel built for only eight passengers, so it was overcrowded like all of the smugglers' boats, and there were no serviceable life vests. Shortly after they left the shore, high waves engulfed the boat, causing it to capsize and hurl everyone on board into the dark, rough water.[29] Alan's mother, who did not know how to swim, hung on to the overturned boat while his father tried to hold both children's heads barely above the water for three solid hours. After his strength gave out, the older brother slipped from his arms and drowned. He then handed Alan over to the mother so he, himself, could regain some strength, but in the end, the mother and Alan both drowned.[30] The father was found semi-conscious after washing up on the beach the next morning.[31]

The *New York Times* report the following morning stated that the "image of this lifeless child . . . his round cheek pressed to the sand as if he were sleeping, except for the waves lapping his face . . . galvanized public attention to a crisis that has been building for years."[32] Suddenly like a bolt of thunder, it seemed the attention of the entire world was directed to the enormity of the refugee crisis that had overtaken Greece and its Aegean islands and was tearing the village of Molyvos apart. German Chancellor Angela Merkel was particularly moved by the event and announced that Germany, already the largest refugee host country in Europe, would take fifty thousand additional refugees.[33] In Canada the news unleashed widespread criticism of its Department of Citizenship and Immigration's insensitive handling of refugee sponsorships, which prompted Prime Minister Trudeau to announce that Canada would accept twenty-five thousand Syrian refugees immediately.[34] In Greece, as in the rest of Europe, the tragedy and the photos made extensive press headlines, but the coverage reflected the country's serious discord over refugees and immigration with left-leaning newspapers focusing on the human toll, while conservative newspapers stressed the cost of the refugee crisis on Greece and its economy.[35]

Molyvos and the north shore of Lesvos felt the effect of the international attention almost immediately. The outside assistance that everyone had been calling for was finally about to arrive; it seemed like only a matter of days, even hours, before dozens of NGOs and hundreds of volunteers from all over the world began to descend on Molyvos, providing the much-needed help. But at the same time this would present challenges that no one could have anticipated.

13

The Starfish Foundation

September and October 2015

News of the crisis was broadcast worldwide and that, in turn, triggered the arrival of NGOs, reporters and camera crews, and large numbers of volunteers. After months of futile attempts to draw attention to the refugee crisis and the urgent need for outside help, Molyvos was suddenly thrust into the global spotlight. The area was flooded with news teams from all over the world. They were everywhere—on street corners, in the harbor, and even on the beaches trying to film landings and interview both refugees and volunteers. Between September 2015 and February 2016 Lesvos became the destination for an estimated fifteen thousand volunteers, and of that number, approximately 1,500 of them went to Molyvos specifically to work with Melinda.[1] Donations of all kinds, both money and supplies, also began pouring in.

Melinda had never wanted to handle any of the money that came in to help cover the costs of feeding and clothing the refugees. Right from the start she had asked all donors either to purchase supplies themselves and bring them directly to her or deposit their donations, regardless of size, in the open accounts that she had set up at local supermarkets and pharmacies. Even the members of the group, who came together earlier that spring to help her create some order amid the chaos and contributed fifty euros each as seed money, were expected to comply with this request. Melinda was adamant about it because she knew that it was against the law for her to accept donations and then make purchases on her own with those funds. At the same time, given the prevailing negative attitudes toward her for helping the refugees, she also hoped to avoid accusations of fiscal malfeasance. As it turned out, however, nothing she did ever protected her from the rumor mill; from the beginning there was already talk of her supposedly pocketing money.[2]

Now she was not only receiving increasingly large amounts of money in donations, but she also had a growing workforce of volunteers who required far more organization and supervision than she had ever dealt with before. She came to realize very quickly that she would have to establish some kind of official and legal structure to manage her expanding operation. Otherwise the chance for errors could increase the risk of inadvertent mistakes or falling prey to questions and criticism.[3] Once again, just as she had done back in March when the refugees began to arrive in such large numbers, Melinda united the original group of friends with whom she had worked so closely since 2008 hoping that, together, they could figure out what to do.

During their deliberations the group kept referring to First Stop, the small organization they had created several years earlier. Its basic mission was to provide the most important and immediate needs of the refugees when they landed: food, water, shelter, dry clothing, and one other need that they had not originally anticipated—information: where they were located and where the refugees' next destination would be. Those same objectives still guided the work that Melinda did every day, but on a much larger scale, and it became clear to everyone that the same mission should remain in place going forward.[4] This time around, however, the new and far more pressing circumstances required them to "professionalize" by creating a formal and workable structure that, first and foremost, would enable them to collect and disburse money legally. At the same time, they wanted that structure to facilitate the establishment and maintenance of a reliable pipeline through which they could obtain and distribute the food, water, dry clothing, and shelter that were so desperately needed.[5]

According to Dionisis, the group's initial meetings were "very difficult" because everything seemed to point almost unavoidably toward the formation of an NGO, and some were very reluctant to become involved with that kind of organization. No one in the group had any direct experience with NGOs other than Ilektra through her political science major at the university, and she was particularly opposed because she disliked what she had learned about how they operate. The group was in accord that they wanted Greece and the EU to intercede in the growing crisis, but they were wary of large outside groups that were unfamiliar with both the area and the situation and might impose themselves in ways that would further disrupt life in Molyvos. Stratis had such negative feelings about NGOs that he vowed not to work with Melinda if she started one, a threat that he made good on. He admitted that he "judged her hard" in that regard, but in the end he agreed to help her, just not as a part of her NGO. Stratis became focused largely on using his boat to help the Coast Guard. Even Dionisis was uncomfortable being involved with an NGO, but the challenges of handling large sums of money legally and the responsibilities associated with having volunteers working with them were so great that he saw no viable alternative. Despite their misgivings and concerns, everyone in the group, except for Stratis, banded together with Melinda as their leader and proceeded to form their own NGO. They "baptized" themselves as the Board and, as a body, began to make official decisions.[6] The Starfish Foundation (*Asterias* in Greek) was officially granted nonprofit status by the Greek government on October 5, 2015.[7]

Whenever anyone asks Melinda how she chose the name of her NGO, and whenever tourist groups are visiting Molyvos who are interested to learn about her efforts, she always tells the "Starfish Story" that she heard as a child:

> One day a man was walking along the beach when he noticed a young girl picking something up and gently throwing it into the ocean. Approaching the girl, he asked, "What are you doing?" She replied, "Throwing starfish back into the ocean. The surf is up and the tide is going out. If I don't throw them back, they'll die." "Young woman," the man said, "don't you realize there are miles and miles of beach and hundreds of starfish? You can't make a difference!" After listening politely, the girl bent down, picked up another starfish, and threw it back into the surf. Then, smiling at the man, she said . . . "I made a difference for that one."[8]

The story resonated with her because, during the entire crisis, she felt like the girl who rescued the starfish one by one. She believes that her individual efforts, along with those of the local people and friends who helped her, "blossomed into Starfish because of the lack of Greek governmental resources and the failure of nations and aid agencies to respond to the emergency in Molyvos early on."[9] She and this handful of people were left entirely alone in the face of what felt like a massive refugee invasion. She knew that it was impossible to fully address all of their needs or save everyone's life, but she and her helpers did their best and saved as many lives as they could, often one at a time. When volunteers began to arrive, knowing that they were likely to feel overwhelmed by the number of refugees and their life-or-death needs, Melinda always shared the starfish story with them, hoping it would inspire them to persevere, just as it had for her.[10]

The Starfish Foundation was very much an extended family affair whose origins went back nearly a decade to 2008, when Melinda and the very same group of friends first came together to help refugees. That same group also responded to her call for help only a few months earlier when it became clear that their friend's honorable undertaking had become too much for her to handle alone. Now they were together once again, inspired by her "just get the job done mentality" and her commitment and ability to lead.[11] They were ready to help her take on this next major challenge. Her husband, Theo, and their children, who all shared their mother's sense of duty, also played an integral role. Everyone involved knew that Starfish would put their self-reliance and endurance to the supreme test because they had already witnessed and experienced firsthand the magnitude of the crisis and the demands that it had made on them. Yet it is doubtful that they were all fully aware at the time of just what they were getting themselves into or the physical, social, and psychological price they would all pay.

In a way Starfish was actually born in the so-called Sandwich Factory because the food made there became the emblem of Melinda's efforts to provide what the refugees needed most upon their arrival in Molyvos. Up to this point, she had relied primarily on donations from locals, tourists, and volunteers, but now that Starfish was officially an NGO, it was legal to actively seek funds. Of course, this involved writing grant proposals and all of the related follow-up that the administration of grant monies entails. In addition, as the news of the refugees in Greece became more widespread and volunteers began to arrive in mounting numbers, integrating those new volunteers into the Starfish operation required specific experience with personnel supervision, skills that few on the Board had. NGOs already on the scene provided some general advice and training in the writing and administering of grants and in personnel management and evaluation, but trying to balance both sets of responsibilities—taking care of the refugees while learning how to handle these additional administrative tasks all at the same time—proved to be truly daunting. Fortunately, as it turned out, many of the new volunteers were already experienced in these areas, and Starfish was able to benefit from their collective skills and expertise.[12]

Nevertheless this new operation placed significant additional strain on Melinda and those working closest with her. When Michael and Tim returned to Molyvos in September, the deliberations leading up to the formation of Starfish were in full swing, but they could already tell that Melinda would not be able to sustain the additional level of stress that Starfish would put on her once it was officially formed. Tim convinced her to hire someone to manage and oversee the administrative work of the Foundation. Up to this point, everyone working with Melinda, including Melinda herself and her family, had been serving as unpaid volunteers, and he believed that offering some form of modest stipend to a qualified person would result in a more solidly run organization. At the same time, having a paid administrator would free Melinda to take care of the critical daily tasks that required her attention and energy. Luckily there was no need to look very far to find such a person. Emma Eggink had come to Lesvos in July 2015 to take part in a summer program at the University of the Aegean and, while there, began working with Melinda as a volunteer. Her organizational and leadership skills soon impressed everyone, and three months after her arrival, the Board asked her to become the program manager of Starfish.[13] Tim's fundraising efforts generated enough money to also provide modest food stipends for a core of volunteers, which enabled them to extend their stays. This incentive was an important factor in Emma's decision to remain and assume this administrative role.[14]

Starfish created additional responsibilities for those involved, but being a small, locally based NGO also enabled it to act far more quickly and independently than the larger organizations like UNHCR and the International Rescue Committee (IRC) that came from outside of Greece. While those NGOs were entangled in the whole process of applying for permits to operate in the country, Starfish was able to move ahead and undertake initiatives with much less delay. Accepting and deploying volunteers was one of them. The first real volunteers in Molyvos had been tourists who were already there for vacation, but as the news reports about the refugees spread, people from all over the world were prompted to consider traveling to Greece to work as volunteers. By simply going on Facebook, they could find information about volunteering opportunities and end up working for Starfish.

By the time the 2015 tourist season was nearing its close, the tourists were being replaced by Starfish volunteers from all over Europe and as far away as the United States and Australia. Among them were employees of all kinds of business enterprises and students and faculty from colleges and universities. Many were affiliated with civic organizations or church groups of all denominations. Some were political and social activists for whom this kind of volunteerism was an avocation. Most of the volunteers were between twenty and thirty years old. Some who acted independently had simply left their jobs while others took vacation time from one week up to two months.[15] It was not uncommon for volunteers from the United States to say that they wanted to help because they felt that their country's involvement in Iraq, Syria, and Afghanistan was "responsible for much of the conflict and terror which led to the crisis."[16] One American volunteer learned about Starfish on Facebook and was so eager to become involved that she simply packed and left for Greece with no set plans.[17] She was not the only one to do that. Once volunteers landed at the Mytilene airport, they could ask almost anyone, including airport personnel, local police, taxi drivers, or car rental agents, about Starfish and be immediately directed to the harbor of Molyvos and the Captain's Table, where they met Melinda.

That October, Melinda was "bombarded" with anywhere between forty and eighty volunteers on any given day.[18] When describing Melinda, one of the volunteers, a twenty-year-old from Denmark, said, "She's taking phone calls every second, running everything. She's like a mother to the volunteers under her command, as well as to the thousands of refugees who pass through the island."[19] Another volunteer reported that "between cooking and greeting customers, Melinda seemed always to be on the phone regarding supplies, buses, and whether another group of refugees had been rescued by the Coast Guard. On top of that, people like me show up and ask to help in some way."[20] In fact volunteers showed up at the restaurant on a daily basis.

Knowing very well that the volunteers who came to Starfish would face stressful challenges and confusion, Melinda required that they all attend an introduction and training meeting where they learned about the refugee populations they would serve and the story of their journeys to Lesvos, the kinds of duties expected of them, and the difficulties they might encounter. Each volunteer was assigned to one of the three daily work shifts, 11:00 p.m. to 7:30 a.m., 7:00 a.m. to 3:30 p.m., or 3:00 p.m. to 11:30 p.m., and was given a specific assignment. They were all instructed to communicate with each other using WhatsApp on their smartphones and advised to stay connected in order to receive notifications of refugee arrivals, duty assignments and changes, and other general instructions. The meetings for new volunteers were held at the Captain's Table every Monday, Wednesday, Friday, and Saturday. Those arriving on a day when there was no meeting had to wait to attend one before they could begin, but as soon as each meeting was over, Melinda would immediately set them all to work.[21]

Assignments varied according to the situation at any given time, but with refugees arriving by the thousands each day, many of the volunteers prepared food in shifts that ran around the clock and, even then, struggled to keep up with the demand. Two volunteers, one from the United States and one from Norway, reported that they made 750 sandwiches during their very first shift. A supply of sandwiches was often gone through so quickly that volunteers had to start all over again and make more before their shift was over. One of the principal tasks of the volunteers who worked in the parking lot was to distribute food. Each refugee received a turkey and cheese sandwich, plus a banana or another fruit, and a bottle of water. Female volunteers covertly distributed sanitary napkins for the women and diapers for the babies. Other volunteers were assigned to the harbor where, day and night, they helped refugees who had just been rescued by the Coast Guard. Starfish always tried to ensure that every refugee had a sleeping bag.[22] Since the worst cases were always brought to the harbor, the volunteers needed to be prepared to perform CPR, calm those who were frightened, wrap those suffering from hypothermia in emergency blankets, place the dead in body bags, and comfort survivors, including newly orphaned children. Sometimes, right when volunteers thought their shift was over and they could relax or get some sleep, the Coast Guard would bring in another group of refugees, or they would be called to deal with yet another emergency.

The creation of Starfish also enabled Melinda to finally attend to one of the largest and most intractable problems that Molyvos faced in the crisis: where to hold the massive number of refugees while they waited for the buses to take them to Moria. The meeting with the school officials in late August in which they insisted that Melinda remove the refugees from the parking lot, along with the installation of the barbed wire fence that followed only a few days later, became a personal call to action. She had pressed that the refugees congregated there on their own and not because of her; however, the school officials had presented her with a challenge from which she would not back down. She believed that something definitive had to be done. Furthermore with the approach of winter and the change in the weather only three months away, she also knew that the sea would get rougher and bring more traumatized people and more deaths.[23] Staying true to her instincts to get on with it, Melinda decided that the time had come to take matters into her own hands and see to it that the refugees were moved from the village.

The campground, a municipal plot of land, had originally seemed like the ideal place for a refugee holding area. The mayor of Lesvos had given his approval, but the public outcry was so strong that the approval was withdrawn. The parking lot by the bus stop, also municipal, was supremely controversial because of its connection to the public school, and the installation of the barbed wire fence had put it totally off-limits, even after Ute cut a hole in it. There was, however, one other option that had not yet been explored.

High on a bluff about halfway between Molyvos and Petra, where the road rounds its first wide bend, leaving Molyvos behind in the distance, there sits a modernistic structure of steel girders supporting a huge platform with a sweeping view of the surrounding hillsides and the sea below that accommodates a swimming pool, dining and bar areas, and a dance floor that can hold as many as two thousand people. Since its opening in July 2014, Oxy Club has had the reputation of being the hottest discotheque in all of Greece, and during its season that runs from early June until the end of August, it attracts crowds of young vacationers to Lesvos from all over Europe. At night the rays from its large and colorful strobe and spotlights extend far out across the water, and some say that the music from its powerful amplification system can be heard into the morning hours from more than two miles away.

As a local resident and a parent of socially minded young adults, Melinda was familiar with Oxy. She was also well aware that the property was privately owned, outside of municipal boundaries, and therefore free of any jurisdiction of the village. She passed by it almost every day and knew that its large parking area, located right along the main road, could offer ample space for large numbers of refugees to be fed, given dry clothes, and provided with shelter while they waited for the buses. There was also plenty of room for buses to pull in, load, and return to the main highway for the run over the mountains to Moria. It was far enough outside of Molyvos that refugees would have no need to come into the village itself or the harbor. Melinda also knew that the club had already closed for the season and would not reopen until the following June. It was as close to ideal as any place along the north coast.

It just so happened that Melinda was acquainted with the owner, and less than a week after the parents closed the school parking lot, she asked him if he would allow Starfish to use Oxy's parking lot as a refugee holding area. To her relief and delight, he agreed, and the very next day she sent a team of Starfish volunteers to Oxy to erect awnings that would provide shade. Next, to free the village of refugees altogether, Melinda arranged for a fleet of buses to pick them all up and transport them to Oxy, so everything was done expediently, and no refugees were left to walk the great distance along the road.

The UNHCR, as it turned out, was somewhat "upset" by the move to Oxy because its staff members did not think that Melinda should have gone ahead and made all of the arrangements without their involvement. They claimed that, since they paid for most of the buses at the time, she should have asked for their permission. For her part Melinda saw the matter quite differently. As far as she was concerned, the UNHCR had little to do with the movement of refugees other than to pay for the buses and the drivers. The real challenge with the buses was getting the crowds of refugees on board, and neither the UNHCR nor MSF who helped fund the buses had ever sent any of their staff members to aid them. They left it to Melinda to develop a reliable and workable procedure for loading the buses, and she and her volunteers were always the only people there to do it. Therefore, from her perspective, this left her completely in charge of the buses and, by extension, free to decide to move the refugees to Oxy without asking the UNHCR for permission.[24]

Melinda was not one to be easily intimidated, and now that she had Starfish, her own locally based NGO, she had both the flexibility and the support system that gave her the strength and the resolve to make critical decisions and tackle problems. In its first month alone, Starfish sheltered, clothed, and fed more than ninety thousand refugees at Oxy.[25] Over the next three and a half tumultuous months, she charted a course of action that would define Starfish as an organization and shape the direction of her own life.

14

Oxy Refugee Transit Camp

October through December 2015

The peaceful November morning was shrouded by a light fog that had drifted in from the sea and cloaked the Oxy refugee transit camp in a reddish-blue haze that would eventually melt away in the warmth of the daytime sun. Tents of varying sizes were clustered together, some of them bearing the logos of the aid organizations that had erected them. A large one bearing the sign of the UNHCR appeared to be set aside as a place where refugees could sleep sheltered from the elements, but on this particular morning, there were so many refugees at the camp that the tent was not large enough. Hundreds of refugees were in sleeping bags or rolled up in blankets on large pieces of cardboard or mats that had been laid next to each other on the ground. Portable toilets were placed here and there. Clothes were hung or spread out to dry everywhere: on any ground area where people were not sleeping, on tent and tarpaulin support ropes, on the fences that protected the camp from the highway, and even on the guardrails on the other side of the road. Tables had been set up in various places. Some looked like they might be changing stations for babies. At others, several people, presumably volunteers, arranged items of clothing for refugees to take. The few refugees who were not asleep or sitting quietly could be seen walking slowly, even aimlessly, among the sleepers or standing on the opposite side of the road, looking over the cliffs toward the sea.[1]

A reporter from one of the many media organizations that had come to Molyvos sat in a large tent with a Syrian refugee, a young woman traveling alone, who had fled her native country. She'd first gone to Egypt, then to Turkey, and just the day before had made the crossing to Eftalou. When the reporter asked her how she was feeling, she replied simply, "Sad." She was hoping to go to Sweden to study and work and then have a family. Seated nearby in that same tent was a man who had also traveled by himself. Many of his family members had died in Syria, and others were still there. Another man was from Afghanistan where he'd worked as a translator. He told the reporter that he left his country because of the fighting and killing. First he took a taxi and then rode in all kinds of vehicles—anything that was available and moved. Finally he ended up walking across Iran and Turkey until he got to the coast where he paid smugglers for passage in a rubber boat to the north coast of Lesvos. The trip from Afghanistan to Turkey had cost him about $1,500, and he paid $800 to the smugglers for the crossing to Lesvos. He said that he was very happy to be at Oxy because everyone there helped the refugees, but he intended to go to Germany where he had relatives who had been living there for thirty years. When the reporter asked him what he wanted in his future, he replied, "Peace. Peace will be enough for me. I want to live in a peaceful place with no war."[2]

Less than twenty-four hours after Melinda got the go-ahead from Oxy's owner, her team of thirty Starfish volunteers was already at work readying the parking area for the arrivals. They climbed up the cliffs directly in the back of the lot, anchored hooks into the rocks, and tied ropes to secure the tarpaulins that they hung to create shelter from the late summer sun and the fall and winter rains that would soon come. They set up two medium-sized tents: one to provide privacy for women and children, and the other for the distribution of food and clothing. Starfish volunteers also prepared booklets in Farsi and Arabic that contained general information for the refugees, including where they were, what to expect, procedures to follow, and what their next steps would be. Neither Greece, the EU, nor any of the larger NGOs that were present on the island had such a site for refugees, and once it was open the NGOs moved quickly to collaborate with Starfish and offer their services at the Oxy location.[3] The UNHCR set up a large tent where people were protected from the elements, another for storage, and several smaller ones from which food and bus tickets could be distributed. Not long after it opened, trucks began to deliver bread and food supplies directly to Oxy so volunteers could prepare sandwiches on-site. Women and Health Alliance International (WAHA) also set up a tent where they provided daytime medical care. In addition, for the first time since May, when the Coast Guard crew stopped registering refugees at their office in the Molyvos harbor, Starfish was granted the authority to begin processing all of the arrivals before they boarded the buses to Moria. A separate tent was set up for that purpose.

The large open area on the eastern end of the parking lot was set aside for buses. The tents were all placed together toward the western end, and any open space that was left around them was normally filled with people sitting or sleeping. There were always lines at the tents where food, clothing, and bus tickets were handed out and where refugees were supposed to register. Electric hookups were generally unavailable, so the only lighting after dark was what filtered down from the floodlights mounted on the steel towers and the large platform of the nightclub on the hill above the parking lot. When the winter rains began in November, Melinda arranged for bulldozers to come in and level off the parking lot to provide better drainage.[4] The need for a refugee holding area had been so urgent when Starfish commenced that Melinda's number one priority was to get the site up and running as quickly as possible, leaving little time for anything other than immediate functionality, not outward appearance. One volunteer who worked at Oxy described it as a "ramshackle refugee camp" that grew bigger every day. He wrote, "A new tent for women and children goes up. A medical bus is parked. A children's play tent is born. But it's not enough. The rains are coming, the winter is coming, and the people will not stop. On a clear day, two, three, four thousand people come through."[5]

Nevertheless the organization that Starfish established at Oxy, "ramshackle" as it might have looked to some, was strong enough to hold up in the face of that fall's onslaught of refugees. In late October, almost immediately after its opening, six thousand passed through in one twenty-four-hour period, and "every single person ate, drank, had shelter, and all those who needed it received medical care."[6] From then on, over the next three months, Oxy became the only major field operation and reception site on the north coast that provided food, water, shelter, medical facilities, and buses for more than 130,000 refugees. They also attended to the victims and survivors of two devastating shipwrecks.[7]

Once Oxy was open no one had to witness the sight of refugees walking from Molyvos to Mytilene any longer. All refugees were transported from the beaches to Oxy and from Oxy to Mytilene in buses paid for by the UNHCR, MSF, and the IRC. Intent upon keeping refugees from the village, Melinda worked with the Kempsons and the volunteers at the beach to set up designated areas along the beach road where the refugees could wait for buses to take them directly to Oxy. It took some time to get this arranged fully, and until then volunteers and locals involved with Starfish did what they could to provide some transportation, at least for the most infirm and vulnerable.

Ute's house was located along the road to Eftalou where, for months, she had watched all of the refugees making their way, first to the Molyvos harbor and then to Oxy, on foot. Every morning after Oxy opened, before she left to go to her shop, she went first to the beach, filled her car with refugees, and drove them to the camp. Families always wanted to ride together to avoid getting separated, and if she could not take an entire family in one trip, she was always willing to go back for the others.[8] Robin and Robert Jones had always offered rides to the refugees, even before the days of the caravan and the repeal of the transportation ban, and they continued to do so until buses from the beach to Oxy came regularly. During those trips they could tell from the way the parents held their children and whispered to each other as they pointed to the throngs of other refugees on the road that the reality of their situation was sinking in. When the car pulled into Oxy and they had the first glimpse of their surroundings, the exuberance on their faces for surviving the crossing was erased by the grim realization that they were not in Germany or Sweden as the smugglers had misled them to believe they would be.[9]

By the time Oxy opened up, as many as thirty or more boats were arriving steadily at any one time, day or night, and volunteers working on the beaches did all they could to prevent boats from capsizing in the surf and rescue passengers when the sea was turbulent and their boats crashed against the rocks. The smugglers did not allow refugees to bring any standard luggage in the dinghies, only plastic garbage bags and backpacks, but most of the bags were lost by the time they arrived. Backpacks seemed to survive the crossing a bit better than the plastic garbage bags—probably because they were strapped on—but like the refugees themselves, they, too, were dripping wet. As a result, when refugees finally got to Oxy, most of them were still completely soaked and wearing the same wet clothes they had landed in. Given those circumstances, getting everyone changed into dry clothing was a high priority, and one of the first tents that Starfish volunteers set up was designated for that purpose.

When they got off the bus, one of the first things the refugees did was remove their soggy shoes if they had not lost them at sea, put them in rows to dry in the sun, then choose a pair from the rows of shoes that those who arrived before them had left to dry. It became a kind of shoe exchange. Ute described the whole scene as "surrealistic," with the still-warm fall days and blue skies forming the backdrop for thousands of people shivering cold and sopping wet, surrounded by drying clothes and shoes.[10] Needless to say, fashion was not on anyone's mind when hundreds of soaking people were waiting in line to be given something dry from one of the clothing tents. Volunteers working in those tents would hold up pants, shirts, or blouses that looked to be about the right size for each of the waiting refugees, and soon they would be seen wearing them around the camp, perhaps not eagerly or stylishly, but contentedly. Many of the children ended up with t-shirts bearing American logos. Even though hundreds of people might be standing in line, volunteers reported that no pushing or shoving occurred while these items were distributed.[11] The pressing demand for dry clothing and shoes for the new arrivals meant these articles were always in short supply, especially the latter. Melinda had managed to find an empty house in Molyvos where the supplies donated to Starfish from all over Greece and Europe could be stored. It was stuffed from floor to ceiling with everything imaginable, and volunteers made multiple trips there daily to fill their cars and bring everything to Oxy.

Back when all the refugees still congregated in the school parking lot, Melinda developed a system for refugees to board buses using tickets with colors and symbols that helped ensure that everything remained orderly and that those who arrived at the parking lot first were also the first to leave. The tickets turned out to be so effective and reliable that Melinda trained the volunteers from Starfish and other NGOs to use them at Oxy, where she also set up a similar system for the distribution of food.[12] Loading buses in the parking lot had been challenging, but the enormous number of refugees at Oxy took the process to another level. Sometimes families of as many as twenty-five people all clamored to board a bus together at one time to avoid being split up. Volunteers learned quickly that, in order for the ticket system to work effectively, they had to keep everyone calm, and the best way to do that was to smile and be calm themselves. Robert Jones, who was often involved with loading the buses at Oxy, found out that "if you smiled, it would stop a panic." When the refugees noticed the volunteers smiling while they helped them board the buses, they almost always smiled back, which, in turn, started a chain reaction that caught on and continued.[13]

The tension associated with the boarding of buses at Oxy was due to much more than just the refugees' eagerness to quickly get on a bus without being separated from family or fellow travelers. The issue of national origin became another significant factor that made the volunteers' task of loading the buses all the more challenging. That summer before Oxy opened, the Greek government opened a second refugee camp, Kara Tepe, on the northern outskirts of Mytilene, several kilometers south of Moria. This was done in an attempt to relieve the severe overcrowding that plagued Moria, but the creation of that second camp generated tension all on its own—Greece established Kara Tepe for Syrians. When Kara Tepe first opened, all refugees were still transported to Moria, where they were registered, and Syrians were then taken to Kara Tepe. However, once new arrivals could be registered at Oxy, Syrians were transported directly from there to Kara Tepe, and all the others were taken to Moria. Greece's creation of two separate camps, one for Syrians and the other for everyone else, forced governmental agencies—particularly Frontex, the European Border Patrol and Coast Guard Agency—as well as the volunteers overseeing the loading of the buses to deal head-on with the critical and highly charged distinction between "refugees" and "migrants."[14] This was not the first time that it had arisen. Smugglers in Turkey were well aware of Syrians' status as refugees, and it was what prompted them to advise non-Syrians to throw their documents overboard before they landed so they would not be carrying proof of their national identity. Needless to say, thousands obeyed hoping to be able to pass as Syrians and thus avail themselves of the protections conferred on refugees. They soon learned how problematic that could be.

Protocol II of the Geneva Convention of August 12, 1949, provides protection for the victims of wars taking place within their own countries that, according to the United Nations Independent Commission of Inquiry (UNICI), reach the "threshold" of "non-international armed conflicts." They can be full-blown civil wars or internal armed conflicts that spread beyond borders and engulf neighboring countries. They can also start internally and then grow to such an extent that other countries are either called upon or forced to intervene.[15] When conflicts reach this threshold, the people who find themselves forced to flee for fear of persecution, torture, and even death are deemed "refugees" because once they have left their home countries, it is not safe for them to return. All signatories to the Geneva Conventions are required to grant the same economic and social rights offered to other resident foreigners, and they cannot be forced to return to their home countries.[16]

Migrants, on the other hand, do not have the same status as refugees. They might come from countries where there is violent political unrest or severe social and economic hardship that threatens their safety and their lives in ways that compel them to flee. However, if their home countries have not been officially designated as locations of "non-international armed conflict," they cannot be considered refugees. As a result, regardless of their circumstances, they are deemed to have left their country by choice in search of enhanced personal and economic opportunity and can, ostensibly, return home safely. Receiving countries, therefore, are not bound by the same international regulations for migrants as they are for refugees and are instead allowed to act in accordance with their own immigration laws and procedures, which can include the right to deport them.[17]

In July 2011 the UNICI determined that the fighting in Syria had reached the "threshold of non-international armed conflict," thereby granting official refugee status to all Syrians who flee their country and guaranteeing them the rights and protection required by the Geneva Conventions.[18] When Greece opened Kara Tepe for Syrians in 2015, it was, for all intents and purposes, acting under those requirements. All other groups—the thousands of Afghans, Pakistanis, and Iraqis pouring into Molyvos at that time—were officially deemed migrants.

Out on the beaches, where volunteers helped people get from the dinghies onto the shore, the distinction between Syrians and non-Syrians, refugees and migrants, was completely blurred. As Robert Jones points out, "We could not deal with such differences there."[19] However, the same was not true at Oxy where the differentiation fueled serious discord that turned into open conflict when non-Syrians realized that the volunteers loading the buses were intentionally separating them according to nationality. Only Syrians were allowed on the buses going to Kara Tepe, and everyone else was forced to take the buses going to Moria. It generated enormous resentment among non-Syrians, particularly Afghans who arrived in very large numbers. They all saw it as granting unmerited special status to Syrians when they, too, had fled violence and persecution in their countries and were unable to return home safely. As one Afghan refugee put it, "Every day the wars in Syria, Iraq, and Afghanistan are getting worse. It's not fit for living anymore, and that's why we came here. We are refugees; we are not migrants."[20] In the meantime everyone had also heard that Moria was seriously overcrowded, dangerous, and unsanitary, while Kara Tepe was cleaner and better maintained, and that generated even greater resentment. However, what most of them did not know was that by the end of October, conditions at Kara Tepe had also deteriorated to the point where two thousand refugees were in a place originally set up for six hundred, with only one functional toilet and no working showers.[21]

Meanwhile the volunteers overseeing the loading of the buses at Oxy had difficulty understanding or explaining anything because they were unable to speak the refugees' languages, and with everyone doing whatever they could to appear Syrian, it was extremely difficult for them to control who got on which bus. There was, however, a Palestinian woman from the United States who worked for the UN at Kara Tepe and was responsible for verifying the nationality of everyone getting off each bus. She could tell, simply by speaking with them and hearing their accents, which refugees did not belong in Kara Tepe, and as soon as she identified them, they were removed from the camp and sent to Moria.[22]

As the number of arrivals continued to increase, the backlog of asylum applications outpaced all efforts to process them.[23] In addition, countries in the EU—responding to both the economic crisis and the growing anti-immigrant sentiments at home—began closing their borders and creating barriers to immigration in an effort to reduce the flow of refugees. Fearful that a crush of refugees would be stuck in Athens unable to move toward their desired destinations in northern Europe, the Greek government reduced access to ferry service out of Mytilene, causing even larger numbers to congregate in the port where there was neither enough space nor adequate sanitary facilities. Anger and frustration turned into violent demonstrations, and despite the concentrated effort to process refugees' papers and fill all available spots on the limited number of ferries bound for Athens, the backup grew massive and began to spread well beyond the port area. To make matters worse, a strike in November by the ferry operators brought transportation to the mainland to a halt, leaving thousands of refugees stranded. Soon tents began to appear everywhere in Mytilene's public parks and every part of the city, from the harbor all the way up the hillside to the castle.[24]

With arrivals at Oxy exceeding three thousand per day, it became impossible to process such large numbers of people. They couldn't have done it even if there had been enough buses to transport them to Moria and Kara Tepe. Moreover both camps would have been hard-pressed to receive them. Oxy was conceived originally as a daytime transit facility, but in time and out of necessity, it became an overnight camp because more often than not, at least a thousand refugees ended up spending the night.[25] Volunteers had to walk around with garbage bags to collect the enormous and ever-growing accumulation of trash generated by so many people. To complicate matters further, human waste was everywhere because of the limited number of functional toilets. Had the volunteers not focused vigilantly on garbage pickup, Oxy would have become unsanitary and uninhabitable.[26]

Matthew Vickery, when describing Oxy in Aljazeera.com, stated that the refugee crisis in Lesvos "is often portrayed in mere numbers, which may be inevitable considering the record numbers at play, but at Oxy, numbers have taken a back seat to a light, almost happy atmosphere," and he attributed that to Melinda and her volunteers.[27] Given the conditions there at the height of Oxy's operations, Vickery's description might seem paradoxical, but when Ilektra speaks of Oxy, her words echo his, "It was a big experience, a wonderful thing that we—the core group of people who set it all up—built from zero to a very high level. We had no experience doing anything like that, but we did it with love. From nothing, we created a small, caring society, and we made it work. Then there were all the volunteers who did an amazing job, each one playing an essential role. Without them we wouldn't have been able to do anything of that magnitude; it was just too big. Unless a person has been involved directly in an effort of this magnitude, you just don't understand it."[28]

Some NGOs gave supplies or money, but the Starfish volunteers did all of the work. They often put in twenty hours a day without sleeping or even pausing to rest; they tried "to make this part of the refugees' life as good as possible." They created a playroom for kids and a space where women could breastfeed their children. Sometimes they broadcast music throughout the camp, and clowns and musicians were even brought in to entertain the children.[29] Since the volunteers had no expertise, they worked together to figure out what to do and how to do it. Ilektra and some others on the Starfish Board kept telling Melinda to make the volunteers take breaks because they were getting seriously exhausted, but their commitment was so strong that she rarely succeeded in persuading them. Even Ilektra herself worked all day helping her mother in her shop in the village and then went to work at Oxy for eight or nine more additional hours.[30]

Linguistic and cultural differences posed challenges. The refugees came with a whole set of culture-based beliefs and practices that were unfamiliar to most of the volunteers. Everything had to be explained, yet since most refugees did not understand English or Greek, volunteers had to find ways to communicate even the simplest things. Ilektra observed that the volunteers tended to have a "Western idea" of doing things that the refugees had never experienced. She notes, "If a practice is not part of your culture, you have a difficult time interpreting it and will even view it with distrust." There were more general differences involving manners of dress and observing specific dietary customs, but many of the differences were gender-based, such as always giving priority to women and children or following certain hygienic practices. All sandwiches were made with cheese and turkey, no pork, yet many refugees were skeptical of what they were served. The volunteers knew that they would need to help women with their periods. They bought the necessary supplies and put them on tables where the women were free to take what they needed. Still nobody touched them. Finally some Muslim women from one of the NGOs, knowing that the women would not publicly accept them in front of the men, began distributing them privately.

Robin Jones remembers one day seeing a little girl sitting alone in a corner wearing the same wet sneakers and top that she had on when she got off the bus. She was shivering and her lips were turning blue. It was November, and the air and sea were frigid when she had made the crossing only a couple of hours earlier. Robin tried to get her to take them off so she could dress her in some dry clothing, but the girl cried and begged her to stop. All of a sudden she realized that the girl was preadolescent, that the clothes she had on, as wet as they were, were all that was left of her traditional garb, and that she would not remove them in the presence of men. Robin and other volunteers stretched a large sheet around her to conceal her from others and then she was able to change into dry clothes. In retrospect Robin says that it makes her sad when she thinks about the respect the refugees needed and deserved but did not get in the chaos of the moment.[31]

Ilektra recalls when one of the volunteers at Oxy came to her with an elderly man who wanted to be taken back to Turkey. He had become separated from his wife and children when he boarded the boat in Turkey. After he had landed in Eftalou, his family called him on his cell phone to tell him that they had not been able to get on the boat and subsequently had decided not to go to Greece after all. Not knowing how to handle an unusual situation like this, Ilektra made some phone calls, but failing to obtain any reliable information, she told the man that when he got to Moria, he could try to look for someone wearing the UNHCR vest and tell them that he needed to go back to Turkey. The grateful man kissed Ilektra's hands for helping him, and he went on his way. There was no way for her to ever know what happened to him.[32]

Volunteers at Oxy had a great deal of compassion for the children who had to leave everything behind when they fled their countries and arrived with only the clothes they were wearing and their families—if they were lucky. If they were unaccompanied, their families, likely fearful that they would be killed, had forced them to flee their homelands and start out alone. Then there were some children whose families had perished during the long overland trek or drowned in the sea during the crossing, sometimes only a few hours before they arrived at Oxy. Theirs was a heart-wrenching story of profound physical and emotional suffering, which some were too young to even fully comprehend.[33] It was important, therefore, to create experiences that would brighten the children's spirits. Ute chose to work with boys and girls between three and five years of age because she felt that, in some small way, she could help them understand what had happened in their lives and think about a future that was different from their past. Once they had changed into dry clothing, they seemed content to just play, so Ute brought with her all kinds of materials and items from her home. The children came to her in waves. One or more groups would arrive from the beach, and another group would leave with their families to board a bus to Moria or Kara Tepe. That was the way it all worked, and volunteers had to adapt to these sudden arrivals and departures.

Even though children from different countries were in her play groups, they all gravitated toward similar things. Whether she brought materials to construct things or paper and crayons to draw pictures, the girls made houses and the boys made guns, usually very big ones. Ute said that, after she had been working with small children for a couple of weeks, she began to ask the boys to imagine that they lived in a safe place without guns and to build something they would like to have in their new life. It took a while for them to think about this, but sometimes the boys would end up playing together with the girls, drawing houses instead of guns.[34]

Robin Jones had already begun painting with the children on the beach back in the spring when she and her husband, Robert, first started to help with the landings. It had been so successful that, after Oxy opened, Robin decided to hold watercolor painting classes for the children to help pass the time while they rested or waited to board the buses. She fashioned paintbrushes by cutting a bunch of sponges into little squares, and she cut all the watercolor paper she had at home into squares on which they could paint. As might have been expected, the children spilled water and paint all over, so Robin wanted to find a different medium. One day, while shopping in a toy and art supply store in Kalloni, she happened upon markers and tablets of paper that could be used for drawing without all the mess associated with watercolors. She immediately bought everything the store had in stock. Having what she describes as "the very American penchant for Ziploc bags," she also bought enough of them to make packages for each child to use.[35]

Equipped with her new supply of materials, she spread a large table-cloth on the ground outside of one of the tents in which families gathered to rest and catch their breath from the boat crossing. If the weather was unfavorable, she moved her "art class" inside. Families would arrive, get dry clothes and something to eat, and then the wait for the buses to Kara Tepe or Moria would begin. Since no one knew when the next bus would come, Robin was aware, as was Ute, that the children might have to leave right in the middle of their drawing. It could be three minutes; it could be an hour or more. Nobody knew what to expect. To attract the children's attention, she laid markers out on the cloth "like candy" hoping to entice them to come over. It usually took only one or two of them showing initial interest, along with motioning to others with a smile, to get a group together. The parents, cautious and very protective, would approach with their children but then hang back and watch. Robin says that, before long, "it all just started flowing into this moment of joy with the children eagerly engaged in drawing, using their packet of multicolored markers." Everything they drew was fresh in their minds; their drawings revealed that they were processing what had just happened to them. They used many bright colors to draw tanks shooting at people, trees, birds, flowers, the sun, boats filled with people floating on blue water, flags, hearts, houses, and mountains. Seeing how happy their children were, the parents expressed their gratitude to Robin with hugs and smiles.[36]

This same scenario was repeated over and over again each day as more families arrived at Oxy, and Robin and Robert ended up with countless drawings in their possession. Given the enormity of what they faced working at Oxy, it was only later—after their return home to California—that they had the time and energy to inspect what the children had drawn. With the help of a psychologist, Debra Linesch, chair of the Department of Marital and Family Therapy at Loyola Marymount University in Los Angeles, California, they gained important insights into the children's thoughts and feelings at that time. Linesch observed that their drawings of Iraq, Afghanistan, or Syria, and even the guns, revealed what normalcy was to them. Most of them probably had never seen an open body of water, but a blue stripe almost always appeared in their drawings, depicting the separation between where they were and where they had come from. They drew what Lesvos looked like to them from the boat out at sea, with its mountains and villages. They provided, sometimes graphic, depictions of the war that they had observed. It was all there. Robin said that the whole experience working with the children at Oxy was so vivid for her that she can remember each child who made a drawing.[37]

Dina says that Oxy was "beautiful" because, to her, it was a place where people responded as best they could to a never-ending wave of refugees that relied on them: "As volunteers, we were all the refugees had; no other form of aid was available. We couldn't imagine what it must have been like for them to make the terrifying crossing and then discover that they were not where they had thought they were actually going. On top of that, they had to experience the shock of so few people being there to help them."[38] When the volunteers had a moment to pause, they realized the absurdity of the moment they were all sharing together, and they would say to themselves and each other, "Isn't this nuts?"[39] Ilektra remembers the day when there were some six thousand people at Oxy all at one time. She says, "It was unbelievable; there were people everywhere. Small children were walking in the road. Local people were driving on the road and yelling very angrily at the refugees out the windows of their cars." She was terrified that "something really bad" would happen, although she wasn't sure what that something might be exactly. Fortunately nothing ever did.[40]

Robert Omar Hamilton, one of the Starfish volunteers at Oxy, wrote in his article published in *Guernica* that it was almost like being robots because, with thousands of refugees arriving continuously, they all found themselves doing and repeating the same things over and over again: "Welcome to Lesvos. You're in a transit point in the countryside. We're all volunteers here working to help you get to the government camp in the south of the island. Here's a bus ticket. The bus leaves tomorrow morning. You'll get your papers from the government there. When you have your papers, you can continue on to Athens. Here is a ticket for food. There are dry clothes in the tent behind us. There are blankets in the big tent. Welcome. Hello. [Smile. Smile.] Hello. Welcome to Lesvos. Is this your daughter? Hello! Would you like a biscuit? Here you go. Sir, you're in a transit point in the countryside . . ."[41]

Even when dealing with seriously injured refugees, Hamilton sometimes felt as if he was working and talking without being truly aware of what he was saying or of the degree of trauma that he was witnessing right in front of him: "This refugee's boat missed the beach and crashed on the rocks. He jumped out to try and steer it away from danger. The waves pushed the boat up over him, pushed him down under the water, pushed him back down onto the rocks. He can't move his legs. We need a wheelchair. We'll get you to the hospital, sir. It will just be temporary, God willing. You'll be fine tomorrow, God willing. Does anyone have a car?! We'll find someone to drive you to the hospital." Yet somewhere deep inside he suspected that the trip to the hospital would take hours and that the refugee might actually die from the injuries, but he couldn't bring himself to go there because the reality of it might be far too much for the refugee—and for him—to cope with. Hundreds, if not thousands of times, volunteers told the refugees, "When you get to Moria, you'll be able to buy a ticket for the ferry to Athens and then go on to Europe." They were all aware that there would be a long wait to get that ticket and that both camps were unsanitary, chaotic, overcrowded, and filled with riot police. There were reports of fights, tear gas, and panic, but in those moments, the volunteers didn't know what else to say. The reality was all just too much for them to contemplate, and they couldn't help but ask themselves, "What are we doing here? Where are we sending these people?"[42]

Jack Rowland, another Starfish volunteer at Oxy, made a video recording of himself at the end of a long day in which he had seen busload after busload of people come in from seven in the morning until well after midnight. He said that he felt "physically, mentally, emotionally broken" and thought it was due to a lack of sleep and working fourteen-hour days. "We just have a lot of people to help and we're short-staffed. It's so busy. Buses bring groups of refugees in from the beach where they have just landed, and as soon as they have unloaded and headed back to the beach, more buses arrive. They just never stop." That afternoon, a potentially volatile situation erupted between Afghans and Syrians, but he said that it was diffused when they "started a game of limbo that turned into a tug of war between the two, and the Afghans won." He added with a laugh that it ended up being "quite fun." Although he was exhausted, he said, "You really can't let yourself get down when you see all the refugees smiling."

On that particular night, Rowland was worried that people were going to die because the temperature was below freezing. There were not enough buses to take the huge number of refugees that had landed that day to Moria and Kara Tepe, and as a result, hundreds had to spend the night at Oxy. He said, "The tents were all full, and the refugees who came in really late, all of them wet, are having to sleep outside where there's no cover from the wind whatsoever. They've got sleeping bags, but it's so cold." He talked about trying to get them to dance to keep warm. "There was even a point where the Pakistanis, Afghans, and Syrians were all doing the macarena together, but it just got colder and darker, and you heard people crying. You hand out water and food, but you just have to sit with them when they're crying and when they're sad."

He talked about sitting with one of the women who had just arrived: "I asked her if she was okay, and she replied, 'No. My home is dead. Syria is dead. It doesn't matter who wins, Assad or ISIS, as they call it. They've killed my country, and I can never go back,' and she just burst into tears.

None of them wanted to leave their countries. They just wanted to live happily. She started to tell me about her garden and how she was named after a daisy that grew there. She told me the names of the flowers that grew in her garden and that she'll never see it again. It made her happy for a little bit just to talk about it, but she's just so sad that she will never be able to go home again." He ended the recording by saying, "It's been a very emotional day, and I'm going to get some rest now."[43]

Everyone who worked with the refugees during the crisis said the same thing: Whatever situation they encountered, they simply did whatever they had to do, and they learned as they went along. They were all completely in the moment. It was always "all hands on deck."[44] Because of the vast number of people who needed to be tended to, Ilektra found she functioned best if she simply focused on what had to be done and just did it: "I wanted to give out water, a sandwich, and wish them good luck because that's what they needed. They needed help right then and there, and that's what I could do. I hope they at least felt that some of us understood that they were trying to find a new and safe life and that we were willing to help them a little bit along the way. Hopefully one day they'll succeed and have a good life in the future, and that's a good thing."[45] Robin Jones used to walk through Oxy, trying not to step on people's hands and feet. As she went, she would bend down to people's eye level to say, "Hello" and ask them if they were alright. She did this intentionally because she realized at the time that volunteers simply could not offer that kind of individual attention.[46]

Robert Jones said that he could feel the "exhaustion from dealing with the unknown," and he knew that all of the volunteers felt it too. At times, they thought they couldn't continue to deal with the terrible reality of it all, but there came a point where the work became addictive. "They lived off the beauty of the refugees actually surviving the trip and arriving on the beaches, and they would get dewy-eyed with relief that the refugees were all in a safe place and that they had been able to help them. Then, in the rare but extreme moments when no refugees came, there was an emptiness, a hole." In those times, a kind of "refugee fatigue" would set in, but then more refugees would arrive, and they would go out and do it all again. Although Robert hesitated to use the word "addiction," he said that it was the best way he could describe it. "It was a serious responsibility for the volunteers, one that also had a significant impact on each and every one of us."[47]

In a second video that Jack Rowland made on the eve of his departure—at the end of his two weeks as a volunteer at Oxy—he told a story that he hoped would encourage others to go there and help. It was a story that another volunteer had told him when he first arrived, and he believed it was one to remember when faced with something like this: "When you help a thousand people, a thousand more come, and what we do is just a drop in the ocean, and it can get on top of you, and you never really feel like you're doing enough and you're not making a difference, but we hope to help a lot of starfish. It's a merry band of volunteers, and we're making a difference. Send sleeping bags if you can; send money if you can. Oxy is a hands-on charity. It's not going to the big organizations with bonuses to people at the top. Get on a plane if you can, turn up in Molyvos, ask for the Captain's Table, and they'll point you in the right direction."[48]

20. Lines of refugees at Oxy wait to register or obtain food and bus tickets. The dance platform of the Oxy Nightclub is in the background. © Robin Jones.

21. Clothing hangs to dry on the guard rails along the road at Oxy. © Robin Jones.

22. Robin Jones (*center*), in the yellow volunteer's vest, helps children draw pictures with colored markers in one of the large tents at Oxy. © Robin Jones.

23. Young refugee shows his drawing that he has just done of war in his homeland. © Robin Jones.

15

The Calamitous Shipwreck

October 28, 2015

On October 28, 2015, at around five in the afternoon, Peggy Whitfield, a British volunteer working for Starfish at Oxy, was busy handing out bus tickets to waiting refugees when her cell phone buzzed with a WhatsApp message. It read: "First boat has ten unconscious children." In her diary, where she made entries almost every other hour that day, she wrote, "Like so many things here in Lesvos, it starts with a WhatsApp message," but this time seemed somehow different. She dropped everything she was doing and hurried to the harbor "armed with nothing but a desire to help, a handful of emergency blankets, and a dim memory of CPR training undertaken over a year ago." As she headed down the road that led to the harbor, an ambulance sped up the hill toward her carrying one of the unconscious children from that first group of ten; this was to be that day's first of many runs to the hospitals in Kalloni and Mytilene.[1]

It was a chilly, cloudy day with rough seas, the kind of weather that, in the past, had caused the number of refugee crossings to decrease until spring, but that had not yet happened. In fact refugees continued to arrive in record daily numbers, leaving the volunteers at Oxy and on the beach to worry about how they were going to manage when the wind and cold of winter actually began. Eric and Philippa Kempson, together with one of the volunteers who was working with them at the time, were standing on the beach near their home in Eftalou, watching as a large double-deck wooden boat carrying approximately three hundred refugees approached the shore.[2] The men were all standing on the upper deck while the women and children rode in the enclosed lower deck, where they were partially protected from the wind and the heavy spray that washed over the boat each time it hit a wave. Suddenly they saw the top deck collapse onto the lower deck, and within seconds the entire boat disappeared beneath the surface of the water.

The scene was not entirely new to the Kempsons. In the last eight months they had been there when boats crashed against the rocks, capsized in high waves, or sank when a vessel's rubber or plastic material ripped apart. They had seen many casualties, and while the loss of life always horrified them, more often than not, if the boats were anywhere near the shore, they usually managed to guide the passengers to safety. That afternoon they stood frozen in place because they had never before witnessed a vessel of that size capsize with such a large number of passengers on board. Several moments later they began to see life jackets popping up on the sea's surface, but there was no sign of the boat. They quickly alerted everyone in the area, and soon the Coast Guard cutter and its crew, along with many fishing boats and privately owned crafts, appeared on the scene to begin pulling refugees from the water and transporting them to the Molyvos harbor. Nobody was prepared for a tragedy of this magnitude, and it required several hours and many trips back and forth before all of the refugees floating on the surface, alive or dead, were brought to shore.[3]

News of the accident quickly gripped the harbor. Although it had become fairly commonplace for the Coast Guard boat and crew to leave suddenly on something other than a routine patrol mission, it always generated anxiety because everyone knew from experience that they would soon return, bringing injured, dead, and dying refugees whom they had pulled from the sea. That afternoon, when people in the harbor saw fishermen and private boat owners, even those who had just returned from their day on the water, suddenly leave their slips and head out around the sea wall, they sensed that something dreadful had happened. By the time Whitfield reached the harbor, rescue boats had already started to come in from Eftalou, and people, "faces pale and drawn," were running everywhere. Some were taking injured children from the arms of the Coast Guard crew members and fishermen, who handed them over from their boats. Others were trying to remove children's wet clothing so they could quickly wrap them in emergency blankets to get them warm. Whitfield watched men disassemble tables from the harbor's restaurants so they could be used as stretchers and bodyboards on which to carry refugees to an "impromptu medical clinic" that was set up on the harbor pavement and then to ambulances whenever they arrived.[4] Perhaps the most sobering sight for her was the dead bodies being carried in people's arms and on tabletops to a place on the pavement outside of the fray, where they would be picked up later and put into body bags if enough of those could be found.

In her diary Whitfield described what happened when she reached the wharf and one of the Coast Guard crew suddenly handed her a child who was foaming at the mouth and whose lips had turned blue because she was not breathing: "I pull her clothes off and wrap her in an emergency blanket. Where is the doctor? They are all busy with other children. I tilt her head to try to check her airway, but her jaw is clamped shut from the cold. I hold her face. No response. I start chest compressions. The nearest medic is doing the same to a little boy, whom I later learn is her brother. Their father is pacing back and forth between them. I check for her breath again. Nothing. So I turn her around onto her front and try to knock the seawater out of her. Still nothing. More chest compressions, more foam at her mouth, still no breathing. I turn her again and strike her from behind once more. This time she vomits, but her breath is weak and ragged. Finally a doctor comes. It's been barely a minute, but it felt like hours. My body floods with relief as he takes over. She and her brother will survive, but many did not."[5] Daphne Tolis, a Greek documentary filmmaker who was also there, described how she watched two Afghan brothers, ages three and seven, both suffering from severe hypothermia, being resuscitated next to each other. One survived; the other did not. It was the first time she had seen a child die.[6]

As the afternoon and evening wore on, rescue boats bearing their human cargo—the dead and the survivors—kept arriving at such a steady pace that every available spot at the piers was occupied, and just as soon as one boat pulled away, another one was waiting to take its place. Little room was left for the larger Coast Guard boat to maneuver as it made repeated trips to and from Eftalou, and the number of smaller vessels entering and leaving the harbor created such congestion that it was no longer possible for boats to dock. Getting the injured—particularly the women and children suffering from hypothermia or close to death from serious water inhalation—off the boats and into the hands of volunteers and medics as quickly as possible was critical. Some survivors could walk on their own, but even they were desperately cold and wet and needed immediate attention. Trying to remove the dead from the boats and place them where they could be identified by the survivors also required quick action. There was no time to wait until a slip or a spot at the pier became available—refugees had to walk or be carried across other boats, sometimes several in a row, to get onto the pier.[7]

By six in the evening, Whitfield reported that they had so many children "teetering on the brink of life and death" that their supply of oxygen in tanks had started to run low. Fortunately a team from Frontex had been able to make its way to the harbor with an ample supply, but for her, the next few hours were "a blur of emergency blankets, car runs for dry clothes, food distribution, and howls of grief from mothers of missing babies and from men who can't find their wives." She and several other volunteers began to look after the children who had lost their parents when the boat sank. They hoped that many of them would be found, but they also knew that some of them were probably lost forever. In her diary she wrote, "The smallest ones don't understand, but the teenagers understand all too well. I don't know what to say to them. I just distract them and keep them warm. We try to hide our tears from them." Later that evening the harbor became so overrun that the village of Molyvos opened a church and a hall situated in the harbor where the traumatized refugees could find shelter. Here Starfish volunteers would have a place to distribute food. Still there was not enough space for everyone, and some people were forced to spend the night outside. Whitfield continued, "I see mothers and fathers reunited with their children, but relief is tainted with the despair of those who are still searching for loved ones."[8]

Unable to get out to where the large boat had sunk, Eric and Philippa Kempson rushed to the harbor and positioned themselves near the Sea Horse café to assist with survivors. It was utter bedlam. Shortly after a boatload of refugees—mostly children—had been brought in, Eric spotted a Coast Guard officer standing in the middle of the chaos "crying his eyes out." Around him lay dead children and some survivors who were all in need of immediate medical attention. When Eric approached, the officer told him, "I've got dead children everywhere."[9] Melinda, who knew the officer well, said that that he "lost it that day; he just couldn't cope. He kept saying with utter desperation in his voice, 'What do I do now? What do I do now?'"[10]

Ute witnessed the entire scene unfold that day from her shop windows. Many of the injured and dead were laid on the pavement. The memory that affected her most was of a mother who had fled Syria with her three children after her husband was murdered. All of her children drowned, but she was on the deck of the Coast Guard boat and saw the crew pull them from the water. Ute watched the mother follow the crew as they carried her children's dead bodies from the boat to the pier and lay them on the ground in front of her shop. She says that the sight and the piercing sound of the mother weeping over her dead children is something she will never forget.[11]

Like Ute, Dina vividly recalls her encounter that day with a mother who had been separated from her four-year-old son. Dina's role as a volunteer had always been to remain on the front lines with Melinda, but the emotional toll of events began to affect her health, so she pulled back and took over the managerial responsibilities in the Starfish office. While she was on her way to the office that afternoon, she saw the crisis in the harbor and rushed over to try to be of help. She found a mother who was deeply distraught because she had become separated from her son, and she was sitting with her when a volunteer came over to say that her son had drowned. Dina's eyes well up with tears when she describes that moment, "The scream of that mother when she was told that her son was dead, I will never forget . . . the scream."[12]

Melinda found herself in the middle of the entire scene helping to direct movement on the pier as refugees came off the boats, all the while doing what she could to ensure that volunteers had the necessary supplies. Molyvos had no resident doctor, and the only hospitals on the island of Lesvos were in Kalloni and Mytilene. As everyone who worked on the beaches knew all too well, doctors were always scarce, if any were available at all. Melinda said that, almost miraculously, on that day when the need was at its greatest, a few doctors from the Boat Refugee Foundation, a Dutch NGO, appeared "as if from out of nowhere." They moved among the masses of refugees to help volunteers with those who were in serious shape and close to death. Melinda was trying, desperately and unsuccessfully, to resuscitate one of the children who had nearly drowned, when one of the doctors instructed her to hold the child upside down and hit him on the back to make the water come out of his lungs. Never having done anything like this before and feeling unsure, she kept asking the doctor if she was doing the right thing. Four years later, when she recalls the scene in the harbor that day, she grows clearly upset. She says, "It was so overwhelming that when I close my eyes, I can still see it!"[13] When Eri talks about the events of that day, she says, "I've seen Melinda weep about this so many times, but there was nothing I could really do to help her because I was in the same situation."[14]

At around two the next morning, Peggy Whitfield, still on duty, encountered an Iraqi family—a husband and wife and their two sons, aged eight and three—trying to sleep on the harbor pavement. They had survived and been brought in earlier that day. Whitfield learned that the wife was thirty-five weeks pregnant and that she and the family had been in the water for hours before being rescued. When the woman told her that she could feel her baby kicking, Whitfield decided that she could not let them spend the remainder of the night on the cold harbor stones, and she took them to where she was staying and put them to bed. When morning came, the family shared their story. They had paid $3,000 each for their voyage from Turkey to Lesvos, more than double the normal price, because they were told that the large wooden boat they were on was the safest kind. After the boat was well out on the water, it began to creak and nails began to spring from the timbers. Then it fell apart entirely. The husband and wife managed to find a life ring and kept their children close. They told their boys, "Today is not the day we are going to die." The woman explained that while she was swimming "she felt the limbs of drowned people brushing against her belly." One of her sons was scared of sharks, but as long as they swam she continued to reassure him that sharks like the one in *Jaws* did not live in those waters. She promised him that, as soon as they got to dry land, the first thing she would do would be to buy him the roller skates he had always wanted.[15]

Children were on everyone's mind, and they were the focus of much of the relief effort in the harbor because they were the most vulnerable to the water and the cold, and every endeavor was made, even amid the mayhem of that day, to try to reconnect families. The next day, when things had calmed down a bit, volunteers took the ten remaining children who had survived, albeit separated from their parents, to the hospital in Mytilene for observation. Hospital staff took pictures of the children, and the volunteers brought the pictures back to Melinda in the hope that she could use them to locate their parents. To her surprise and joy, she was able to reunite all ten children with their parents. She says, "It was as happy an ending as one could hope to have after a day like that."[16]

After the accident, divers and lifeguards from the Barcelona-based NGO Proactiva Open Arms—which had just been organized earlier that month—assisted with the search and rescue operation that extended the length of the coast from Skala Sykaminias all the way to Petra, where nearly thirty bodies washed up two days later. The Coast Guard estimated that forty-three people died that day and that thirty-eight remained missing, but it was very difficult to get accurate figures.[17] The search for the dead continued for more than a week with only partial success, and dead bodies washed ashore for quite a time afterward.[18] The problem was that no one could ever be sure whether all the bodies were from the October 28 incident because bodies of refugees who had drowned at sea, washed up all the time.[19]

The events of October 28 were captured in the short Oscar-nominated documentary *4.1 Miles* made by the Greek filmmaker Daphne Matziaraki.[20] Inspired by the work of Molyvos-based Greek Coast Guard boat captain Kyriakos Papadopoulos, Daphne traveled from her home in the United States to Lesvos to film him and his small crew as they rescued refugees from the water. When she arrived in Lesvos, she reported that "there were just four Greek Coast Guard boats, each with four- or five-person crews, and one helicopter from the European border patrol" on the whole island. Most of the Coast Guard crew did not have CPR training, and boats lacked the basic equipment to deal with search and rescue emergencies. They felt alone and abandoned, and the captain thought the entire world was turning its back on the crisis. About Captain Papadopoulos, Matziaraki said, "He is a truly honorable man who has a real sense of responsibility; he cannot afford to lose one person—and the people and the children that he does lose really haunt him." Prior to October 28, he had already saved thousands of refugees.[21]

After some time in Molyvos, Matziaraki was able to gain permission, which was rarely granted, to accompany the Coast Guard crew on the boat when it went out to pick up refugees. It so happened that she was there on October 28 and rode the Coast Guard boat with Captain Papadopoulos and his crew, including Melinda's friend Eri Grigorelli, as it made its rescue missions. The film contains authentic raw footage, but scenes of dead people—particularly dead children—were cut.[22] The film captured the brave heroism of the crew and the captain, who at the end of the day, when he was preparing his report, stated, "When I look into [the refugees'] eyes, I see their memories of war. They come from war. They escape the bombs that fall on their homes. And we see these families in the Greek sea. Losing each other in the Greek sea. In the sea of a peaceful country because of the way they have to cross."[23] Papadopoulos, hailed as a national hero for rescuing thousands of refugees and migrants, died suddenly of a heart attack on October 9, 2018, at the age of forty-four.[24]

The tragedy of that October day had a profound impact on everyone. No one who witnessed it or was in any way involved remained unscathed. Refugees experienced the terror of their sinking ship as the collapsing top deck crushed passengers on the one below before plunging into the Aegean. The Coast Guard and everyone who came forward to assist with the rescue, both on sea and land, were unable to save everyone, making the loss of life during this single event frightening. The number alone of parents who lost children and children who lost parents was horrifying beyond imagination. In fact the most excruciating memories that volunteers have of that day are the sounds of mothers and fathers mourning their children and the heartrending cries of the orphaned children. Melinda has some painfully vivid memories. She remembers a girl, perhaps twelve or thirteen years of age, hunched on the stones of the pier. The girl had lost every member of her family when the boat sank, and she was screaming in agony. Melinda says that the girl remained there and wailed for a full forty-eight hours. Among the refugees also on the scene were two siblings, a brother and sister, who watched their entire family, parents and grandparents, drown. Another woman on that same boat lost all but one of her children. She lay there on the pier, banging her head against the cement, shrieking for hours. Although she had one remaining child who was still alive, she would not go near him. She needed medical treatment but refused to leave the pier, her bloodcurdling screams piercing the night. Four years later, Melinda is still haunted by the sound.[25]

16

Blessings and Burdens

Volunteers and the NGOs in Molyvos

October and November 2015 saw the average number of refugees increase to a staggering four thousand and sometimes six thousand per day, with still no sign whatsoever that the volume of boat crossings from Turkey would decrease. Local authorities estimated that, in the forty-eight-hour period between October 21 and 22 alone, arrivals exceeded fifteen thousand.[1] On the evening of November 6, standing on the beach at Eftalou against a backdrop of crowds of refugees disembarking from rubber dinghies, Lindsay Hilsum from the United Kingdom's Channel 4 said, "They want to come now because the seas are calm. There are many children, and people feel they need to come now because the weather will get worse."[2] At roughly the same time, volunteers working on the beach were told by refugees that, because of the rush to cross before the weather changed, departures from Turkey were so backed up that they were forced to wait for as long as ten days for their boat to leave.[3] This stoked everyone's fears, both on the beach and at Oxy, because they all wondered how they were going to provide safety and protection for this massive number of refugees when the weather conditions worsened in the winter.

The drop in the volunteer workforce that was caused by the departure of the season's tourists had been replenished by newly arriving volunteers from all over the world. All in all, from October on, thousands of volunteers came to Lesvos in response to the news of the crisis that was being reported live from Molyvos each day.[4] More than two thousand came to work with either Starfish or the Hope Project, and large numbers also joined with other NGOs. By the beginning of November, at least a dozen international

NGOs with their volunteers were at work in Lesvos, but Starfish remained the hub of Molyvos's refugee operation on the north coast. Melinda quickly set the Starfish volunteers to work providing food and clothing, coordinating medical attention, and assisting the Coast Guard in the harbor with the refugees who were in critical condition. Most of her volunteers actually did double duty by also handling the daily operations at Oxy where they registered and provided food, water, shelter, and basic medical care to the thousands of refugees who stayed there while they waited to be transported to Moria and Kara Tepe.[5]

The Kempsons and their volunteers maintained their steady, around-the-clock schedule on the beaches, helping to guide boats to shore and getting the passengers safely on land. Dozens of them also worked at the Kempsons' seaside home unloading and storing supplies that were sent directly to the Hope Project by people from Sweden, Norway, the Netherlands, and England. Their compound had become a kind of nerve center for what was happening at the beach. Boxes of supplies of all kinds—emergency blankets, clothing, diapers, baby clothes and bottles, ladies' hygiene products, tents, sleeping bags, food, fruit, and medical kits—were stored under the canopy by the garden, under trees, on tables, on the ground, everywhere. Some of the medical kits were set aside to be taken down to Moria where they were desperately needed. Eric's studio, where he normally worked on the wood carvings for which he was so well known, became shoe storage. Crates of water were stacked on the patio by the back door of the house. It was common to go through sixty or more in one day. Their daughter, Elleni, organized and maintained an inventory of everything. Once a volunteer team working at the beach had distributed their carload of supplies, one of them would drive back up to the house where another team of volunteers was waiting to reload the car with boxes full of fresh supplies, and the driver would return directly to the beach to meet the next wave of boats. Meanwhile the volunteers at the house would set about refilling the empty boxes that they would then load into other cars, already waiting in the driveway. This cycle went on around the clock as the refugee boats kept coming.[6]

There were also scores of independent volunteers with no NGO affiliation who took it upon themselves to travel to Lesvos on their own and at their own expense. As soon as they landed in Mytilene, they rented cars or vans, filled them with bottled water and other supplies, and headed to the beaches. Once there, they spent their time driving back and forth on the coastal road between Eftalou and Skala Sykaminias, always on the lookout for boats heading toward the shore and landings in progress. Sometimes they could easily pull over and quickly leave their cars on the side of the road, but oftentimes they had to scramble down steep embankments, carrying their supplies to where boats had come ashore.

For the most part, the volunteers who showed up in Molyvos were both capable and deeply committed to helping the refugees. However, along with their geographical, cultural, linguistic, and political diversity came varied styles of working and interacting, as well as their often-competing notions of organization and supervision.[7] Melinda and the Starfish Board had anticipated such diversity, as had Eric and Philippa with the Hope Project, and they established guidelines and standards for their volunteers that enabled them to embrace and accommodate the differences within their organizations. Above all, they insisted that their volunteers respect the village and its people, and they tried to help them understand that the locals' livelihoods and the space they called home were dramatically impacted in ways that outsiders might not see. Residents of Molyvos admittedly had mixed emotions about the refugees and were frightened by their numbers, but many reached out generously to help in one way or another, whether it was with dry clothing, food, water, something for the children, or a bed for the night. They had also endured the effects of the refugee invasion on their local economy and the way they went about their daily lives. Melinda and Eric both wanted to ensure that the volunteers and workers who came from the outside understood this and that they treated the local people and their property with the utmost respect.

Ilektra, who encountered many of the Starfish volunteers at Oxy, found it remarkable and admirable that people would leave their home countries where there were no refugee problems and travel all the way to Lesvos to help. "I'm not sure if I would do such a thing," she admitted but then added, "Of course, not everyone is in a position to do that because of money, job, or family." At the same time, she also observed that many of the independent unaffiliated volunteers and the volunteers and staff who arrived with the larger NGOs were not held to the same standards of conduct as those who came to work with Starfish or the Hope Project. They showed little understanding or appreciation of the extent to which the people in the village had already been caring for the refugees long before anyone from the outside even knew about the crisis. Ilektra found their desire to help the refugees commendable, but she saw that they lacked empathy—that they "didn't care about the place itself"—giving rise to misunderstandings and hard feelings among the people in the community that were not easy to overcome.[8]

Melinda was inclined to be less circumspect: "A lot of the volunteers just came in and did whatever they wanted to do without asking what was actually needed," she says, referring to independent volunteers who landed in Mytilene, rented cars, filled them with cases of water, and arrived in Molyvos, only to find that Melinda already had plenty of water but was in desperate need of shoes. Given the enormity of what Melinda dealt with, she says, "It was frustrating when they would just show up without first trying to find out what was needed before making purchases. People just felt that they could do whatever they wanted, and sometimes that wasn't helpful." At the same time, not wishing to seem ungrateful, she always pointed out that, in spite of the problems, the volunteers shared a serious commitment to humanitarian ideals: "They cared, and they found kindred spirits in the other volunteers who also cared."[9]

It may have been that sense of kindred spirits that inspired volunteers to keep coming back. This was the case with many volunteers who worked with the Kempsons' Hope Project. One such volunteer, a medic from Norway who had only been in Eftalou for less than twenty-four hours, was tending to a fifteen-year-old boy who had endured the entire trip to Lesvos covered in shrapnel wounds. Eric had carried him off the refugee boat and laid him on the beach next to his mother. When the nurse looked at the boy and noticed that his whole torso had turned black, she knew right away that he would not make it to the hospital. He only lived for three more days. It was this nurse's first time as a volunteer, but despite what she experienced on that first day of her first trip, she chose to come back seven more times. Five years after the height of the crisis in Molyvos passed, volunteers still return to the Hope Project warehouse to help. Eric says of those volunteers, "They just keep coming back because they can't get it out of their system," but he goes on to say that the volunteers who were there in the late fall of 2015 were all severely affected. "They've never been 'right' since that time. They saw too many bodies, too many deaths, too much misery. Too much went on. It was like a war zone."[10]

There also was a darker side to the volunteer story, one that was unforeseen amid the profusion of dedication and goodwill—one that caused its own share of problems. Not all volunteers arrived on truly charitable or altruistic missions. There were volunteer groups from various religious organizations who came to the beaches intent upon converting the refugees to Christianity and whose aggressive behavior impeded landings and endangered many lives. Some of them actually ventured out into the water and tried to board the boats to give Bibles to the refugees even before they had landed. Others remained on the beach and preached to them rather than offering water, food, or dry clothing. At times, competing religious groups even fought with each other in an attempt to gain access to the refugees. More often than not, Eric and Philippa found themselves all alone as they tried to tactfully handle what Eric referred to as the "religious wars."[11]

There also were what Eric refers to as "traffickers": people posing as volunteers who came to the beaches trying to pick up babies and children. He tells the story of one incident on the beach after a boatload of refugees had landed: He saw a volunteer, someone he had not seen before, sitting on the beach with her back to him. At first he assumed that she was sitting there overwhelmed by what she had just experienced, but when he walked over to her, he discovered that she was hiding a baby next to her. She had come to the beach looking for a baby and had "stolen" one from a boat that had just arrived. Another instance involved a baby who came in on one of the boats with her parents and suddenly went missing while the children were being handed to volunteers and carried to the beach. Nobody knew how or when it had happened. They frantically searched everywhere for the baby. Finally, seven hours later, she was found in a chair in a restaurant in Kalloni. "No one knows to this day how she got there."[12]

The dark side of people's behavior was not limited to volunteers; it extended to reporters as well. Long before any NGOs arrived, camera crews and journalists pitched in with the tourists to help on the beaches. Reporters who showed up in Molyvos that summer, like the tourists, were generally quick to lend a hand, and their involvement was often a critical factor in the saving of lives. Indeed, had Franck Genauzeau, the reporter for France 2, not boarded the refugee boat—albeit clandestinely—to report on one of the crossings, the entire boatload of refugees might have lost their lives when the motor stalled, leaving them stranded in the channel in the middle of the night. There was also a BBC reporter who drove a refugee to the medical center in Kalloni in his car after the man's leg had been torn apart during a landing. Had the reporter not been there, that refugee might very well have bled to death on the beach. However, once the news about the crisis in Molyvos became more widely known, reporters began to show up in large numbers, all vying for the most sensational stories. Some of them were very aggressive, particularly independent reporters with no recognizable press affiliation. They flocked to the beaches as refugees were landing, and in their rush to film a rescue in progress, they elbowed volunteers and medics out of the way. Still other reporters, seemingly employed by news organizations with a particular bias, were observed screaming "Taliban" at the refugees or yelling at them to go home. Eric refers to such reporters as "vicious paparazzi" but quickly tempers his remarks, noting that they always tried to work cooperatively with the press because they wanted legitimate reporters there to keep the world informed about what was happening.[13]

The police were always a factor in the way the refugee drama transpired in Molyvos. In the days before the repeal of the law forbidding the transportation of refugees by vehicle, their role was an unpopular one that generated great tension in the community because they were enforcing a statute that many deemed inhumane and unjust. Eric claims that, despite the tension back then, the police were not really enemies; they understood how very difficult the situation had become for everyone, including themselves. He says, "Often the police simply didn't want to know about a lot of the things we were doing because we were breaking the law," and he proceeded to tell how, one day, while he was talking with a policeman, Philippa drove by with a refugee in their car, which was, of course, illegal. The policeman said, "Eric,

I didn't see that," and they both laughed. Once the volunteers, cameramen, and reporters started coming from all over the world, the police stepped up to the challenges imposed by the completely unfamiliar and ever-changing situations and conditions. Except for the volunteers specifically working for either Starfish or the Hope Project, it was impossible to keep track of who was there or what the outsiders were actually doing. However, when dark and terrible things happened, like child abductions and people interfering with the safety of rescue operations, the police always intervened to establish order, make arrests, and remove wrongdoers from the island.[14]

Even from back in the days of First Stop, everyone involved with the refugee crisis knew that, sooner or later, additional help from Greece, the EU, and international aid organizations would be needed, and it was more or less assumed that their help would come in a timely manner. They only had to look at the reports from places around the world where disasters struck to see that the United Nations, the Red Cross, and other NGOs were usually on the scene to provide money and personnel. Their well-crafted advertisements in the media offer plenty of evidence of their presence and effectiveness. It seemed to everyone that this was a crisis that certainly warranted their attention. International aid organizations such as the UNHCR and the IRC were in Mytilene in early 2015 but failed to set up any operations in the north where the majority of refugee landings actually took place.[15] Melinda spoke numerous times to both organizations about the acute need for their help in Molyvos. Michael and Tim made international contacts continually, hoping to bring attention to the situation, and Eric Kempson's videos that he posted online were more than ample testimony of the turmoil being caused by the refugee onslaught on the northern beaches. Even Greek Coast Guard ensign Chrisafis Theofilos made multiple requests to the Greek Coast Guard headquarters in Athens for additional assistance and supplies. The fact that help did not come when the situation began to reach crisis proportions was at first perplexing, then inconceivable, and ultimately infuriating. People couldn't figure out why it took so long for the NGOs stationed in Mytilene to extend their operations to the north and why other NGOs were not coming to Greece at all. It felt as if they were downright ignoring what was happening in Molyvos. Ensign

Theofilos stated publicly that he and his crew felt abandoned, and this certainly mirrored the feelings of people in Molyvos. Over time, with the uninterrupted masses of refugees overrunning the village and no outside help forthcoming, their feelings turned into utter panic.

The first major established international NGO did not arrive in Molyvos until late July when Doctors Without Borders/Médecins Sans Frontières (MSF) came in. They immediately joined together with the UNHCR and the IRC in Mytilene to provide funds for buses to transport refugees to Moria. By that time, the refugees had already converged by the hundreds, and even the thousands, in the school parking lot, and while the availability of buses did help to alleviate some of the crowding and reduce the number of refugees being forced to make the trek to Moria on foot, in the opinion of many, their arrival was already too late.[16]

A few other smaller NGOs started to appear in September and October. Among the earliest to arrive was Proactiva Open Arms, the Barcelona-based NGO devoted to search and rescue operations at sea that was actually set up that October in Lesvos; their volunteers began working right away on the beach alongside the Kempsons. Proactiva had two fully outfitted boats and a team of rescuers, all of whom were young, strong, and trained to work in the most challenging locations. They were equipped to tow boats with broken motors and bring up boats that had sunk. The rescuers were also trained to save refugees who had fallen into the water and rescue people from inaccessible areas of the beach located next to cliffs—often these refugees had to be brought up on ropes. Eric said that Proactiva frequently called him in the middle of the night to ask him to help with boats that had come in. He would shine their battery-powered spotlights on the cliffs while they climbed the ropes, carrying refugees in their arms.

IsraAID, an Israel-based NGO that also carries out search and rescue all over the world, came to the north coast at about the same time as Proactiva. Their team was made up of Palestinian and Israeli doctors, and they—along with Lighthouse Relief and later the UNHCR—set up their base of operations in Skala Sykaminias. Eric and Philippa claimed that IsraAID, like Proactiva, was one of the best NGOs to come to the north coast. The Palestinian and Israeli doctors worked together in teams, and they went straight to the beach to assist with landings and provide medical services that had been completely unavailable in the past because the nearest doctor was in Kalloni. The Palestinian doctors had a calming effect on frightened and injured refugees because they were able to communicate with many of them in Arabic, and the Kempsons enjoy describing the look on refugees' faces when they realized that at least one of the doctors taking care of them was an Israeli Jew. In that particular time and place, the work of IsraAID's doctors offered a vision of what could be achieved through international cooperation and rapprochement. Following Proactiva Open Arms and IsraAID came the Dutch Boat Refugee Foundation, the Norwegian A Drop in the Ocean Foundation, the Greek Red Cross, Islamic Relief, and Greenpeace, among others, but few were active in the north much before December.[17]

The long-awaited arrival of NGOs in Molyvos, like the large-scale arrival of volunteers, was welcomed. The NGOs brought money that was badly needed. Qualified and reliable volunteers made their way to the area as a result of their presence, raising the awareness of the refugee crisis to a global level. This certainly enhanced the resources that flowed to Starfish and the Hope Project. Yet, for the locals, particularly those who had been most closely involved in helping the refugees, the NGO presence and the actions of their staff members also opened an unforeseen and exasperating chapter of conflict and resentment that ultimately threatened to overshadow much of the valuable assistance they provided. In the minds of many who were there at the time, the conflict and acrimony that their actions provoked placed the efficacy of some of the large and well-known aid organizations in doubt.[18]

Stratis Kabanas goes right to the heart of the matter when he says, "The refugees overran the village, but the NGOs ran over us."[19] Reports by outside observers and one from the IRC itself indicated that "tensions between established international NGOs and local volunteer organizations flared occasionally, especially when professional providers began running programs in areas that, until then, had largely been the province of volunteers."[20] In its own report, the IRC acknowledged the tension somewhat obliquely by referring to a "need for greater coordination of response activities and better collaboration among responders, stakeholders, and local communities."[21] The locals saw the whole situation from quite a different perspective, to put it mildly, and they were decidedly unequivocal when voicing their opinions. Once again Stratis sums up their sentiments sincerely and passionately when he explains, "The NGOs moved in with their staff to help, and when they did, they took over roles that had been filled by local people and started bossing the locals around. They just came in and ran over us. They should have helped the locals to help the refugees. We locals knew how to deal with it. We already had dealt with it. We had experience, but the NGOs passed over the locals." Nevertheless he said it with an undertone of bitterness that was shared by many others in the community.[22]

To some, this might seem like nothing more than a petty struggle between the larger centralized organizations and the local volunteers who resented what they saw as NGO interference and hubris rather than helpfulness. However, their resentment can be seen as both sincere and justifiable considering the frightening, months-long struggle that the locals endured in the face of the endless waves of refugees and the effectiveness of their efforts that were born when they had no one to rely on but themselves.

Everyone involved at the local level agreed that it took far longer for the NGOs to get to Molyvos than it should have. For their part, NGOs claimed that they were not allowed to operate in Europe under their existing charters and that their applications to move into Greece got caught up in red tape, thus delaying their arrival. Melinda acknowledges that Greek bureaucracy can be exasperating, but in the same breath she also wonders how smaller outside organizations, such as international church groups, were able to come in and begin working within weeks when it took the larger NGOs months.[23] The mayor of Lesvos at the time reported that, by the end of 2015, over eighty NGOs were operating on Lesvos, but only thirty were registered with the municipality. According to him, some of the NGOs worked cooperatively with the municipality, but many others were "just doing their own thing," and that created such feelings of distrust that many viewed their presence as "disruptive rather than useful."[24]

People's frustrations turned to anger almost immediately when the NGOs started to mistreat and insult local people who, for months, had already been working hard to help the refugees. One day in September when Michael Honegger went to the beach at Eftalou to help, just as he did every day while he and his partner Tim were in Molyvos, he happened upon some people from the IRC who screamed at him and told him that he could not be there. Apparently by that time, the IRC had put itself in charge of the north coast and did not want anyone else around. Stratis had a similar encounter on the beach when a man from one of the NGOs approached him and asked what he was doing there. Stratis responded indignantly, "I'm Greek. I'm from here. I sail these waters. I live here by these beaches. What are YOU doing here?" Stratis was livid that the man, who was not from Lesvos and had only recently arrived with the NGO, implied that he did not belong on the beach helping refugees.[25] Hotel owners became upset that NGO personnel did not respect their properties. The owner of one hotel complained that they walked all over the grounds and parked their cars wherever they wished without asking permission. This particular owner had been helping refugees from the very beginning.[26] He lodged them in some of the hotel's guest rooms and laundered their clothes at his own expense, and it troubled him to be disrespected by people who had no idea how much he had done long before they arrived.[27]

The Kempsons no longer remember how many times they were confronted by NGO representatives on the very beach where they oversaw hundreds of landings before the NGOs had even acknowledged that there was a crisis. Eric claims to have seen UNHCR staff out on the beaches only twice. On one of those two occasions, an arriving boat flipped over in the waves and people fell into the sea. Everyone there, even reporters, ran in to help. As Eric trudged out of the water dripping wet and with a child in his arms, he noticed UNHCR staff members standing on the beach doing nothing. When he asked them why they wouldn't go into the water to rescue people, one of them replied, "It's not our protocol." Eric finally figured out that anyone out on the beach wearing a vest from either the IRC or the UNHCR and assisting directly with a rescue was an unpaid volunteer, not a staff member. The two organizations provided money for the buses to transport refugees, but paid staff members did not help load the buses, nor were they required to help with the beach landings. That was left to the volunteers who received no compensation for their work.[28]

Many of the locals considered the UNHCR to be the worst of the NGOs, but the reputation of the Red Cross was not much better. One day while Michael was in Mytilene, he came upon a Red Cross representative standing on a street corner. He went up to her and asked, "What are you providing for the refugees?" She replied, "We have prepaid phone cards they can use to call a loved one back home for three minutes." Incredulous, Michael said, "Call a loved one? Have you seen the refugees when they come on shore? They take out their cell phones all carefully wrapped in plastic and make calls and take selfies. Haven't you seen them charging their phones in town? All the cafes have charging stations that they use." The Red Cross representative responded, somewhat dumbfoundedly, "No wonder nobody wants my calling cards." Michael thought to himself, "Oh my God, the Red Cross. The refugees need blankets! They need hats! They don't need a phone card!"[29]

Not only were the NGO staff members' attitudes seen as laissez-faire when it came to hands-on involvement with rescue operations but also their general demeanor in public was viewed by many as a flagrantly inappropriate display of privilege and prestige. One observer, a member of the Coast Guard crew who had carried out daring and dangerous rescues at sea, said it was "horrible" to watch paid NGO staff "eating big elaborate meals of fresh fish in the harbor right in front of the refugees and the unpaid volunteers." She claimed that NGO staff members were earning more than adequate salaries and had expense accounts that enabled them to live well while in Molyvos, drive the fanciest cars that local rental agencies had available, and enjoy a regular regimen of expensive meals while their unpaid volunteers who did all of the hard work languished. She also said it was well known among the volunteers that NGO staff members often partied through the night and either overslept or were extremely hungover the following morning.[30]

It also seemed unclear to local observers what the large NGOs actually did for the refugees, if anything. When they arrived on the north coast, they brought with them an entourage of paid staff members who stayed at local hotels and dined in local restaurants. They set up office headquarters and erected tents, and yet it was reported regularly that their staff members were rarely seen, except when a promotional video—during which they were even known to physically push people out of the way—was being shot.[31] One day, five boats came in on a part of the beach where the only way to the road was a path up a very steep escarpment. About two hundred refugees had gone up the path and were standing by the road when all of a sudden a group of police cars and vans with flashing lights appeared. Eric and one of his volunteers carried a child up the path, and when they arrived at the top, a woman "popped out of one of the cars and announced that they were the UNHCR and that they were 'on the beach.'" When the woman blocked Eric's way forward, he saw a film crew up ahead shooting a video of the UN high commissioner and his staff members all wearing UNHCR vests. It became immediately clear to him that they wanted it to appear as if the UNHCR was alone on the beach and in charge. In a similar vein, the IRC turned up with prominent media personalities to make promotional videos. Sometimes the film crews actually asked refugees—who were in the process of getting their families off the boats—to stop and pose so they could get a shot of their vested volunteers helping to bring refugees ashore.[32]

The NGOs' help was badly needed, and their arrival was eagerly anticipated, but once they arrived in Molyvos, local volunteers working with the refugees observed that the demeanor of the NGOs' staff members did not match the gravity of the situation, nor did it bear much resemblance to the image they tried to project to the world in their promotional materials. Their highly polished videos, which generated a wealth of donations, all of a sudden seemed intentionally deceptive—as if the fundraising was done for no purpose other than to finance an elaborate and expensive bureaucracy. Paid employees who rarely saw a refugee paraded extravagant lifestyles, bullied locals who had already done so much for the refugees, and left the hard work to unpaid volunteers, many of whom had come to Molyvos at their own expense. Some outside observers even pointed derisively to the UNHCR logo on the tents at Oxy and said that they were there in name only, while the entire burden of responsibility for running Oxy rested on Melinda and the volunteers of her local low-budget Starfish Foundation.[33]

It was also known locally that volunteers from the large NGOs were sent out to the beaches without adequate materials and supplies. Eric Kempson did not mince words: "The big agencies came in here, put up a tent, claimed that it was their operation, and they didn't do anything. They make millions in donations, but the people suffering are being taken care of by unpaid volunteers. They're being fed by unpaid volunteers. They're being clothed and given medical treatment all by unpaid volunteers. They are coming to me for emergency blankets, baby clothes, and medical supplies because they don't have any. They're using the funds for administrative costs, and the money isn't getting to the people who need it."[34]

The IRC conducted its own study of the Lesvos refugee crisis and published a report titled "Learning from Lesbos: Lessons from the IRC's Early Emergency Responses in the Urban Areas of Lesbos between September 2015 and March 2016." The report's author acknowledges that the prolonged process of registering to operate on Lesvos delayed the IRC's response and that there was a serious "need for greater coordination of response activities and better collaboration among the responders, stakeholders, and local communities."[35] It was further noted that this was particularly true in Molyvos.[36] The author also claims that the report incorporates input from a broad range of participants, but the description of events in the report and conclusions drawn contain errors, and they differ considerably from the locals' portrayal of much of the NGO's involvement during that time.

Surprisingly the IRC report states that "the first boat came ashore . . . on April 27, 2015 . . . by the Aphrodite Hotel," when in fact the migration had already reached crisis proportions in Molyvos well before the beginning of April of that year, leading to the Coast Guard's decision to end registrations in Molyvos in May.[37] One is left to question whether the IRC was completely unaware of those first five tumultuous months of the crisis between November 2014 and March 2015, or whether it chose to overlook them. Also surprising is that there is one lone reference to refugees walking in all kinds of conditions from the beaches where they landed to Molyvos harbor to register. According to the report, this should not have occurred because the IRC had made arrangements with the municipality to provide ample bus transportation, and it blames the resulting "humiliating parade" of exhausted refugees through Molyvos on the locals giving them "inaccurate information."[38] It does not mention that the MSF and the UNHCR also provided money for bus transportation, and it fails to acknowledge that buses were in such short supply at first and their schedules so wildly erratic that it led to dangerous overcrowding in the Molyvos harbor and the school parking lot, leaving endless lines of refugees to wait for hours to board the buses, if and when they arrived. Finally there is only a brief reference to the entire period between May and September when refugees had no choice but to make the grueling trek all the way to Moria on foot, not to mention the clear distinction made between the NGO's professionalism and the local volunteers' lack of experience.[39] All in all, the people who had been on the ground working with the refugees for most of that year found the report's inaccuracies, omissions, and its hauteur difficult to tolerate, if not downright insulting.

Robin and Robert Jones both recognized the importance of the NGOs' role in Molyvos, but they nevertheless found themselves "in a state of disbelief when organizations such as the Human Rights Watch, Save the Children, the IRC, and the Human Rights Campaign claimed that their resources were being delivered directly to where they were actually needed most." Robin further underscores her own perspective, saying, "Having lived through this kind of event and observed the actions of the big organizations, I would say that the big 'whatevers' may be too big to ensure that the money and the personal assistance get to where they are most needed, . . . or maybe they fail to see refugees as human beings."[40] Michael Honegger and Tim Smith are not so tactful. They make it clear that they were "furious" with the NGOs.[41] Stratis was too: "The NGOs should have come here to help the locals help the refugees, but that's not what happened. They came and immediately started telling us what to do and how to do it, and they created a negative feeling. When they came here, they should have learned more about the area and found out who has been helping and what they have been doing. We felt occupied. It was an invasion, and it was all about money for the NGOs."[42]

So it's understandable why Eric and Philippa Kempson were so appreciative of the work of Proactiva and IsraAID because, according to them, those two NGOs "didn't make shiny videos; they just saved lives."[43]

17

Cleaning the Beaches and Weathering the Community's Bitterness

Fall and Winter 2015

An aerial photograph of the north coast of Lesvos taken in October showed that the beach was strewn with life vests, rubber boats, clothing, and other debris that were left on the shore after the refugees reached Oxy.[1] In the early months of the crisis, the Kempsons and the volunteers who worked with them made a point of cleaning up the beach as much as possible after each landing. However, when autumn came and the number of landings exceeded a thousand refugees each day, the accumulation of debris became so immense that individual efforts like theirs proved futile. At times, abandoned orange life vests, silver-colored emergency blankets, and the remains of black rubber dinghies numbered in the tens of thousands. They mixed with wet mounds of unsalvageable clothes and food all along the water's edge as far as the eye could see. Some of the rubber boats remained largely intact, but most of them were either slashed by the refugees as they approached the beach or torn apart when they slammed against the rocks and the cliffs along the shoreline, leaving large remnants floating in the surf or buried in the sand and rocks.[2] Hulks of wooden and metal boats, some intact and some in pieces, lay caught in the surf or in the rocks where they had run aground. Masses of fishing nets also lay submerged several hundred yards off the coast where they were brought down when boat motors became entangled in them after falling off.[3] Refugee landings continued at a staggering pace, bringing mountains of trash with each wave of new arrivals and each change of tide. Removing this vast amount of debris became an unending effort that had to be repeated over and over again throughout the fall and winter months of 2015 and 2016.

That fall Starfish volunteers began the cleanup of the western end of the beach, starting in Molyvos and going halfway to Skala Sykaminias. It became an ongoing effort with groups of volunteers working every day in at least two shifts in the morning and the afternoon. Starfish volunteers donned wet suits and cleaned the entire harbor of Molyvos on both sides of the sea wall. In doing so they also brought up trash that had been lying at the bottom of the harbor for years. ECO Relief, the environmental cleanup and upcycling arm of the Lighthouse Relief Project, cleaned the western half over to Skala and the more difficult rocky areas of the coastline that were inaccessible by road; everything had to be hauled up the steep cliffs using ropes and pulleys.[4] A crew of Scandinavian divers came with special equipment and worked in the water to bring the fishing nets, motors, and other sunken debris up to the surface, and they disassembled many of the larger wooden boats, piece by piece.[5] Assisting in all of this were local volunteers and municipal workers, and the village of Molyvos provided the trucks.[6]

Sometimes it took as many as seven people an entire day just to dig out the remains of a single rubber dinghy that had become trapped in the sand and rocks. They were so heavy that, in order to remove them from the beach, they had to be cut into pieces and packed in bundles along with other rubbish that was collected from the water and the surf. The bundles were then picked up by teams of volunteers working in the water and placed onto rafts that they floated along the shore. Once a raft was full, they floated it to a spot near one of the beach access lanes and transferred the debris from the raft onto municipal trucks. At the same time, volunteers working on the beach loaded debris that they had picked up from the sand onto the trucks, and everything was hauled up the lane to the coastal road. There it was transferred to waiting garbage trucks and taken to a dump located in the hills above Eftalou.[7]

The cleaning of the beaches produced an unanticipated side effect for the Kempsons. Everyone who worked with the refugees had long felt the rancor of those, particularly from the village, who were opposed to providing any form of assistance. In the village it certainly impacted the lives of Melinda and the volunteers with Starfish, but the animosity extended beyond the village to the beach, where the Kempsons were also victims of vicious

CLEANING THE BEACHES

personal attacks for their involvement. Looking back Philippa believes that some of the insensitivity and mean-spirited behavior directed toward them stemmed in particular from the fact that the vast majority of the landings took place along the beaches and not in the village. Consequently people in the village did not witness the extent of the daily misery that refugees and volunteers endured on the beach. Philippa thinks that the amount of human suffering on display every day might have tempered their hostility had they been there.[8]

Philippa's feelings about this were borne out in the fall of 2015, when the village sent municipal workers to the beach to assist the volunteers with the clean-up. Refugee arrivals were at their peak at that time, and the workers witnessed scores of landings. They watched while volunteers guided boats to shore, often struggling to prevent them from overturning in the waves or crashing against the rocks; they saw firsthand how the volunteers helped families and the injured come ashore, soaking wet and freezing cold. It was not what they or anyone they knew in the village had ever imagined, and it affected many of them so deeply that they started joining in to help. They already knew about the condition of the boats and the faulty life vests; they had come across plenty of them in the clean-up. However, their involvement with the actual landings brought them into direct contact with the refugees themselves, especially the children and their parents and those in wheelchairs. As soon as they started interacting with the refugees, they began to admire their courage in the face of such trauma. Not only did they learn what the refugees were like but they also discovered that no one was getting sick or dying from diseases that the refugees were rumored to be spreading, nor were they getting blown up by the "terrorists" who were purported to be among them. This changed the villagers' attitudes to such an extent that a good number of them even began going to the beach as volunteers outside of their regular work hours. For the first time, Eric and Philippa felt as if they had "friends in the town," but it did little to heal the larger division between the two sides.[9]

To say that Molyvos was split asunder by the refugee crisis evokes biblical passages from Isaiah in which the entire earth is violently shaken and broken up.[10] At first glance that may seem like an exaggeration, but when considered in the context of the village and its surroundings, it is understandable that the people most affected by what was happening, regardless of which side they were on, would perceive the rift in such a dramatic way. Like the crisis itself, the local conflict in Molyvos began on a small scale and then escalated. At first it involved a basic difference of viewpoints between those who feared the refugee intrusion and the impact it would have on their livelihoods and those who felt compassion for the refugees' plight and decided to help. Melinda and her family were the first to feel the effect of the conflict early on, but by March 2015 the negativity grew to such an extent that, after the Kempsons started helping the refugees, they too felt the brunt of it. Throughout that spring and summer, as the numbers of refugees grew larger and their impact on tourism became undeniable, the conflict gained momentum, and everyone associated with Melinda and the Kempsons became the targets of local people's ire.

The number of tourists traveling to Molyvos began to decline precipitously, ultimately dropping by as much as 80 percent as the crisis intensified, and it remained that way with little improvement through the summer of 2018. This left locals who depended on tourism without adequate income, and to make matters worse, it was happening at a time when the Greek economy was also in free fall. The result was both panic and anger, with people's reactions growing ever louder and more vociferous.[11] Sentiments often were aired in public hearings that, ironically, were organized to foster understanding and bring the two sides together. Dionisis tried to create therapy groups in which people could talk about the issues and speak calmly without fighting. Members of the Starfish Board, of which he was a part, organized meetings to explain to everyone what they were trying to accomplish at Oxy. There were also sessions in which representatives of the two opposing sides talked and led discussions. At times, the attendees seemed to understand the divergent points of view, but in the end the polarization in the community overpowered the discussions, and nothing was resolved. One of the meetings had to be adjourned after only five minutes because it had deteriorated into a shouting match that could not be brought back to order.[12] Timothy Smith felt that the tenor of the conflict reached an all-time low when a woman at one of those public hearings screamed that the refugees should be shot before reaching the beaches, and when "a local travel agent turned his hose on refugees to keep them from resting on the sidewalk outside his office."[13]

Dina, who was part of Melinda's team from the beginning and attended those public meetings to offer support for the refugee relief efforts, was deeply disturbed by what she heard and saw. At the same time, she also understood how people felt. "It's fear," she says. "When you have fear of losing your business that is very successful and that you've worked for many years to build, and when your business provides food for your family's table, I understand the fear of losing it, the worry . . . but I don't understand why you have to be so horrible to another human being or say that they are pigs and they can drown or that people should get guns and shoot them. How can you say that about another human being? That I can't understand."[14]

Dionisis attributed the source of discord within the community not so much to the local citizens themselves but rather to a relatively small group whom he refers to as the "powerbrokers": local businessmen who governed the area's tourism. These men controlled the tour operators who brought the tourists to Molyvos, filled the hotels and guest houses, directed tourists to bars and restaurants, dealt with car rentals and car rental agencies, and provided the clients for all of Molyvos's stores and galleries. Since tourism drives the local economy at every level, these powerbrokers wield enormous influence—social as well as economic—throughout the region. According to Dionisis they were the most threatened by the crisis—at first because of the immediate loss of business and profits due to the enormous refugee presence in Molyvos that kept tourists away. As it turned out, however, the refugee influx was not to be their only worry. Starting that fall, after the regular tourist season had ended, the arrival of employees of NGOs and other international agencies, along with reporters and technical crews from media companies worldwide, began to generate a kind of alternate tourism. Hotels and restaurants were all full, and it was difficult to find a rental car. In fact business in Molyvos started to boom, but those "alternate tourists" had made their reservations directly over the internet, thus bypassing all of the standard tour operators that the powerbrokers controlled, depriving them of what would have been their normal share of the profits. It became an immediate cause for alarm because they knew that if this practice were to continue and become more widespread, they would lose their leverage over the area's entire tourist industry, and they had to do whatever they could to put a stop to it.

They began their offensive by launching a campaign of "bad propaganda" against everyone who was actively helping the refugees, all with the intent to tarnish their reputations and incite antagonism against them. Local newspapers and radio stations began to report malicious stories about how Melinda, Ilektra—because she was on the village council—and all of their associates locally, along with the Kempsons, were responsible for the area's economic and social problems. They also were accused of pocketing money from donors and even receiving unlawful payments from foreign sources for helping the refugees. The accusations were groundless, but once they were broadcast in the media, they began to take root in the community. Then these powerbrokers further bolstered their campaign by using their power and influence to coalesce public sentiment, not only against their original targets but the entire relief effort. Residents of the village grew too intimidated to speak out. Instead they chose to remain quietly "in the center" and look the other way. The antagonism grew to the point where the staff and volunteers working for the NGOs, as well as reporters and camera crews, were targeted to such an extent that they felt so unwelcome—even unsafe—that they pulled out of Molyvos and moved to Skala Sykaminias and Mytilene. By the time spring came, there was no one left in town. Mytilene and Skala were booming, but Molyvos was empty. In many respects, their wholesale opposition to anything related to the refugees backfired.[15]

Robin and Robert Jones were saddened by the rift in the community that they had known for so many years as both year-round and seasonal residents. They always acknowledged that there were people, many of them their friends and neighbors, who "would just as soon this whole thing had never happened," but like Dionisis, Ilektra, Dina, the Kempsons, and everyone who was targeted in the bad propaganda campaign, they maintained that the bitter anger toward the refugees and those who helped them was born out of fear—fear for their businesses, fear of what the future might hold, and certainly fear of the powerbrokers. They honestly believed that the antagonism was not universally shared and that many of the towns-people just preferred to remain quiet rather than overtly taking sides. It also concerned them that narratives about this time period would become unfairly and inaccurately focused on the villagers' prejudices toward the immigrants and on "how bad it was in Molyvos," not on the reality that everyone was just overwhelmed by the never-ending "ocean of humanity" that descended on the village.[16]

Nevertheless the animosity that grew out of the crisis caused a deep and bitter split in the social and psychological fabric of Molyvos, and it inflicted personal pain and hardship on the people who sincerely believed that they had no other choice but to help the refugees. Eri Grigorelli refers to this as "the drama behind everything else that happened."[17]

For Dionisis it got to the point where, whenever he went into the street or to the market, people confronted him about what they had seen or heard about him in the media or the village's various social circles. Even neighbors with whom he was friendly and who spent time in his home grew antagonistic. The harassment spilled over into the high school in Petra where he taught and where he ran international exchange programs and organized opportunities for students from the school to interact with the refugee children at Oxy. Parents, faculty, and administrators responded by accusing him of trying to destroy the school and the local community by being involved with the refugees, and they opposed any initiative that involved interaction between their children with those at Oxy. Finally, in what appeared to be a retaliatory move, they closed down the exchange program, saying that they "didn't want it anymore." He says, "I tried not to be angry because as a teacher, I have to have a balanced perspective to transmit to the students," but it became clear to him that, even though he was trying to do what he thought was right, he was making enemies in the process. Not wanting "to keep living as an enemy of society," he left his position at the high school in Petra, gave up his home in Molyvos, and moved to Mytilene, where he began teaching high school mathematics.[18]

As a member of the Molyvos village council, Ilektra was frequently the target of people's wrath, and she claims that she lost most of her friends as a result of the bad propaganda attacking her for helping the refugees. People in town held a great deal against her, including her campaign to open the campground as a holding area, her support for the portable toilets being set up in the parking lot, her membership on the Starfish Board, and finally her work at Oxy. The hostility toward her was so intense that she developed PTSD and had to be hospitalized for treatment in Athens. She, like Dina, understood the townspeople's reactions to the refugee crisis and its effect on their lives. She respected their right to have their own opinions, even though they were in dramatic opposition to hers, but she felt as if they were foisted upon her in such a way that she could no longer live in Molyvos. "I couldn't have fights all day with the village," she says. Unable to tolerate the way they treated her, she moved to Mytilene and became much more contented, but she notes that she would leave Lesvos altogether and return to Athens if her work as an asylum officer did not compel her to remain.[19]

Dina lost her sense of community spirit and began to feel the hostility directed toward her as the split deepened. Although she was not originally from Lesvos, she had lived in Molyvos for several years and thought of it as home until she was identified as a member of the group that helped the refugees. From that time on, she was subjected to the same animosity as the others, and with a mix of anger and sadness, she grew less and less "attached" to Molyvos. Both she and Ilektra remained strong-willed and unflinching when their sense of justice was challenged. She says resolutely, "Since my role in the refugee crisis, some people don't even say good morning to me, and it has hurt me a lot, but I speak my mind when I feel like I'm right, and I will stand up and defend myself. One day when I did that, I was almost physically attacked by someone from here. It took me a while to face this person, but now when I see him, I say good morning first, because I've concluded that the way he views my involvement with the refugees is his problem, not mine." Like everyone in their original group, Dina eventually needed to seek psychological help to overcome the PTSD that resulted more from her treatment at the hands of the townspeople than from everything she went through with the refugees.[20] Eventually Dina left Molyvos and moved to France.

Eri found herself in a special predicament because, as a member of the Coast Guard crew, she was expected to remain nonpartisan. However, with the Coast Guard office in the harbor next to the Captain's Table, her work with Melinda inevitably became public knowledge, and she ended up embroiled in the conflict. People in the village denounced her publicly, saying that the refugees would not have come if she and Melinda had stopped feeding them and giving them dry clothing. They did this whenever she wore her uniform, even though they knew that she was risking her life when she went out on the Coast Guard boat and pulled drowning refugees out of the stormy sea. After a while she refused to acknowledge any of them because of the way they treated her and the other members of her group: "They didn't understand that I hadn't invited the refugees to come here, that I was just being a humanitarian, and that I really didn't have a choice." Finally Eri requested a transfer from the Molyvos office because she was too hurt and worn down by the attitudes of the townspeople.[21]

No one felt the pain of being targeted more acutely than Melinda and Eric and their families. They were seen as the ring leaders, largely because their commitment was so impassioned and their efforts prodigious and unwavering, far more so than anyone else. Dionisis called Eric's involvement with the refugees "a great story," one of a very strong-minded man and his equally steadfast spouse, both imbued with compassion and generosity and an uncompromising sense of justice.[22] They had lived in Eftalou for sixteen years, set up a very successful studio, and enjoyed the respect of those who knew them and the quality of Eric's art. Nevertheless as soon as they began their rescue efforts on the beach, they, too, were blamed for the refugee crisis and started to incur enormous animosity in the form of verbal abuse and threats of physical harm. They were shunned by almost everyone, and it seemed as if the whole village wanted to fight Eric because they felt he was doing something wrong. People attacked him on Facebook and threatened to ruin his business. Some of the threats were so formidable that he and Philippa had to obtain orders of protection.

Like Dina and Ilektra, Eric refused to back down when he felt wronged, but there was one difference: he was fearless when speaking his mind. Of Eric, Ilektra says, "I can't do what he does or say what he says. I mean, I can, but then I have to go to the village where we make our lives. I don't have the strength to endure the negativity that Eric has."[23] Eric acknowledges that he is probably safer living in his off-the-road compound in Eftalou rather than in Molyvos: "I have enough problems, but at least I live out here where I have the security of the private road leading to my house. Anyone [attacking me] would have to get back down that road to flee a crime scene." The restaurant at the intersection of the coastal road and the road leading to Eric's house offers a level of added security because anyone coming to hurt him would have to pass the restaurant on the way in and out. Eric also has the phone number of a Coast Guard security police officer who works in Petra and who promised to protect him. He and Philippa say, "He has always looked after us. He can get to our house in five minutes. That's why we're still here. Otherwise, with all these threats, we would have left the area."[24] Since that time, the Kempsons' landlord refused to renew their lease, and they have moved closer to Mytilene and the Hope Project warehouse.

Melinda has lived in Molyvos since she was three years old. Her stepfather was a highly respected local sea captain, and Melinda and her mother ran a popular restaurant in the village before she and Theo married and opened the Captain's Table. Together they raised their family in Molyvos. Over the years she has also been someone on whom others depended to collect clothing and distribute it to villagers in need. None of this warm, fuzzy history shielded her from the bad propaganda and the resulting anger, and it has been particularly devastating for her, Theo, and their children. Eric admits, "Melinda has a lot on this town, but she has hidden her anger and bitterness." He adds, "I have shouted mine" and then goes on to say, "I don't know how she even lives there; I wouldn't."[25]

Right from the start, witnessing all of the activity at the Captain's Table, people openly blamed Melinda for the crisis and held her personally responsible for the refugees' presence. By extension, when tourists started to cancel hotel reservations and the volume of tourist business began to decline, she was blamed for destroying the economy and the livelihood of Molyvos. Then came the accusations that she was accepting money from Turkey and Syria to bring the refugees there and pocketing donations that tourists and locals had given to buy food and supplies. Even though she created Starfish to make all financial transactions legal, those accusations kept coming. Speaking of those times, Melinda says, "For two years, I would only walk from my house to the restaurant and back. I wouldn't leave the harbor or go up into the village. I wouldn't go anywhere, for that matter, because of what people were saying about me. Last year [2017], I walked through the harbor with a friend, and she told me that people were saying hello to me, but I didn't even realize it. Before I left the house to go to Pirates—a bar in Molyvos—for the first time, I played 'I Will Rise' by Katie Perry really loud on my laptop and screamed the lyrics at the top of my voice. When I was finally seated at Pirates, I watched as people walked by without even saying hello. I felt really awful. I felt excluded. It's been very difficult for me." For his part Theo confesses that he has been "very much affected" to the point where he would like to leave Molyvos: "I would very easily leave yesterday, not today, not tomorrow, yesterday. But we can't really leave because we have the restaurant, and I have to work for at least five more years in order to get our money out of it. However, I'm very disappointed with the people here."[26]

A sadness and lurking uneasiness have permeated their lives. Even with the crisis at an end and no more refugees in the streets of Molyvos, they have found it difficult to shed the feeling that certain neighboring business owners still eye them disapprovingly—if not angrily—whenever they walk through the harbor. Anyone watching them can see the stiffness of their gaits and the way they avoid eye contact with passersby. One of the Starfish volunteers who worked very closely with Melinda and Theo for the duration of the crisis—and even remained after the height of the crisis had passed in order to work with unaccompanied minors at Moria—talks about the anger among the townspeople. He says, "At some points, I feel like this village is my house. I have been here for a long time, and I have many friends from here. But I can always leave. The people here don't scare me. I don't get sad about myself." Pointing toward Melinda and Theo, he says, "I get sad about this family and the other families who helped the refugees." As he mentions the names of those families, both Melinda and Theo spontaneously let out a sigh of affirmation that speaks volumes about what they have seen personally and what the families who worked closely with them have had to endure because of the townspeople who made their lives so difficult.

In October 2023 the Captain's Table closed permanently after twenty-nine years of operation.

18

Oxy Closes

December 2015

The scene on the beach that fall and the early winter months heading into 2016 was not unlike what it had been when Eric and Philippa first began to help with landings back in February—except now refugees were landing by the thousands each and every day, and there were far more volunteers than before. In fact the sea was dotted with boats coming at a rate of at least thirty an hour, and the volunteers working with the Kempsons had been joined by volunteers from the numerous NGOs that were operating in the area as well as the many who had come to Molyvos independently. They stood together at the edge of the water and motioned with their arms or waved red flags or life vests in the air to catch the attention of the refugees steering the boats, hoping to direct them to safe landing spots. At night they waved flashlights, their cell phones, or sometimes a lantern. As soon as a boat was within wading distance from the beach, several volunteers rushed out to grab its sides and pull it in until it rested firmly in the sand.

On days when the wind was incredibly strong and heavy waves crashed onshore, the volunteers had to learn to deal with challenges that the Kempsons and their veteran helpers had faced hundreds of times before, namely how to keep the boats steady and guide them to land without capsizing. At those times it took volunteers working in teams to keep the flimsy rubber boats from becoming victims of the waves that would cause them to rise and fall violently while water spilled over the edge and screaming passengers were thrown into the sea.[1] Few of the new volunteers who arrived that fall and winter had ever been in a situation like this, but fortunately the majority of them were young and had the strength and stamina to stay upright in the waves and turbulent surf that threw them about much like the boats themselves.

In December 2015 a young high school teacher named Hasan Oswald flew from New York City to Mytilene where, like many of the independent volunteers, he rented a van, filled it with boxes of food and crates of water, and drove to Molyvos to "help and learn." Once there, he spent his time driving on the coastal road and stopping at places on the beach where boats were landing. So many boats were constantly arriving that he was always busy. In addition to helping refugees, he used his cell phone to film and narrate numerous videos of the gripping situations that unfolded in front of him. At one of the stops he captured a scene in which a refugee woman, probably in her midthirties, was on her knees on the beach being consoled by a volunteer and weeping uncontrollably because she believed that her young son had perished during the crossing. What Oswald was able to capture in the video, but the mother could not yet see, was her son, safe and running toward her with arms outstretched screaming, "Mama, Mama!" When the mother spotted her son, she embraced both him and the volunteer in her arms and wailed, "Thank you! Thank you!" It was a moment of pure joy and relief.[2]

In another of Oswald's videos, a child wearing a life vest was standing alone on the beach crying, "Mama!" A volunteer approached him, put his hand comfortingly on the child's shoulder, and together they searched the beach area until they found his mother lying barely conscious on the sand while a medic wrapped her in an emergency blanket.[3] This story's outcome is deeply uncertain; we do not get to see the ending. However, these two videos convey the brutal reality and raw emotion that were so much a part of each landing. Families who had the good fortune to arrive together on calm seas were able to kiss the ground, give thanks to their God for a safe crossing, take selfies, and call family members back home. On the other hand, though, there were some whose trip from Turkey to the beach at Eftalou ended in misery, disaster, and heartbreak. The volunteers witnessed it all firsthand.

In a night landing that Oswald also filmed, the many flickering lights that could be seen in the darkness affirmed that the sea was full of boats, but the group of volunteers he had joined was focused on one particular boat that was not too far out and whose signal they had spotted several minutes earlier. They waited, and as soon as signals started coming at regular intervals, they all rushed to the spot where they expected the boat to land. The volunteers waded into the water to guide the boat in, and the children were then handed to the volunteers, who carried them to shore before the adults began to disembark. This time, however, it was dark and the volunteers had to work with whatever light they had available from flashlights and cell phones. The water was choppy, with strong waves coming in one after the other, and the beach was very stony with pockets of deep water that made the landing dangerous. Many people—passengers and volunteers carrying children—fell into the water and were submerged in the deep pools or the pounding surf. Just when it seemed that the waves had quieted and people could steady themselves, another wave washed in and threw them off balance. Gasping children were pulled to the surface by the volunteers and taken to shore, where they were quickly wrapped in emergency blankets. One elderly man, clearly unable to walk, was lifted from the boat. Once on land, he grabbed the arm of one of the volunteers who had helped him and kissed it in gratitude. Other volunteers can be seen holding emotional, frightened, and chilled refugees in their arms, providing comfort and warmth.[4]

The Starfish volunteer who stayed in Molyvos to work with unaccompanied minors at Moria spent most of the fall and winter of 2015–16 out on the beaches because the number of arriving boats was so high that he frequently ended up working around the clock with little to no chance of sleep. It was often his inclination to work on more isolated sections of the beach where the steep terrain made access difficult and where there were fewer volunteers to help the refugees. In those spots he was usually alone, especially at night. There were always so many children, people who could not walk or who had narrowly escaped drowning and were too weak to move, and young men his age with serious wounds from war, all of them dripping wet. He carried them on his back, one by one, up the steep hillsides from the beach to the main road. At one point he developed pneumonia with a high fever, but he kept going. He didn't feel that he had the choice to stop.[5]

Robert Omar Hamilton described one of his days as a Starfish volunteer when he was assigned to the beach rather than Oxy: "Half an hour after I arrived, I was waist deep in the sea when a man handed me a baby from the waterlogged dinghy. We waded onto the land, weighed down by bags. I handed him back his child, and he stood still for a moment, dazed. I squeezed his arm and then his head was on my shoulder, and we were both crying."[6]

Oxy closed at the end of 2015. By that time both the UNHCR and the IRC had established themselves all over Lesvos. Notwithstanding the anger and resentment that their actions fomented among the locals, the two NGOs began to carry out their planned professionalization of operations that placed them in charge of overseeing the largest share of the rescue efforts on the island. The UNHCR focused on the south around Mytilene, and the IRC opened up a camp, Apanemo, near Eftalou, from which they managed all operations along the north coast.

After the last busload of refugees bound for Mytilene left Oxy, the tarpaulins and tents were taken down and all vestiges of the large refugee holding center were removed. Suddenly this singular spot that Melinda had created in her courageous effort to spare Molyvos and offer food, dry clothing, medical attention, and a moment of respite for more than two hundred thousand refugees who passed through Oxy was no more. It returned to being the nightclub parking lot, almost as if the refugee center had never been there. An eerie silence settled over the area where, for four of the most turbulent months of the entire crisis, Melinda's friends, neighbors, colleagues, and thousands of volunteers had come together to offer their help to people whose lives had been totally and brutally upended by war and death. Dionisis says regretfully, "We can't find a way to speak about Oxy in a historical way because it's not there anymore; it's just an empty space, and all that remains are some numbers and some stories but very few pictures or other artifacts. Everything else was lost."[7]

With Oxy closed, Starfish moved into a somewhat different mode. Melinda and the remaining Starfish volunteers continued to take care of shipwreck victims who were still being brought into the harbor of Molyvos by the Coast Guard, distribute clothes and supplies to refugees in other parts of the island, and provide personnel to work with the growing population of unaccompanied minors living in Moria.[8]

After the start of 2016, refugee arrivals continued unabated with more than forty-six thousand arriving in January and February alone.[9] In a statement issued on March 16, Dimitris Vitsas, the Greek minister of migration, called for the ongoing refugee crisis to be resolved. In a clear reference to Alan Kurdi, the Syrian boy whose dead body had washed up on the Turkish beach in September, he stated, "We can't tolerate losing children in the Aegean Sea. [We must find] the solution to protect people, to implement safe procedures and safe routes for migrants and refugees."[10] To that end, on March 18, EU leaders signed an agreement with Turkey that was aimed at stopping the flow of refugees from Turkey into Europe and ending the smuggling that had put thousands in danger. Under the terms of that agreement, refugees seeking asylum were to be placed in the camps, and migrants entering Greece from Turkey were to be deported to their home countries.[11] The deal also provided Turkey with $6.6 billion in aid to help pay for looking after the refugees who remained there. In addition the EU agreed to resume negotiations with Turkey on membership in the EU.[12]

The signing of the agreement resulted in a massive decline in the number of refugees entering Europe. It effectively closed down the Balkan route overland and the sea routes leading to the Greek islands of the Aegean, but it did not stop them from coming into Greece altogether.[13] As Eric Kempson says, "The press coverage stopped; that's what's stopped. But the boats have not stopped."[14] In the first week of April 2016, only two weeks after the signing of the agreement, the UNHCR reported a total of 1,276 refugees making the crossing, but all except a few of them were intercepted before they reached the beach at Eftalou. Spotters from organizations such as the Lighthouse Relief Project that kept watch all along the coast reported the presence of any refugee boats in Greek waters to the Coast Guard, whose crews picked them up at sea and arranged for them to be taken directly to Mytilene and placed in one of the refugee camps. As a result refugees all but disappeared from Molyvos. In addition, when cleaning the beaches along the north shore, ECO Relief sought "to remove all visual reminders of the migration . . . in order to support the local residents and encourage the continuation of tourism."[15] When Robin and Robert Jones returned to their home in Molyvos that spring, not only were there no refugees, but they found that the beaches had been so thoroughly cleaned that, by comparison to the state it was in when they left, there was very little that reminded them of what had happened there. In fact they felt that the beaches were almost "too clean." Robin says, "Something gets lost when there are no remnants of such an event."[16]

What is left in Molyvos, however, are the memories that remain in the minds of all those who witnessed one of the largest human migrations in modern history. Those memories will live forever in the hearts and minds of all the locals and volunteers from all over the world who, together, gave generously and selflessly of their time, energy, and personal resources so that the thousands of refugees would have a first stop where they could be fed and cared for before they set out on the next leg of their arduous journey toward safety and freedom.

There were times, particularly during the spring and summer before any outside help arrived, when it seemed to everyone involved as if the enormity of it all might destroy them. In some very important ways, their lives in Molyvos were permanently altered. However, Joel Hernandez, who at the time was working with the Humanitarian Academy at Harvard University, wrote that, during the height of the crisis when it seemed as if Molyvos and its entire way of life might unravel, "Melinda McRostie and Eric and Philippa Kempson, along with their odd crew of volunteers, preserved the social order in Molyvos and channeled refugees in and out of the community in an organized fashion. . . . Given the immense number of refugees and the small number of volunteers, this was no small accomplishment."[17]

24. The "dump" in the valley in the hills above Eftalou where all debris from the beaches and roads was deposited. Courtesy of Nelson Mondaca.

25. The author stands in front of a ten-foot-high mound of debris—inner tubes, life vests, deflated dinghies, and remnants of clothing. Courtesy of Nelson Mondaca.

Epilogue

Reflections on the Story of Molyvos

It was late in the afternoon on our last day in Molyvos. My husband, Nelson, and I had been there for two weeks while I interviewed people who had been at the center of the refugee crisis. Early the next morning, we would be leaving for our flight from Mytilene to Athens and then directly on to New York, but we still had one more place to visit, which we had saved for this last day. The week before, when we talked with Robin and Robert Jones, they asked us if we had gone to "the dump." Strangely enough this was the first time since we arrived in Molyvos that anyone had specifically mentioned the dump; not even Melinda or the Kempsons had brought it up. Everyone I interviewed had talked about the incredible amounts of debris that accumulated—remnants of boats, life vests, motors, and everything else left behind in the wake of the refugees—and the extraordinary effort required to clean the beaches and the roadway. However, no one said much of anything about their disposal other than a vague reference to a place somewhere in the hills above Eftalou, and I hadn't thought to inquire further. Robin and Robert not only talked about the dump but insisted that we would find going there an unforgettable experience. For them, it seemed that it was a kind of culmination of the refugees' story. They thought the place should be preserved as a memorial to what had happened in Molyvos: "Lest we forget, lest we forget."[1]

To get there we followed the now-familiar coastal road that winds around in the back of the castle and passes the beachside hotels before it leads to Eftalou. Robin and Robert had cautioned us to watch carefully to avoid missing the turnoff. We drove slowly past the hotels and some open fields where sheep were grazing before we spotted the inconspicuous, almost invisible, intersection where the stony dirt lane branches off the asphalt road and begins its ascent along the slope up to the peak of the rise high above the sea. As we neared the top, the dirt roadway simply faded into nothing but a grassy trail. The only clues that indicated we were headed toward the right location were pieces of orange fabric, shreds of black rubber and plastic, remnants of simple cloth, and shoes with their worn-out laces that had all become entwined in the bent and rusted mesh wire fence that lined the trail and fluttered in the wind that blew up from the sea.

When we crested the hill, we found ourselves looking down into a large, shallow valley, an indentation in the surrounding hills. And there it was! The valley—some 150 feet down the slope from where we stopped our car—was filled with massive orange and black mounds ranging from fifteen to thirty (or more) feet in height. Everything was there: thousands of black dinghies, hundreds of boat motors no longer worth stealing, shoes of every size and style, articles of tattered clothing, deteriorating emergency blankets whose now-crinkled silver surfaces reflected the late afternoon sun, and hundreds of thousands of orange life vests. These mountains of debris had all been brought there by the teams of volunteers and municipal workers who cleaned the beaches. We sat there in awed silence for quite a while before getting out of the car. Then we walked slowly toward the hills of debris that held the memories of everything we had learned about the story of Molyvos.

The dinghies were indeed made from plastic, not rubber, just as the volunteers all claimed, and the torn seams, readily visible, confirmed that the glue holding them together could not withstand the heavy loads of passengers and the power of the waves. A sudden gust of wind blew across the nearest pile and stirred a large piece of plastic, its torn edge revealing the gaping hole of a dinghy. During our conversation with Dina Adam shortly after arriving in Molyvos two weeks earlier, she recalled watching as the boats made their way across the open water from Turkey, as if they were in a convoy, and thinking, "My God, there are people in those boats." For a moment it was as if the chill and the sound of that wind across the mound were conveying the refugees' heart-throbbing fear as they boarded those boats and their terror when the plastic gave way and they were thrown into the cold, dark, churning water. So many boats. Piles of them. So many people. All desperate to get away. So many dreams. So many unknowns. We felt as if memories of them were suspended in that valley in the hills overlooking the very sea that the refugees crossed and the beaches where they landed.

Life vests lay everywhere, each one a testimony to a refugee's existence. We couldn't help but wonder who might have worn it. Was it a child whose parents, fearing the future, had made the excruciating decision to leave everything behind and begin their life-threatening journey into a huge unknown aboard one of those boats—maybe the one with the gaping hole? What caused them to flee their homelands? How did they feel at the time? What were their hopes and aspirations for themselves and their children? After all, in the words of Warsan Shire's poem:

> . . . no one puts their children in a boat
> unless the water is safer than the land[2]

It was while wearing those life vests that the refugees felt sheer terror when waves approached and crashed over their boat, when they were tossed about in the dark with nothing but a few faint lights along the shore to guide them, and when they discovered that their vests were filled with pillow-like stuffing that didn't buoy them up but, instead, pulled them below the surface of the water. How did each of those life vests get to shore? Did the person who wore that one there survive the trip and land or did that person drown and the vest slip away to eventually wash up on the beach? Where are the survivors now? Are they trapped in one of the refugee camps, waiting while they seek asylum? Are they somewhere on another monumentally difficult road still in search of a welcoming destination, or have they arrived in the promised land of their dreams? Are they alive or dead?

The Joneses referred to this spot up in the hills as "the dump." Others have too. In some media reports, it has been referred to as the "life jacket graveyard."[3] Whatever name it was called by, it disclosed, visually and ineluctably, the magnitude of the story that unfolded in Molyvos and on the beaches below. I have since learned that the entire site is now empty. Everything has been removed: all the life vests and rubber dinghies, the boat motors, and the bags of refugees' belongings that were left behind on the beach. Melinda says that many in the area are relieved to have all of it gone so they can finally move on from the trauma of those times, but their sentiments are not necessarily shared by the locals and volunteers who came forward to help the refugees. They tend to regard the site as hallowed ground because they were all there in body, mind, and soul. Everything that lay in that shallow valley gave voice to the stories of the refugees and Molyvos and its residents. In many ways it embodied the story of humankind's search for safety and freedom at any cost.[4] For me, when I was there and the wind stirred the life vests and the remnants of the plastic dinghies, it felt as if their stories of anticipation, determination, strife, terror, suffering, death, hope, and even happiness were being carried by that April afternoon's winds.

This particular story of Molyvos and its refugee crisis draws to a close in early 2016 with the shutdown of Oxy, the start of the IRC's supervision of refugee operations on the north coast, and the signing of the agreement between the EU and Turkey that was intended to stop the massive influx of people. However, the story does not simply end there. Although refugees have continued to arrive, the number of boats landing on the north shore of Lesvos has declined significantly, and everything is now handled by the Coast Guard and Frontex. This leaves Molyvos and the beaches largely free of refugees, except when boats make it across the Mytilene Strait without being detected by the spotters positioned along the coast. Although tourists to the area might never see a refugee, as Matina Stevis-Gridneff wrote in the *New York Times* in March 2020, "For the Greeks, the migrant crisis of five years ago has yet to end. The problems it saddled the country with have persisted and wrung almost every drop of generosity from a people who prided themselves on their compassion."[5] Among the most pressing problems were the refugee camps, Moria and Kara Tepe, that remained so dangerously and unmanageably overcrowded that, realistically, neither camp was safe for human habitation. Moria, the larger of the two, became particularly problematic.

The governments of the EU countries that were once receptive to refugees, such as Germany and Sweden, were shaken by serious political backlash from anti-migrant groups that caused their leaders to reverse course.[6] As Europe essentially became closed to refugees, Greece's local and national governments were at a loss as to what to do because there was no place for the growing number of refugees to go. Not only were they barred from reaching their desired destinations in northern Europe, but the restricted flow into Europe left them stuck in Greek refugee camps. In turn, overcrowded conditions in holding areas on the mainland, Athens in particular, meant that many being held in Moria and Kara Tepe were forced to remain there. Consequently Moria, originally a short-term transit point where refugees came to register before leaving Lesvos, became a "bottleneck," with people stranded for months to a year or more, waiting for their asylum applications to be processed.[7] At one point in 2018, Giannis Mpalpakakis, the camp's director at the time, referred to Moria as "the most crowded place in the world if you divide the number of residents by the square meter[s]."[8] Meanwhile the quality of life there continued to deteriorate, and residents, desperate to leave, began staging protests that made local and international headlines. One such protest took place in Mytilene the day before we went there to interview Ilektra and Dionisis. Another had taken place only three weeks earlier, just before we left the United States, in which two refugees threatened to kill themselves by strapping their bodies to an electric pylon. These reports all reverberated intensely throughout Molyvos because of the potential impact they could have on the area's still-fragile tourism.

By February 2020 the number of people being held in Moria waiting for their asylum applications to be processed grew to nearly twenty thousand. Refugees had to stand in long lines for up to eight hours a day just to be fed because there were no cooking facilities anywhere in the camp. At the same time, doctors from MSF claimed that the amount of food being delivered to the camp was inadequate and that the meals fell "below minimum calorie requirements."[9] The stench from the existing bathrooms and latrines—none of which were properly cleaned or maintained—spread throughout the local area. This continued to fuel the frequent and ever-growing number of angry protests staged by camp residents, along with locals living in the nearby town of Moria, and Greek right-wing anti-refugee groups.[10] They complained that there was no support from either their government or the EU.[11]

In March 2020, when the COVID-19 pandemic swept across Europe, the entire continent braced for the worst by initiating extensive preventive measures to control its spread. Lesvos, faced with the added worry of what to do in case of an outbreak in Moria or Kara Tepe, imposed a mass quarantine on the camps, and police cordoned off both areas to prevent any of the refugees from leaving. Fortunately, even surprisingly, it was not until September 3 that the first case of COVID-19 was announced in a statement issued by MSF.[12] Nevertheless with such staggering numbers under lock and key in squalid conditions for so many months, it was what Marco Sandrone, the Lesvos project coordinator for MSF, described as a "time bomb ready to explode."[13]

And explode it did! At midday on Tuesday, September 8, Reuters reported that the number of COVID cases at Moria had doubled to thirty-five within a forty-eight-hour period and was expected to increase.[14] Then that very same night, a raging fire, fanned by high winds and exploding gas canisters, destroyed most of Camp Moria, leaving no place for its inhabitants to go other than the streets and roads of the immediate area. The next night, on September 9, there was a second fire, and this time around, the extent of the blaze was so vast that it could not be stopped. Everything was destroyed: the parts of the main compound that had been spared the night before, the entire overflow area outside of the camp's walls where the refugees lived in tents, and the camp's water system. Moria was no more. Widespread belief festered among aid workers and others closely associated with Moria that the fire was deliberately set by angry camp residents. However, residents claim to have seen local Greeks, angry members of right-wing groups, setting fires in the camp on both nights.[15]

For a time chaos reigned as thousands of refugees anxiously milled about, wondering where they would stay, how they would eat and care for themselves, and very importantly, how much longer their quest for asylum and the departure to their hoped-for destinations would be delayed. The EU acted quickly and, within weeks, a new temporary camp, Mavrovouni, also known as "Moria 2.0," was put in place on a treeless tract of land at the edge of the sea near Mytilene. At first many refugees were hesitant to move there for fear of again being stuck under another imposed lockdown similar to what they had experienced in Moria before the fire. They also feared that the new camp's barren location right next to the water, where they were directly exposed to the hot summer sun and the chilling wind and rains of the winter months, would create unfavorable living conditions. Ultimately they were given only one choice: to be placed in Mavrovouni, and in May 2021 they were joined by the residents of Kara Tepe when Greek authorities closed that camp as well. At the very same time, COVID-19 began to make its appearance in Lesvos with some three hundred cases reported among the island's residents. Fortunately, and perhaps even miraculously, despite the existing conditions in Mavrovouni, the number of cases there never reached significant proportions, largely because of the handwashing and mask distribution programs that were carried out by Melinda and her Starfish volunteers.[16] Nevertheless the Greek Council for Refugees ultimately declared that conditions in the camp were "not fit for human dwelling."[17]

Then came the summer of 2021 and the collapse of the NATO-led mission in Afghanistan that added further to the already existing social, political, and diplomatic tensions surrounding refugees. America's withdrawal of its troops triggered an exodus of Afghans, many of whom had worked or fought along with the United States for twenty years and now faced certain imprisonment or death under the newly installed Taliban regime. In the relatively brief period between April 2021, when U.S. president Biden officially announced the troop withdrawal, and July 2021, Afghan migrants entered Europe at a rate of as many as 30,000 a week. They fled first into Iran, then crossed into Turkey and made the 1,400-mile trek to its land and sea borders with Greece.[18] Turkey currently holds 3.6 million Syrian refugees and an additional 400,000 migrants from other countries within its borders—more than any other country in the world.[19] Now it faces a new influx, but this time, the majority are Afghans rather than Syrians.

Turkey has profited, at least indirectly, from the smuggling of refugees across the Mytilene Strait to Greece's islands since 2015, and as part of the March 2016 agreement with the EU, Turkey has received payments for keeping Europe-bound refugees confined within its borders. Turkey's president Recep Tayyip Erdogan has often called the terms of the agreement inadequate and insists that the West provide his country with more military backup in its conflicts with Syria and more aid to help pay for the refugees staying in Turkey. In the meantime the massive refugee presence has started to take a huge toll on Turkey's economy to the point where President Erdogan has publicly stated that his country is "under no obligation to be Europe's refugee depot," and he has begun to look the other way while refugees leave Turkey and head for Greece.[20] His threats to violate the terms of the 2016 agreement and open the borders to allow the refugees being held there to cross over into Greece have always made people nervous because they know that it could very well lead to a repeat of what happened in 2015, or worse.

Since the borders along the land route have all been effectively closed, large numbers of Afghans have taken to the sea in smugglers' plastic dinghies, many of them headed to Lesvos, as always, because it is the shortest route. However, Europeans who fear that a renewed onslaught of Muslim refugees will fan the flames of the far right that threatened the balance of power in 2015 are definitely not in any mood to take them in.[21] This leaves Greece with the continued and unwanted burden of being the refugee depot on the EU side of the Aegean.

At the height of the crisis in Molyvos, Greece remained committed to the terms of the Geneva Conventions in spite of the mixed attitudes toward the refugees, and when the Coast Guard spotted refugees at sea in Greek waters, they rescued them and brought them to one of its refugee camps. As a result, since 2015 Greece has struggled with more than one hundred thousand refugees housed for extended periods of time in its overcrowded refugee camps—Moria and Kara Tepe being two prime examples—while other European countries did little to share the burden.[22] The population of asylum seekers and refugees housed in Lesvos in late summer 2021 dropped from its high of approximately 20,000 before the fire in Moria in 2020 to an approximate 6,355 who now reside in Mavrovouni.[23] Nevertheless it is safe to say that the Greeks are simply worn out, especially with little support from the EU, whose countries are all too willing to let Greece keep the refugees so they won't venture any farther into Europe. Reflecting his country's weariness, Greece's minister of migration and asylum declared that his country will not be the "gateway" for refugees to Europe again.[24]

Things are not the same as they once were; attitudes have hardened. Where there was once compassion and acceptance, even a spirit of welcome, especially during the earlier waves of migration, there is now exhaustion. Rather than rescuing refugee boats at sea and bringing them safely to land, as they did in 2015, the Greek Coast Guard is being accused of pushing refugees back to Turkey. Although the Greek government denies it, there is a constantly growing number of reliable reports and complaints that Greece is not only apprehending boats at sea but also physically and brutally removing asylum seekers who have reached its islands by forcing them into life rafts and towing them into Turkish waters. As might be expected, many who were involved with the relief effort, particularly Melinda and the Kempsons, have expressed disappointment and frustration that the Coast Guard and the Greek government have forsaken the spirit of philoxenia to pursue this callous approach without allowing asylum cases to be heard. Raphael Shilhav, an EU migration expert for Oxfam International, a confederation of charitable organizations dedicated to disaster relief and migration advocacy, has observed that, despite "mounting national and international pressure, Greece is still continuing with pushbacks." He goes on to note, however, that "the EU is standing idly by."[25]

In the meantime the Russian invasion of Ukraine on February 24, 2022, immediately catapulted the EU into yet another refugee crisis that—less than two months after the start of the Russian onslaught—saw more than two hundred thousand Ukrainian refugees crossing into the EU daily, a number that surpassed the crisis of 2015–16 by hundreds of thousands.[26] While the EU welcomed these asylum seekers with open arms, the magnitude of the migration has nevertheless raised questions about individual nations' capacity to accommodate the refugees if the war in Ukraine is prolonged.

There were two sets of players in the story of the refugee crisis in Molyvos between November 2014 and March 2016. Of course, one was the refugees. The other was that small group of locals who initially and courageously banded together and eventually, joined by large numbers of international volunteers, responded as directly and as fully as was humanly possible to the waves of refugees that inundated their village and their lives. Theirs is a story of intensely personal and sometimes herculean efforts, stoicism and tenacity, fearlessness in response to terrifying challenges, bravery in the face of suffering and death, grit and endurance when confronting extreme animosity, boundless compassion, and limitless dedication to helping people whose needs exceeded their own.

While writing this book, I have continued to wonder what would have happened if Melinda, her family and friends, and Eric and Philippa had not decided to come forward and launch their own relief efforts. Regardless of how much blame for the refugee crisis was directed toward them, the refugees would have come anyway, and Molyvos, Eftalou, Skala Sykaminias, and the beaches of the north shore would still have been overrun. But suppose there had been no one on the beach to help guide the boats ashore, no one to wrap freezing, water-soaked refugees in emergency blankets or provide dry clothing, no one to prepare food and hot tea or offer a reassuring gesture and a comforting smile in the face of fear and tragedy? What would have happened if there had been no brave Coast Guard crew members willing to offer themselves as human lifelines to pull drowning refugees from the water or recover the bodies of family members who had already drowned? What if there had been no one like Coast Guard boat captain Kyriakos Papadopoulos to fret over every person floating helplessly in the water, a man who refused to abandon his search, regardless of whether it was day or night or what the conditions of the sea might have been? What would have happened if fishermen had not been ready to leave the harbor on a rescue mission when the Coast Guard was overwhelmed? What would have become of the refugees making the long trek on foot to Moria if no one had organized the convoy in defiance of the law forbidding anyone to give them a ride? Suppose there had been no Starfish Foundation with all the strength and goodwill of those who helped to create it? Or no Oxy and all the volunteers who brought it to life? Or no Hope Foundation and its tireless team of volunteers? What if the policy of deterrence that called for full-scale refusal to provide humanitarian aid in an effort to keep refugees from coming had prevailed and people had stood passively by? What would the magnitude of human suffering or the number of deaths have been if these local people had not come forward in the months before help of any kind, government or NGO, arrived? It's hard to imagine what would have happened to Molyvos or just how great the tragedy would have been without each and every one of them.

Can we call these people who were so deeply immersed in the crisis heroes? Certainly their deeds were the "stuff" of heroism. Yet none of them laid claim to the title of "hero." When they reflected on what it all meant to them and what they'd learned about themselves and others in the process, they all spoke instead about human interconnectedness and responsibility. In my conversations with them, the word heroism would more likely have been used to refer to the refugees, not to themselves. I came away from those conversations convinced that they all would have eschewed any laurels of heroism.

In a video recording, the fisherman from Skala who pulled a bleeding refugee from the water when he was trying to swim to shore wearing a faulty life vest, said, "For the people we saved, we're heroes. Personally I don't feel like a hero. Why would I? I did what I had to do. Anyone would've done the same. I saved the lives of some refugees once. And do you know what they did, all the people in the boat? They stood all their children in a line and each one came up and hugged and kissed me. It's the greatest joy there is. If the same thing happened again, and I hope it never does, I know I'd go and help again because I'd have to."[27]

Another Skala fisherman expressed the very same sentiment: "The people you saved see you as a hero, but I don't feel like a hero. We didn't have a plan; we just stepped in. You can't watch someone suffering or dying and not feel anything. That's just not how it is. I could be getting on a boat and leaving my home with my baby, and wherever I ended up, I'd want someone there to help me. You can't stand by and watch people drown as if it's no big thing. You have to help people because tomorrow you might be the one in need. We all have to do this; we have to help each other. Not just in cases like this but generally all over the world."[28]

In the article "Drops of Light into the Darkness: Migration, Immigration, and Human Rights," Spyros Orfanos writes about the enormous courage of Coast Guard boat captain Papadopoulos, who, piloting his boat, rescued thousands of refugees. Yet Papadopoulos admitted that he also panicked in the face of it all, that he, too, was scared and could not reassure the refugees. Orfanos states, "He's an ordinary man in extraordinary circumstances who makes a choice to step in to help, not to judge or to question, simply to help."[29] When the filmmaker Daphne Matziaraki talked about her film *4.1 Miles*, she said that Papadopoulos went out of his way to help because he "felt an internal, really huge responsibility."[30]

Matziaraki went to Greece to film Captain Papadopoulos with only her camera, no knowledge of CPR, and absolutely no experience with any kind of emergency such as this one. In fact when she was finally granted permission to accompany the crew on a rescue mission—which rarely happens—she planned to be as invisible as possible on the small Coast Guard boat. As fate would have it, she ended up on the boat on October 28, the day of the worst catastrophe of the entire crisis, when the large wooden double-deck boat with hundreds of refugees on board broke apart and sank carrying many to their death and injuring scores of others. Suddenly and unexpectedly, she was thrown into the thick of this gruesome rescue operation when she was asked to lay down her camera and became directly involved in life-or-death situations, one of them with a dying child. She found herself far outside her comfort zone and completely removed from any area of expertise that she could have claimed to possess, but she said, "The emergency was so big that I had no other option . . . there was no second choice." At the day's end she was left with an underlying question: "How do we act as citizens of the world when another human being needs us?"[31]

Melinda and Theo became victims of a double jeopardy. They, along with their family and closest friends, extended themselves generously and on an almost superhuman scale to help the thousands of refugees in need. Yet business owners and people from the village accused them of escalating the crisis and destroying the local tourist industry by choosing to feed the refugees. When I asked Melinda what made her decide to do this, she said, "This was the thing. People tell me that I had a choice of whether or not to feed them, but I truly don't feel I had a choice. To me there simply wasn't any choice. You see people standing there all dripping wet and cold having fled their countries for God only knows what horrifying reasons and having experienced the crossing of the sea in some flimsy boat or having nearly drowned. How could I possibly feel that I had a choice whether or not to give them food and find them some warm, dry clothing? Sometimes when I was very tired and the refugees just kept on coming, I would think to myself, 'Oh no, not again,' but I just was never able to say no, and I just didn't feel I had a choice." She told me that she was able to cope with everything that was happening because it wasn't happening to her or her children. "We were all safe in our homes in our own country. Even though Greece has its problems, we were safe. That makes me feel so privileged. Sometimes I think, 'My God, I'm just so lucky.' It still isn't easy for me to absorb it all, but it helps me to think about how lucky I am."[32] Even though she became a target of people's hatred and anger for having helped the refugees, she said, "I'm willing to pay the price for doing that. I don't regret it for a moment."[33]

Melinda's work with refugees has not ended. After Oxy closed and the arrival of refugees—even in the harbor—ceased, Starfish was faced with the need to redefine itself. There was a strong feeling among some members of the Starfish Board that its role as a first stop for refugees had ended and that it should terminate its operation, with the understanding that it would start up again if refugee arrivals were to resume on a large scale. Melinda was opposed. She felt strongly that people from around the world had invested in Starfish and that a lot of important work of different kinds remained to be done. Starting with grant money that was awarded to Starfish to help launch community projects, she moved the office to Mytilene and began to steer her NGO into a whole realm of new endeavors designed to benefit both the remaining refugees and the larger community of Lesvos.[34]

When the COVID-19 pandemic hit and everyone feared there would be a potentially uncontrollable outbreak in Moria, Starfish set up and maintained hand-washing stations around the clock at the camp's entrance to help minimize any spread, and that has continued at Mavrovouni. A library with five thousand books in eleven different languages has also been set up for children and adults at the camp. Sadly and alarmingly, animosity toward Melinda and Theo has continued to flare up; one of the more recent occurrences was in late 2020, when angry graffiti was painted across the doors and walls of the properties they own in Molyvos and on the van belonging to Starfish. Among the defaced properties was the one where Nelson and I have stayed each time we've been in Molyvos. Melinda is still being made to pay a price for having helped the refugees, but true to her word and her beliefs, she persists.

Heroism was not what prompted the Kempsons to become involved in February 2015. They saw that the volume of arrivals was increasing and that boats were carrying families with children suffering from hypothermia and in need of serious attention. There were more and more refugees with gangrenous bullet wounds and burns from the wars and with shrapnel sticking out of their sides. At that point they realized that they had to do something. Philippa says, "There was no other choice. You couldn't go down to the beach and ignore what was happening."[35] For both of them no challenge proved to be so great and no circumstances so daunting that they threw up their hands and ran, even when faced with cruel threats or a landlord who refused to renew their lease on the home compound in Eftalou where they had lived for nearly twenty years.

In many ways Eric and Philippa did not miss a beat when everything quieted down in 2016. They continued to go to the beach when they spotted an undetected refugee boat, and they would bring it in and get its passengers safely onto the shore. However, with the IRC placing itself in charge of operations along the north coast, the need for their presence on the beach is no longer as critical as it was before. In fact the IRC doesn't want them there and has attempted to thwart their rescue efforts on numerous occasions.[36] Instead, when their landlord refused to renew the lease on their home in Eftalou, they moved closer to Mytilene in order to focus on their Hope Project warehouse. From this location they continue to distribute clothing, toiletries, and personal care items—even blankets and sleeping bags—to refugees who now reside at Mavrovouni. Remaining true to his work as an artist, Eric also set up a studio in one section of the warehouse where refugees can paint, draw, sculpt, or engage in any number of crafts. The Kempsons rely on refugees to help them in the warehouse, especially when they are not there; they provide a welcoming and trusting environment by speaking the languages of the people they help.

The fiery destruction of Moria and the closing of Kara Tepe placed an additional burden on the Hope Project as Eric and Philippa and their volunteers strove to provide for the displaced refugees, and once Camp Mavrovouni opened, they began going there to distribute food, clothing, and basic medical and hygienic supplies. Up until they were forced to leave their family compound in Eftalou, it continued to serve as a storage area and a base of operations for the Hope Project. On any given day, volunteers—some local and some who have returned to Eftalou numerous times to work with Eric and Philippa—could be found coming and going from the house to the warehouse or from other tasks that they performed as part of the Project Hope team. True to their original commitment, like Melinda, they are still at it, and this work remains a significant presence in their lives.

Naomi Krauz was working as a volunteer with the Hellenic Rescue Team, a search and rescue organization based in Thessaloniki, when she became involved in the crisis on Lesvos. Referring to a rescue where a mother gave birth on one of the dinghies during the crossing, she said, "It is something that stayed on my mind. You have to do something. You see them arriving in wet clothes, dirty, without the things they need to survive. They are people. You can't just stand by and pretend nothing is happening. When we get a call, in thirty minutes we must be on the sea. To help others is and should be a human instinct. I think that is what defines humanity. I hope so." Of his work, Panagiotis Konstantaras, another Hellenic Rescue Team volunteer, explained, "When I see a person in a difficult situation, I must help them. I don't care if they're Christian or Muslim; I help. If my phone rings, I leave my job and volunteer because I know it's a human life. I tell my colleagues who come with me on the dives to pick up the dead not to look at them in the eyes or at their face, but I do because I always want to remember the lives I couldn't save."[37]

A young woman named Marieke was among the many volunteers who came from Holland to work on the beach at Eftalou in November 2015. One of the refugees she helped was an Afghan who told her that he had watched while his mother was shot, presumably by a smuggler, while they were boarding one of the dinghies. The man also bore numerous wounds from having been shot in the stomach before he and his mother left Afghanistan to make their way to Turkey. When Marieke found him wandering on the beach, he was exhausted emotionally and in severe pain. Once she managed to get him seated, he burst into tears, and she simply held him until he had regained his composure and could board the bus for Oxy. She believes that the Western countries, in their quest to control the oil in the Middle East, are largely responsible for the refugee crisis, and she has traveled to Molyvos because, as a Westerner, she wants to do something to help. When describing her experience as a volunteer, she spoke about the need to show generosity and love to people who are suffering: "We are wealthy in Holland," she said. "We have everything, so we can give some away. If you share it, it multiplies. If you give it away, it comes back to you. We all should join together as a world. We are all born. We all raise our children. We all hurt. We all have our religions. We are all the same. We are all humans."[38]

Robert Jones observed that people who were in Molyvos at the time and saw that something needed to be done just stepped up and helped: "This is what people do when we don't have a chance to really think about it. It's who we are as humans. This is what we all do to a degree. This was not a political movement; it was a totally human movement. It was a day-to-day thing that brought out the normalness in people. It ended up showing us who we are as people and how we respond to such crises, and it offers a hopeful picture of humanity."[39]

Sitting prominently on a shelf in the Kempsons' home in Eftalou is a small stone that Eric mounted on a piece of olive wood from his studio. It was given to him by a Palestinian refugee on the beach one day after seven boats had arrived and all the people were safely on land. Eric stood talking with the man and his very large family that had all come together. After Eric had taken their picture and they introduced themselves, the man reached into the black bag that he had carried with him all the way from his home and pulled out this stone. He told Eric, "When I left Palestine five months ago, I took this stone from the ground and put it next to my heart. I've been carrying it there ever since, and I've been waiting to give it to someone special." As Eric told this story, his voice began to tremble, and his eyes welled up with tears. Philippa, equally moved, talked about a day in June when boats carrying several hundred refugees came in all at one time, and she and Eric were struggling with the landings because there were so few volunteers to help them. It turned out that some refugees had died during the crossing. After everyone's nerves had calmed a little, Philippa felt a tug at her sleeve and saw one of the refugee children holding a flower that she had picked for her. Fighting back tears, she told me, "It was the children's gifts that always got to me."[40]

Ute noted that the economic crisis in Greece at that time was causing great frustration and anger. Many Greeks were living in poverty and could not even afford housing. When she and I talked that afternoon in the harbor in front of her shop, she told me that many people she knew—herself as well—underwent a significant change in attitude after seeing the refugees arrive in the village having lost everything and having witnessed the slaughter of their family members and friends back in their home countries. She said that trying to see things from the refugees' side brought out a greater sense of respect and compassion for them as fellow human beings whose suffering was significantly greater than their own. She described a scene that she witnessed when the Coast Guard crew brought the body of a refugee who had drowned to the front of her shop and placed it in a body bag. They had no sooner closed the bag when they were told that they had to open it to take a picture of the body for identification, and this brought a lot of morbidly curious onlookers. Ute had already told me that, early in the crisis, she felt some members of the Coast Guard were too harsh with the refugees, but on this day, she said that the members of the Coast Guard crew, seeing all the bystanders, stepped into position and formed a half-circle around the body to shield it from being seen by everyone there. She was deeply moved by their show of respect.[41]

Ilektra described an encounter one day with a young girl at Oxy: "I heard her calling to me, 'Sister! Sister!' The girl was holding her hand very tight and moaning as if in serious pain. When I looked at her hand, she had only a very small and insignificant bruise, but I put something on it, and she felt better immediately. With everything that was happening in her life, she just needed someone to pay attention to her and take care of her for a little while." Working with the refugees was an experience that she said changed her life for the better because she was able to help people and realize how privileged she is. We talked for quite a while about her work as an asylum hearing officer in Mytilene. Ilektra said that she finds it very difficult because she has to deny asylum to some people. At the same time, she also knows that everyone who comes to her office is accorded "a good interview and a fair decision" because she knows all about what happened to them and what they went through before they set foot in her office. "I have mental pictures of their journey. I have them in my mind in a boat with most of them never having seen the sea before. I see them on the beach or in the harbor totally wet and tired, frightened, cold, and helpless. I see them on the road walking to Mytilene when I passed on my motorcycle handing out water. I see them in Oxy Camp." Then she went on to say, "Sometimes the people who come to me for their asylum interviews are like animals from having been confined in such terrible conditions in the camps. They are accompanied by guards who warn me that they are dangerous. I often dismiss the guards and, instead, give the person a bottle of water." When they see that she has shown them this graciousness, they react appreciatively. One of the men who came to her accompanied by guards spoke four languages and was a serious professional. "They are not dangerous," she insisted. Ilektra feels good about herself and all the work she's done with the refugees over the years, but she said that she also "feels bad about feeling good" when so many people have suffered. Her psychologist tells her that she has every reason to feel good for having helped.[42]

Talking about this time period, Dina said, "I can't help but see the horrible images in my head, the brutal life and death events that played out here, and I always get emotional. Nothing prepared us for what we saw and experienced. However, there were also happy times. I was involved in a rescue once where, thank God, no one died. I was still working at the hotel but also spending a lot of time on the front lines, and I ended up taking care of a lovely three-year-old boy when he came ashore soaking wet. After everything was under control and I was saying goodbye to the refugees as they boarded buses to Mytilene, that little boy saw me and ran to my arms. I just held him there and he was hugging me. I often wonder about him, what kind of life he has now and where he is. To deal with these kinds of emotions, nothing prepares you." One of the lessons Dina said she learned from it all is that "we are lucky to be free people. We are lucky to have the freedom to go wherever we want. I kept thinking this as I saw these people crossing this stretch of water in those terrible boats to get to freedom."

Dina continued, "Looking back, there were so many people from so many corners of the world—not all fantastic—but they all came to help, and it was wonderful to see that if you work for the same cause with the same determination to make something, then you will have success. We had people wet, hungry, disillusioned, emotionally spent. Imagine leaving home, coming across the sea, watching people drown, traumatized. You know that you have to do something. You just want to make these people feel a little bit normal for a while. You couldn't not get involved." Dina suffered in many ways, both psychologically and personally, so much so that she had to step back from her involvement with Starfish on the front lines and ultimately seek psychological help for PTSD. In spite of all that, she proudly and steadfastly said, "I would do it all again!"[43]

Nelson and I spent several hours with Stratis Kabanas seated under a fig tree on his property that he calls "Escape Land" surrounded by his chickens, his beautiful and stately rooster, his goats and sheep, and his dogs. "All mutts," he told us. After I more fully explained the purpose of my visit and my desire to write a book about what happened in Molyvos, we talked about what the whole refugee crisis did to him, what he learned from it, and about our human obligations to one another. At one point in the conversation, Stratis turned to me and asked, "What makes you want to write this book?" Then, as if to answer his own question, he went on to say, "If you want my opinion, I think your book should be about peace and compassion and about how people should understand each other."

It was clear that watching the human suffering and seeing the huge emotional and physical price the refugees paid had an enormous impact on Stratis. He said that it has saddened him, but going out to sea to save refugees from their sinking rubber dinghies, helping them to get out of the water and onto the shore, observing firsthand their almost superhuman determination to find safety, and then feeling their gratefulness for his help has humbled him. It has changed his life forever. This is also why he harbors such a deep anger toward the NGOs. Their help was so desperately needed, but it came way too late, and they were extremely disrespectful toward the locals whose honest and sincere efforts saved thousands of refugees before any NGOs had arrived.

He also believes that it is essential to take a close and comprehensive look at the whole refugee crisis in Molyvos: "We need to set ourselves and our egos aside so we can focus on what the real issues were and to analyze what we did and how we did it. Then we will know what to do the next time. If we don't and this kind of crisis comes again," as he believes it will, "we will end up doing the same things over again and making the same mistakes. If that happens, the negative reactions will be even stronger the next time around. This problem is not mine. This problem is global, and you cannot close your eyes to it. You can avoid it if you want, but it's going to find your kids. We have to do something now. We have to be prepared to act."[44]

This is essentially the same message that a professor at the University of California, Santa Barbara conveyed to his students when he introduced the Joneses, whom he had invited to campus to speak about their experiences in Molyvos. He told the students that what they were about to hear was a dry run for their generation as it deals with the effects of climate change on immigration.

His students had to know what he was talking about because the news media carried reports every day about what was happening along the border between the United States and Mexico and about the deeply rooted political and social discord that centers around the nation's unresolved issues with immigration. In 2020 an estimated 515,000 people fled the countries of the Northern Triangle of Central America: El Salvador, Guatemala, and Honduras.[45] Between the months of October 2020 and March 2021 alone, U.S. Customs and Border Protection recorded more than 396,000 migrant crossings into the United States, legally—through official ports of entry—as well as illegally, compared to about 201,600 during the previous year.[46] Of that number, 3,300 were unaccompanied children, which is triple what it was in 2019.[47] This migration is caused by serious economic stagnation and decline throughout the region, an underlying lack of adequate water resources, political instability, and a prevalence of gangs that act in total and violent defiance of any laws, including extortion from ordinary citizens and physical and sexual exploitation of children. The people are terrified for their lives because the countries in this region have some of the highest homicide rates in the world. The conditions were further magnified by the onset of the COVID-19 pandemic and the hurricanes of 2020 and 2021 that destroyed whole sections of Guatemala and Honduras.[48]

Those numbers were further augmented in 2021 by a surge in the arrival of Haitians from South American countries, where they had been living since 2010, when their country was devastated by an earthquake that killed two hundred thousand people and shattered the country's economy. Always hoping to eventually reach the United States when political conditions favored their migration, they chose the election of President Biden as a signal to begin their trek from South America, crossing the mountainous jungle of Panama's Darién Gap—one of the most dangerous passages in the world—and the countries of Central America to reach the Mexican border.[49] Between January and August of 2021, approximately 24,700 Haitians crossed the border from Mexico to the United States compared to only 1,640 during the last six months of 2020.[50]

In the wake of such large numbers of arrivals, there is serious overcrowding in facilities set up at the border to accommodate migrants, and border agents have been hard put to increase capacity. At any one time, hundreds of families and unaccompanied minors sleep in overcrowded, unsanitary shelters while authorities struggle to find additional space or move them to other centers away from the border where they can stay in more humane surroundings while they wait to have their cases processed.

The Center for Migration Studies of New York stated in 2021 that "the failed strategies of deterrence, interception, detention, and criminal prosecution have never prevented desperate migrants from reaching U.S. borders and territory."[51] Undeterred by the construction of walls or an increased presence of border patrol agents, crossings along the southern border with Mexico continue in record numbers. This, in turn, has given rise to an often acrimonious and alarmingly divisive national debate over immigration that even pervades elections at federal, state, and local levels. At center stage are such hotly contested issues as U.S. asylum and citizenship for undocumented immigrants; the cost of harboring the huge numbers of people massing along our border; the way children are treated at the hands of U.S. Homeland Security; the negative impact that some believe immigration has on employment for U.S. citizens, though there is little evidence of this; and the changing demographic patterns that, in some sectors, has evoked fear of a permanent alteration of the country's national identity. In short the United States has grown increasingly split along the very lines that have challenged European unity in the wake of its own immigration crisis since 2015–16. What will happen with the enormous migration of Ukrainian refugees into the EU as a result of the ongoing war in their country remains to be seen.

Globally, at the end of 2020, there were 82.4 million displaced people—1 percent of the world's population. Twenty-six million of them—the highest number ever recorded by the United Nations—were displaced due to conflict and persecution in their homelands. Among them, 4.1 million were in the process of seeking asylum. The head of the UNHCR said that "the scale of global forced displacement and the response required dwarfs anything ever seen before."[52] These figures add poignancy to the challenge that the professor in Santa Barbara presented to his students and to Stratis Kabanas's warnings that "this will follow your kids" and that "we must be prepared to act."

Joel Hernandez, who was affiliated with the Humanitarian Academy at Harvard University at the time of the crisis in Molyvos, wrote that the humanitarian response set up by Melinda and the Kempsons "deserves study and emulation as an ad hoc model for refugee assistance operations."[53] That is a powerful statement to make about an essentially homespun undertaking that relied upon basic human resolve, compassion, and a willingness to do whatever needed to be done to help people in trouble and prevent what they feared could be a total disintegration of their home community. Even though what they created was rough around the edges, makeshift, and plagued with chaos from myriad unexpected challenges, the fact is that they succeeded in many ways. Most remarkable of all is that they managed to carry on all by themselves without help from any outside, large-scale institutional sources. The help came from friends, friends of friends, tourists, and caring volunteers who made the effort to show up. Even when the large NGOs finally arrived some ten months after Melinda's first encounter with the refugees in November 2014, they expected the locals and unpaid volunteers to provide the real hands-on assistance. The success of this essentially homespun operation suggests that there might be a lesson from what happened in Molyvos on how to more effectively address issues of human displacement and the plight of refugees, and quite possibly some of mankind's other challenges, even ones still unforeseen.

Clearly everyone in Molyvos was gripped by the fear of losing their quality of life as they knew it, and that fear certainly motivated them to act and even turn against each other, but that fear was not foremost in Eri's mind when she encountered refugees in the port for the first time that November morning. Nor was it on the minds of either Melinda or Theo when, in response to Eri's call, they grabbed the large pot to make tea and headed for the restaurant. Their first thoughts were of wet, trembling families with children standing in the harbor after making the crossing from Turkey, and their first acts were to tend to their immediate needs and make them comfortable. They responded to a deeply rooted feeling of responsibility for the welfare of other human beings, and that sense of responsibility was so strong that they could not ignore it. When Eri heard the horrifying sound of people drowning while she was out on the Coast Guard boat, her first instinct was to jump into the water to save them, until her colleagues and the voice of her trainer in her head brought her to her senses. In December 2014, when Melinda received a call informing her that refugee children who had just landed were desperately in need of dry clothing, she was in the intensive care unit of a hospital where her stepfather lay dying. Yet her thoughts turned automatically, almost instinctually, to the suffering children who needed her help. When one of her Starfish volunteers was sick with pneumonia, he still worked day and night at the beach because people were arriving in difficult weather and terrible physical condition. He could not bring himself to stop.

When people, whether they were in Australia or New York, learned from news reports about the crisis in Greece, they felt compelled to board planes, rent cars, travel long distances, and endure physical and emotional hardships just to be of help. Once they were there no one could persuade them to take a break even though they were exhausted, and many returned to Molyvos repeatedly. As Eric says, "They just couldn't get it out of their system." Melinda was routinely called out of bed in the middle of the night to make tea and distribute dry clothing. "How could I not?" she asks. Eric and Philippa felt as if they had no choice but to decide in favor of going to the beach, and once they started, they continued devoting their lives and personal resources to the effort. Philippa says, "You can't just stand by without doing something." Dina was heavily involved until she became so exhausted that she needed treatment for PTSD, as did Ilektra. All of this is what responsibility looks and feels like—albeit a supreme sense of responsibility—because it involved other human beings often in a life-or-death struggle. Every person I interviewed told me that they fully and instinctually embraced that responsibility, that they felt as if they had no other choice, and that they would do it all again.

When we sat with the Joneses on the patio of their Molyvos home that overlooks the Aegean and the harbor, we found ourselves engaged in a far-ranging discussion of human beings' sense of responsibility and what motivates people in such trying times. They were very encouraging when I told them that, in addition to telling the Molyvos story, I wanted to explore what happens within people when they are faced with this kind of event and decide to act. Robin told me that she found it "refreshing because it's part of the story that hasn't really been talked about." Reflecting on her own involvement with the refugees and what she witnessed among volunteers both on the beach and at Oxy, she said, "People want to add meaning to their lives by doing something good. That's what happens in a village." Of course, there is the saying, supposedly of African origin, that it takes a village to raise a child. One can think in literal terms about the village, but a village is also a human collective where people, all kinds of people, band together in shared concern and responsibility for the good of everyone, including themselves. By extension it can be said that it takes a village to care for the infirm, educate its population, ensure protection and provide security, grieve with people over the loss of their loved ones, and bury its dead. Our interconnectedness makes us stronger and more secure because we share the burdens and responsibilities of existence. Spyros Orfanos, when writing about Daphne Matziaraki's film, suggested that "meaning in the world lies in the interconnection of every person in humankind."[54]

This, of course, raises the basic existential question about how one's life may gain meaning. Some philosophers claim that the answer lies in becoming involved, in taking it upon ourselves to act, but they also remind us that acting carries with it the weight of responsibility because when we act, we do so for all mankind. Marieke, the volunteer from Holland, expressed that existential notion when she said that we are all born, we all raise our children, we all hurt, we all die. We are humans. We are part of a common humanity, natives of different countries from different cultures and beliefs, but all humans nonetheless. We are interconnected. We are alike in our humanness, and we have a responsibility to one another. If we look mindfully at each other, we can glimpse a reflection of ourselves, and that can prompt us to act by sharing love, an act born of compassion. When commenting about *4.1 Miles*, Daphne Matziaraki observed that some people feel this huge responsibility, and some others just do not. However, if we try to escape our connections or ignore our responsibility, we do so at our own peril because if mankind is to survive and if we are to find meaning in life, we must all do our part, and somewhere deep inside, we all know it. Sometimes it takes a crisis for us to come face to face with the essence of our human existence.

In Molyvos some of the players seemed to know instinctively that our interconnectedness is what makes us human and that we must respond with compassion if we're to survive. Others learned from the experience that each one of us must do our part, like the girl who threw the starfish back into the ocean one by one. Stratis Kabanas is convinced that action must be rooted in a shared belief in the fundamental good in people: "If you reach out honestly and sincerely, the other person will recognize your sincerity and respond in kind. It takes that kind of basic belief to survive what's happening on a larger scale in our world."[55] It reminds one of what King Solomon meant when he advised his people to "cast your bread upon the waters."[56]

On the evening of December 9, 2015—only a couple of weeks before Oxy closed and the last refugees boarded the buses for the trip to Moria and Kara Tepe—Jack Rowland, a Starfish volunteer, recorded a video of himself as he reflected on his ten days working at Oxy. This is what he said: "I'm really sad to be leaving. I loved every single day. I wouldn't change any of it for the world. It's been the best experience of my entire life. I'm going to miss that sunset and the stars at night, but mostly I'm going to miss the people. All of the volunteers are amazing. We're just a group of freelance volunteers who all just want to make a difference in people's lives, and it's amazing. It's been a pleasure working with everyone involved, and the refugees—all of them—they've just shown incredible love. When you look people in the eye and you listen to their stories, you realize we're all the same, and when you're talking to them, you see yourself reflected in them because we are just completely the same . . . and you really realize it in a place like this."[57]

Robin Jones believes that this kind of story, the story of what happened in Molyvos, should "never stop being told because it is so closely linked to the purpose of being human."

ACKNOWLEDGMENTS

I undertook the writing of this book about what happened in Molyvos between November 2014 and March 2016 because I believed it was a story that needed to be told. As the largest human migration since World War II, it shook the political, economic, and cultural pillars of Europe. By any definition it was an international crisis. Meanwhile, completely unnoticed, in the small seaside village of Molyvos on the Greek island of Lesvos, that same crisis took on a distinctly human drama as the endless tidal wave of desperate refugees landing on its shores threatened to unravel an entire way of local life. Ultimately it would have resulted in an untold amount of personal suffering and death had it not been for individual residents and groups of volunteers working on their own without aid of any kind from outside sources and without making any headlines. Courageously and tirelessly they mounted a relief effort that averted a catastrophe of epic proportions. I didn't want that side of the story to get sidelined, overlooked, or, worse yet, forgotten.

I was not present in Molyvos during the months that are the subject of this book. Nor were journalists who could have provided documentation of the events as they unfolded. That didn't happen until the fall of 2015, after the death of Alan Kurdi finally brought that human side of the crisis to the world's attention and help began to arrive. Therefore in order to tell the story I had to rely on people who witnessed it and were willing to talk with me about what they had experienced firsthand. This proved difficult for some of them because it evoked distressing emotions and painful memories that still cause personal anguish. During my conversations with them, there were tears and expressions of anger and frustration, but overall there was also deep-seated reflection and a palpable sense of responsibility for fellow human beings that brought them all inner peace.

Fortunately some of the individual volunteers who came to Molyvos that fall and winter, people I never met personally, documented their experiences in the form of videos, diaries, or other anecdotal accounts that they posted on social media. To all of them, those with whom I spoke personally and whose recordings and written accounts I was able to access, I owe a huge debt of gratitude. They enabled me to witness the astonishing events and the utterly remarkable courage that was displayed in Molyvos that I hope I have adequately conveyed in the pages of this book.

Michael Honegger and Timothy Smith need to be mentioned first because it all started when they invited me and my husband, Nelson Mondaca, to spend time with them in Molyvos in 2013. They introduced us to their friends, notably Melinda McRostie and her husband, Theo Kosmetos, and their restaurant, the Captain's Table. Michael's and Tim's postings on Facebook during the summer of 2015 and Michael's vivid photographs of refugees landing on the beaches and filling the village's streets alerted us to the crisis and its magnitude long before news media carried any reports. Michael agreed to let me choose photographs for this book from his vast collection.

Needless to say, there would be no story without Melinda McRostie, and there would be no book without her generosity and patience as we communicated on Skype and exchanged emails during the four years in which I was working on the book. She and Theo made me feel welcome when I traveled to Molyvos to conduct interviews, and they spent hours talking with me in detailed, insightful, and, at times, painful conversations about the events that took place, the central role they played in the relief effort, and the formation of the Starfish Foundation. Melinda introduced me to Dina Adam, Dionisis Pavlou, Ilektra Pasxouli, Stratis Kabanas, Erasmia Grigorelli, Ute Vogt, and Robin and Robert Jones, all of whom worked with her during the crisis and graciously offered to be interviewed. Their names will be familiar to the book's readers because their stories fill its pages. Robin and Robert Jones helped me to recognize and articulate the essential humanitarian spirit that motivated the volunteers, and Robin provided me with rare photographs of life in the Oxy Transit Camp. To all of them I remain forever grateful as well as awed by their deeds.

Likewise there would be no story without Eric and Philippa Kempson, and there would be no book if they had not been trusting enough to invite me—a total unknown who was "writing a book about the refugee crisis"—to their home. During our long and deeply absorbing conversation that day, I learned the important details about their personal involvement with the refugees on the beaches and in the camps and about their efforts in creating the Hope Project to raise funds to obtain critical supplies that could be distributed to all those in need. They invited Nelson and me to spend time with them at the Hope Project warehouse near Mytilene and introduced us to refugees working there who, in turn, took us to the tent compound just outside the walls of Moria, where we walked the grounds, spoke with refugees being detained there, and visited their living quarters. Eric provided me with links to the hundreds of videos that he recorded and narrated on the beaches during the landings, and they, along with his and Philippa's personal stories, enabled me to craft several of the most dramatic narratives in the book. I am forever indebted to them and will be forever amazed by their courageous and selfless efforts.

I also relied on video reports by media correspondents who began to arrive in Molyvos starting early in the fall of 2015, when news of the crisis had finally reached the outside world. Of particular value to me when crafting detailed narratives of the refugees' crossings from Turkey were Alex Crawford's September 11 broadcast on Sky News, the AFP News Agency's video that aired on November 5, and the October 18 broadcast of Franck Genauzeau's report on France 24. The personal videos and written reports that were posted on the internet by individual volunteers—those traveling independently and those who came to Molyvos to work for the Starfish Foundation or other NGOs—provided me with details of events and perspectives on the crisis that I would not have had otherwise. I am particularly indebted to Hasan Oswald for his video "Refugees Welcome—Lesvos, Greece," which he posted on YouTube on December 22, 2015; to Jack Rowland for his two videos that were posted on YouTube on December 9, 2015;

and to Peggy Whitfield for her diary entries in "I Spent a Frenzied Night Saving Children . . . ," which was posted on November 4, 2016. The latter formed the basis for much of chapter 15, which chronicles the October 28 shipwreck. Of course, no acknowledgment would be complete without a huge shout-out to Daphne Matziaraki and her short documentary *4.1 Miles*. The links to all of these sources appear in the bibliography, and I urge interested readers to access them.

Harriet Barnett, Robert and Robin Jones, Gregory Molinari, Daniel Gashler, Elsie Rhodes, and Suzanne Mayer patiently and helpfully read all or parts of versions of the manuscript, and I am grateful not only for their insights and valuable suggestions but also for their steadfast enthusiasm and encouragement. My editor-turned-agent, Philip Turner of Turner Book Productions, expertly guided me and offered me the best four-year writing seminar a writer could ever hope to have. His guidance and candor in every aspect of the writing process and his sincere interest in the subject all gave me the confidence to keep going. My best friend of many years, Brian Kaplan, read every draft of every chapter over the entire four-year period in which I was writing the manuscript and provided focused and constructive commentary as well as never-failing encouragement. I could not have completed the book without him.

My husband, Nelson Mondaca, persuaded me to write the book after a conversation we had with Melinda McRostie while we were in Molyvos in September 2017. He observed the way in which her story resonated with me and convinced me that it needed to be told and that I was the right person to tell it. He accompanied me to Molyvos in April 2018, sat in on all the interviews, and together we explored all the locations associated with the crisis. His many photographs, some of which appear in this book, helped me to visualize many of the events, and his ever-present encouragement sustained me throughout. Our three golden retrievers, Jersey, Dakota, and Savannah, kept me company by sitting next to my desk while I wrote and reminding me periodically that I needed to stand up so I could give them treats.

NOTES

PROLOGUE

1. Kadletz, "Philoxenia."
2. Hernandez, "Humanitarianism without Humanitarians."

1. INESCAPABLE MEMORIES

1. McRostie, "Melinda"; McRostie, "Our Father, Giorgos."
2. Lamp, "Beacons of Safety."
3. Kempson, "Our Story."
4. CBC, "Syria's War."
5. Faiola, "Anti-immigrant Golden Dawn."
6. Khazan, "Europe's Far-Right Groups."
7. Stock, "Melinda McRostie Is a Basque Culinary World Prize Finalist."
8. UNHCR, "Operational Data Portal."
9. Ross, "The ECO Warriors."
10. *World Today*, "A Week in the Life of Melinda McRostie."
11. Magra, "Greece's Island of Despair."
12. Robert and Robin Jones, interview with author, Molyvos, Lesvos, Greece, April 26, 2018.
13. Drury, "David Morrissey Helped Rescue Terrified Refugees."
14. Melinda McRostie, interview with author, Molyvos, Lesvos, Greece, via Skype from Cooperstown, New York, April 5, 2018.

2. THE TIDE BEGAN AS A TRICKLE

1. Erasmia Grigorelli (Coast Guard crew member), interview with author, Kalloni, Lesvos, Greece, April 28, 2018.
2. McRostie, interview, April 5, 2018.
3. Hernandez, "Refugee Flows to Lesvos."
4. Deep Space Diver, "Way Out Home, Part 10."

5. Cooper, "Trading Places."
6. Digidiki, "Humanitarianism in Crisis."
7. Stratis Kabanas, interview with author, Molyvos, Lesvos, Greece, April 24, 2018.
8. Grigorelli, interview, April 28, 2018.
9. Kadletz, "Philoxenia."
10. Digidiki, "Humanitarianism in Crisis."
11. IDFA, *4.1 Miles.*
12. Dionisis Pavlou, interview with author, Mytilene, Lesvos, Greece, April 24, 2018.
13. Ute Vogt, interview with author, Molyvos, Lesvos, Greece, April 25, 2018.
14. Pavlou, interview, April 24, 2018.
15. Pavlou, interview, April 24, 2018.
16. Psaropoulos, "Reponses to the Refugee Crisis."
17. Dina Adam, interview with author, Molyvos, Lesvos, Greece, April 21, 2018.

3. IN THE HARBOR AND ON THE BEACH

1. DeLargy, "Europe's Humanitarian Response."
2. McRostie, interview, April 5, 2018.
3. Banks-Anderson, "The Refugee Boats Keep Coming."
4. Banks-Anderson, "The Refugee Boats Keep Coming."
5. McRostie, interview, April 5, 2018.
6. *World Today,* "A Week in the Life of Melinda McRostie."
7. Eric and Philippa Kempson, interview with author, Eftalou, Lesvos, Greece, April 9, 2018.

4. THE REFUGEES

1. Eric and Philippa Kempson, interview, April 9, 2018.
2. Guru-Murthy, "Refugee Crisis: New Boats Still Arriving."
3. UNHCR, "Figures at a Glance."
4. Genauzeau, "Syrian Refugee Crisis."
5. Psaropoulis, "Reponses to the Refugee Crisis."
6. Oswald, "Refugees Welcome."
7. Crawford, "Joining Refugees."
8. Digidiki, "Humanitarianism in Crisis."
9. Psaropoulos, "Reponses to the Refugee Crisis."
10. Crawford, "Joining Refugees."
11. Psaropoulos, "Reponses to the Refugee Crisis."
12. Crawford, "Joining Refugees."
13. Channel 4 News, "Refugee Crisis: Lesbos Struggles."

14. Tanzania, "Lesvos Day 2."
15. Eric and Philippa Kempson, interview, April 9, 2018.
16. Digidiki, "Humanitarianism in Crisis."
17. Crawford, "Joining Refugees."
18. Robert and Robin Jones, interview, April 26, 2018; Adam, interview, April 21, 2018.
19. Eric and Philippa Kempson, interview with author, Eftalou, Lesvos, Greece, April 21, 2018.
20. Genauzeau, "Syrian Refugee Crisis."
21. Vickery, "At the Captain's Table."
22. Kingsley, "Greek Island Refugee Crisis."
23. UNHCR, "Operational Data Portal."

5. THE KEMPSONS ARE STILL ALONE

1. Eric and Philippa Kempson, interview, April 9, 2018.
2. Kempson, "Fourth Boat of the Morning!!"
3. Eric and Philippa Kempson, interview, April 9, 2018.
4. Kempson, "Casualty & No Doctor!!!!!!"; Kempson, "Casualty & No Doctor!!!!!! Update."
5. Eric and Philippa Kempson, interview, April 9, 2018.
6. Kempson, "More Blood Spilled!!!"
7. Eric and Philippa Kempson, interview, April 9, 2018.
8. Channel 4 News, "The British Family Helping Thousands"; *World Today*, "A Week in the Life of Melinda McRostie."

6. ENDURING THE SCREAMS OF DESPERATION

1. Banks-Anderson, "The Refugee Boats Keep Coming."
2. Eric and Philippa Kempson, interview, April 9, 2018.
3. Melinda McRostie, interview with author, Molyvos, Lesvos, Greece, via Skype from Cooperstown, New York, January 18, 2018.
4. Matziaraki, *4.1 Miles*. Matziaraki's film *4.1 Miles*, released in September 2016, won the Peabody Award and received an Academy Award nomination for Best Documentary Short Subject.
5. Kermeliotis, "Daphne Matziaraki's Powerful Short Documentary."
6. Grigorelli, interview, April 28, 2018.
7. Grigorelli, interview, April 28, 2018.
8. Kabanas, interview, April 24, 2018.
9. McRostie, interview, January 18, 2018.
10. Grigorelli, interview, April 28, 2018.

7. THE SITUATION IN THE HARBOR WORSENS

1. Barnets, "Greek Island Community."
2. McRostie, interview, January 18, 2018.
3. Ilektra Pasxouli, interview with author, Mytilene, Levos, Greece, April 23, 2018.
4. Pavlou, interview, April 24, 2018.
5. Grigorelli, interview, April 28, 2018.
6. Adam, interview, April 21, 2018.
7. Adam, interview, April 21, 2018.

8. LOCALS AND TOURISTS

1. Grigorelli, interview, April 28, 2018.
2. Kabanas, interview, April 24, 2018.
3. Vogt, interview, April 25, 2018.
4. Vogt, interview, April 25, 2018.
5. Robert and Robin Jones, interview, April 26, 2018.
6. Jones, *The Refugee Crisis*.
7. Johnnie Walker Storyline, "Ode to Lesvos."
8. Kempson, "Appeal from Government Needed."
9. Michael Honegger, interview with author, Nice, France, via FaceTime from Cooperstown, New York, October 17, 2019.
10. Voutsina, "The Growing Refugee Toll on Lesvos."
11. Eric and Philippa Kempson, interview, April 9, 2018.
12. Robert and Robin Jones, interview, April 26, 2018.
13. Witte, "Tourists Stay to Help Refugees."
14. Timothy Jay Smith, email correspondence.
15. Honegger, interview, October 17, 2019.
16. Kempson, "Angels & Demons."
17. Vogt, interview, April 25, 2018.

9. THE SITUATION GOES OUT OF CONTROL

1. Robert and Robin Jones, interview, April 26, 2018.
2. Kabanas, interview, April 24, 2018.
3. Melinda McRostie and Theo Kosmetos, interview with author, Molyvos, Lesvos, Greece, April 23, 2018.
4. Robert and Robin Jones, interview, April 26, 2018.
5. Kingsley, "Greek Island Refugee Crisis."
6. McRostie, interview, April 5, 2018.
7. Pasxouli, interview, April 23, 2018.

8. McRostie, interview, April 5, 2018.
9. Kingsley, "Greek Island Refugee Crisis."
10. Melinda McRostie, email correspondence with author, March 10, 2022.
11. Kempson, "The Struggle Continues."
12. Kabanas, interview, April 24, 2018.
13. Robert and Robin Jones, interview, April 26, 2018.
14. Digidiki, "Humanitarianism in Crisis."
15. Pavlou, interview, April 24, 2018.
16. Papadopoulou, "How Greece Reported the Migration Crisis."
17. Faiola, "Golden Dawn Rises in Greece."
18. Digidiki, "Humanitarianism in Crisis."
19. Eric and Philippa Kempson, interview with author, Eftalou, Lesvos, Greece, April 19, 2018.
20. Kempson, "Another Tragic Morning on Lesvos Greece."
21. Vogt, interview, April 25, 2018.
22. McRostie, interview, April 5, 2018.
23. McRostie, interview, April 5, 2018.
24. Robert and Robin Jones, interview, April 26, 2018.
25. Pavlou, interview, April 24, 2018.
26. Grigorelli, interview, April 28, 2018.
27. Psaropoulos, "Reponses to the Refugee Crisis."
28. Robert and Robin Jones, interview, April 26, 2018.
29. Eric and Philippa Kempson, interview, April 19, 2018.
30. Melinda McRostie and Theo Kosmetos, interview with author, Molyvos, Lesvos, Greece, April 28, 2018.

10. A LONG, HOT SUMMER

1. Digidiki, "Humanitarianism in Crisis."
2. Kempson, "Tourism & Refugees in Greece."
3. Kempson, "Hot, Dusty, Dirt Road!!!"
4. Harlan, "Migrants Wait in Bread Lines."
5. Harlan, "Migrants Wait in Bread Lines."
6. Robert and Robin Jones, interview, April 26, 2018.
7. Pasxouli, interview, April 23, 2018.
8. Niarchos, "An Island of Refugees."
9. McRostie, interview, April 5, 2018.
10. Pavlou, interview, April 24, 2018.
11. Kingsley, "Greek Island Refugee Crisis."
12. Kempson, "Lesvos Death March Update."

13. Kempson, "Faith in Humanity Restored!!!!!"
14. Kempson, "Lesvos Death March Update."
15. Kingsley, "Greek Island Refugee Crisis."
16. Pavlou, interview, April 24, 2018.
17. Robert and Robin Jones, interview, April 26, 2018.
18. Eric and Philippa Kempson, interview, April 9, 2018.
19. Amnesty International, "Humanitarian Crisis Mounts."
20. Honegger, interview, October 17, 2019.
21. McRostie and Kosmetos, interview, April 23, 2018.

11. SKALA SYKAMINIAS

1. McRostie and Kosmetos, interview, April 23, 2018.
2. Johnnie Walker Storyline, "Ode to Lesvos."
3. Deep Space Diver, "Way Out Home, Part 03."
4. Michael Honneger, email to author, August 19, 2019.
5. Kempson, "Hot, Dusty, Dirt Road."
6. *Word Press*, "Volunteering with Refugees in Lesvos."

12. THE PARKING LOT BY THE SCHOOL

1. McRostie and Kosmetos, interview, April 23, 2018.
2. Honegger, interview, October 17, 2019.
3. Pavlou, interview, April 24, 2018.
4. Honegger, interview, October 17, 2019.
5. McRostie and Kosmetos, interview, April 28, 2018.
6. Pasxouli, interview, April 23, 2018.
7. Adam, interview, April 21, 2018.
8. Pasxouli, interview, April 23, 2018.
9. Eric and Philippa Kempson, interview, April 9, 2018.
10. Pavlou, interview, April 24, 2018.
11. Deep Space Diver, "Way Out Home, Part 03."
12. McRostie and Kosmetos, interview, April 23, 2018.
13. Deep Space Diver, "Way Out Home, Part 03."
14. McRostie and Kosmetos, interview, April 23, 2018.
15. Deep Space Diver, "Way Out Home, Part 03."
16. Honneger, interview, October 17, 2019; Timothy Jay Smith, email to the author, October 7, 2019.
17. Eric and Philippa Kempson, interview, April 9, 2018.
18. Honneger, interview, October 17, 2019.
19. Paxchouli, interview, April 23, 2018.

20. McRostie and Kosmetos, interview, April 23, 2018.
21. McRostie and Kosmetos, interview, April 23, 2018.
22. Honneger, interview, October 17, 2019.
23. Adam, interview, April 21, 2018.
24. Vogt, interview, April 25, 2018.
25. Alan Kurdi's name is spelled "Aylan" in most media reports, but his aunt Tima Kurdi stated that the correct spelling of his name is Alan. See Cole, "The Aunt of the Drowned Syrian Boy."
26. NBC Nightly News, "Stirring Images of Syrian Boy's Body."
27. Barnard and Shoumali, "Image of Drowned Syrian, Aylan Kurdi."
28. Cole, "The Aunt of the Drowned Syrian Boy."
29. Osmandzikovic, "The Drowning of Aylan Kurdi."
30. Barnard and Shoumali, "Image of Drowned Syrian, Ayan Kurdi."
31. Wall Street Journal, "Drowned Syrian Boy."
32. Barnard and Shoumali, "Image of Drowned Syrian, Ayan Kurdi."
33. Osmandzikovic, "The Drowning of Aylan Kurdi."
34. Gordon, "Canadian Government under Fire."
35. Papadopoulou, "How Greece Reported the Migration Crisis."

13. THE STARFISH FOUNDATION

1. Pavlou, interview, April 24, 2018.
2. Grigorelli, interview, April 28, 2018.
3. Pasxouli, interview, April 23, 2018.
4. Pasxouli, interview, April 23, 2018.
5. Eggink and McRostie, "The Starfish Foundation."
6. Pavlou, interview, April 24, 2018.
7. Melinda McRostie, email to the author, March 10, 2022.
8. Eiseley, "The Star Thrower." The original version is about a young boy, but when Melinda tells the story, the starfish thrower is a young girl.
9. World Today, "A Week in the Life of Melinda McRostie."
10. Melinda McRostie, presentation to a tourist group at the Captain's Table, September 21, 2018.
11. Vickery, "At the Captain's Table."
12. Pavlou, interview, April 24, 2018.
13. Eggink and McRostie, "The Starfish Foundation."
14. Timothy Jay Smith, email to the author, October 7, 2019.
15. Pasxouli, interview, April 23, 2018.
16. Vickery, "At the Captain's Table."
17. Word Press, "Volunteering with Refugees."

18. Eggpink and McRostie, "The Starfish Foundation"; *World Today*, "A Week in the Life of Melinda McRostie."
19. Vickery, "At the Captain's Table."
20. *Word Press*, "The Refugee Crisis in Greece."
21. Kofou, "Lesvos Island—My Experience (Part I)."
22. Vickery, "At the Captain's Table."
23. Vickery, "At the Captain's Table."
24. McRostie, interview, January 18, 2018.
25. Vickery, "At the Captain's Table."

14. OXY REFUGEE TRANSIT CAMP

1. Dijksma, "Transit Refugee Camp Oxy."
2. Deep Space Diver, "Way Out Home, Part 12."
3. Eggink and McRostie, "The Starfish Foundation."
4. Starfish Foundation, "Farewell Oxy."
5. Hamilton, "Welcome to Lesvos."
6. Starfish Foundation, "Farewell Oxy."
7. *World Today*, "A Week in the Life of Melinda McRostie."
8. Vogt, interview, April 25, 2018.
9. Robert and Robin Jones, interview, April 26, 2018.
10. Vogt, interview, April 25, 2018.
11. Robert and Robin Jones, interview, April 26, 2018.
12. Eggink and McRostie, "The Starfish Foundation."
13. Robert and Robin Jones, interview, April 26, 2018.
14. Edwards, "UNHCR Viewpoint: 'Refugee' or 'Migrant.'"
15. ICRC, "Protocol Additional to the Geneva Conventions."
16. ICRC, "The Geneva Conventions of 1949."
17. In writing this book, the author used the term "refugee" to refer to all of the people making the crossing to Molyvos.
18. RULAC, "Non-international Conflicts in Syria."
19. Robert and Robin Jones, interview, April 26, 2018.
20. Strickland, "Protest in Greece."
21. Wall, "The Humanitarian Caste System?"; Smith, "Bank Closures, Refugees and Showers."
22. Eric and Philippa Kempson, interview, April 9, 2018.
23. Green, "Understanding the Refugee Crisis in Europe."
24. Honegger, interview, October 17, 2019.
25. Eggink and McRostie, "The Starfish Foundation."
26. Robert and Robin Jones, interview, April 26, 2018.

27. Vickery, "At the Captain's Table."
28. Pasxouli, interview, April 23, 2018.
29. Nomikos, "In Transit."
30. Pasxouli, interview, April 23, 2018.
31. Robert and Robin Jones, interview, April 26, 2018.
32. Pasxouli, interview, April 23, 2018.
33. McRostie and Kosmetos, interview, April 23, 2018.
34. Vogt, interview, April 25, 2018.
35. Robert and Robin Jones, interview, April 26, 2018.
36. Robert and Robin Jones, interview, April 26, 2018.
37. Jones, *The Refugee Crisis.*
38. Adam, interview, April 21, 2018.
39. Robert and Robin Jones, interview, April 26, 2018.
40. Pasxouli, interview, April 23, 2018.
41. Hamilton, "Welcome to Lesvos."
42. Hamilton, "Welcome to Lesvos."
43. Rowland, "Afghan Dancing and Mental Breakdowns!"
44. Robert and Robin Jones, interview, April 26, 2018.
45. Pasxouli, interview, April 23, 2018.
46. Robert and Robin Jones, interview, April 26, 2018.
47. Robert and Robin Jones, interview, April 26, 2018.
48. Rowland, "Refugee Crisis, Completed It."

15. THE CALAMITOUS SHIPWRECK

1. Whitfield, "I Spent a Frenzied Night Saving Children."
2. Westcott, "'It Was Hell.'"
3. Eric and Philippa Kempson, interview, April 9, 2018.
4. Whitfield, "I Spent a Frenzied Night Saving Children."
5. Whitfield, "I Spent a Frenzied Night Saving Children."
6. Westcott, "'It Was Hell.'"
7. Eric and Philippa Kempson, interview, April 9, 2018.
8. Whitfield, "I Spent a Frenzied Night Saving Children."
9. Eric and Philippa Kempson, interview, April 9, 2018.
10. McRostie, interview, April 5, 2018.
11. Vogt, interview, April 25, 2018.
12. Adam, interview, April 21, 2018.
13. McRostie, interview, April 5, 2018.
14. Grigorelli, interview, April 28, 2018.
15. Whitfield, "I Spent a Frenzied Night Saving Children."

16. McRostie, interview, April 5, 2018.
17. Westcott, "'It Was Hell.'"
18. Grigorelli, interview, April 28, 2018.
19. Eric and Philippa Kempson, interview, April 9, 2018.
20. Mazariaki, *4.1 Miles*.
21. Kermeliotis, "Daphne Matziaraki's Powerful Short Documentary."
22. Grigorelli, interview, April 28, 2018.
23. Mazariaki, *4.1 Miles*.
24. *National Herald*, "Heroic Coast Guard Officer Papadopoulos Dies at 44."
25. McRostie, interview, April 5, 2018.

16. BLESSINGS AND BURDENS

1. Digidiki, "Humanitarianism in Crisis."
2. Channel 4 News, "Refugee Crisis: Lesbos Struggles."
3. Kempson, "Disgusting Aid Agencies!"
4. Eric and Philippa Kempson, interview, April 9, 2018.
5. Hamilton, "Welcome to Lesvos."
6. Kempson, "Our House!"
7. Grigorelli, interview, April 28, 2018.
8. Pasxouli, interview, April 23, 2018.
9. McRostie, interview, January 18, 2018.
10. Eric and Philippa Kempson, interview, April 9, 2018.
11. Eric and Philippa Kempson, interview, April 9, 2018.
12. Eric and Philippa Kempson, interview, April 9, 2018.
13. Kempson, "Disgusting Behavior."
14. Eric and Philippa Kempson, interview, April 9, 2018.
15. McRostie, interview, April 5, 2018.
16. Grigorelli, interview, April 28, 2018.
17. Hernandez, "Refugee Flows to Lesvos."
18. Robert and Robin Jones, interview, April 26, 2018.
19. Kabanas, interview, April 24, 2018.
20. Hernandez, "Refugee Flows to Lesvos."
21. Saliba, "Learning from Lesbos."
22. Kabanas, interview, April 24, 2018.
23. McRostie, interview, April 5, 2018.
24. Nianias, "Refugees in Lesbos."
25. Kabanas, interview, April 24, 2018.
26. Nianias, "Refugees in Lesbos."
27. Honegger, interview, October 17, 2019.

28. Eric and Philippa Kempson, interview, April 9, 2018.
29. Honegger, interview, October 17, 2019.
30. Grigorelli, interview, April 28, 2018.
31. Honegger, interview, October 17, 2019.
32. Eric and Philippa Kempson, interview, April 9, 2018; Grigorelli, interview, April 28, 2018.
33. Kempson, "Disgusting Aid Agencies!"
34. Kempson, "Disgusting Aid Agencies!"
35. Saliba, "Learning from Lesbos," 3.
36. IRC, "Learning from Lesbos."
37. Saliba, "Learning from Lesbos," 15.
38. Saliba, "Learning from Lesbos," 17.
39. Saliba, "Learning from Lesbos," 10.
40. Robert and Robin Jones, interview, April 26, 2018.
41. Honegger, interview, October 17, 2019.
42. Kabanas, interview, April 24, 2018.
43. Eric and Philippa Kempson, interview, April 9, 2018.

17. CLEANING THE BEACHES

1. Deep Space Diver, "Way Out Home, Part 10."
2. Kofou, "Lesvos Island—My Experience (Part I)."
3. McRostie and Kosmetos, interview, April 23, 2018.
4. McRostie and Kosmetos, interview, April 23, 2018.
5. Kofou, "Lesvos Island—My Experience (Part I)."
6. Robert and Robin Jones, interview, April 26, 2018.
7. McRostie and Kosmetos, interview, April 23, 2018.
8. Eric and Philippa Kempson, interview, April 9, 2018.
9. Eric and Philippa Kempson, interview, April 9, 2018.
10. See Isaiah 24:19 (King James Version).
11. Stock, "Melinda McRostie Is a Basque Culinary World Prize Finalist."
12. Pavlou, interview, April 24, 2018.
13. Smith, "Reckoning."
14. Adam, interview, April 21, 2018.
15. Pavlou, interview, April 24, 2018.
16. Robert and Robin Jones, interview, April 26, 2018.
17. Grigorelli, interview, April 28, 2018.
18. Pavlou, interview, April 24, 2018.
19. Pasxouli, interview, April 23, 2018.
20. Adam, interview, April 21, 2018.

21. Grigorellli, interview, April 28, 2018.
22. Pavlou, interview, April 24, 2018.
23. Ilektra Pasxouli, interview with author, Mytilene, Levos, Greece, April 21, 2018.
24. Eric and Philippa Kempson, interview, April 9, 2018.
25. Eric and Philippa Kempson, interview, April 9, 2018.
26. McRostie and Kosmetos, interview, April 23, 2018.

18. OXY CLOSES

1. AFP News Agency, "Volunteers Cry for Help."
2. Media Line, "Conversation with Hasan Oswald."
3. Oswald, "Refugees Welcome—Lesvos, Greece."
4. Oswald, "Refugees Welcome—Lesvos, Greece."
5. McRostie and Kosmetos, interview, April 23, 2018.
6. Hamilton, "Welcome to Lesvos."
7. Pavlou, interview, April 24, 2018.
8. Starfish Foundation, "Farewell Oxy."
9. McElvaney, "Rare Look at Life."
10. Strickland, "Protest in Greece."
11. Digidiki, "Humanitarianism in Crisis."
12. Kanter, "Europe Nears Accord with Turkey."
13. Evans, "Europe's Migrant Crisis."
14. Eric and Philippa Kempson, interview, April 9, 2018.
15. Ross, "The ECO Warriors Are Back in Action."
16. Robert and Robin Jones, interview, April 26, 2018.
17. Hernandez, "Humanitarianism without Humanitarians."

EPILOGUE

1. Kipling, "Recessional."
2. Shire, "Home."
3. Lindsay, "Dispatch from the Lifejacket Graveyard."
4. Robert and Robin Jones, interview, April 26, 2018.
5. Stevis-Gridneff, "Vigilantes in Greece."
6. Evans, "Europe's Migrant Crisis."
7. Harlan, "Migrants Wait in Bread Lines."
8. Magra, "Greece's Island of Despair."
9. Harlan, "Migrants Wait in Bread Lines."
10. BBC Newsnight, "Lesbos: Who Started the Fire."
11. Stevis-Gridneff, "Vigilantes in Greece."
12. MSF, "Greek Police Enforce Quarantine of Moria Camp."

13. Kingsley, "Fire Destroys Largest Refugee Camp."
14. Reuters, "Greece Finds 35 COVID-19 Cases in Moria."
15. Kingsley, "Fire Destroys Largest Refugee Camp."
16. Melinda McRostie, conversation with the author, March 6, 2022.
17. Oikonomou and Papastergiou, "Update on the EU Response."
18. Gall, "Afghan Refugees Find a Harsh Border."
19. Stevis-Gridneff and Kingsley, "Turkey Threatens to Open Borders"; IOM, "World Migration Report 2020."
20. Gall, "Afghan Refugees Find a Harsh Border."
21. Bennhold and Erlanger, "Why Europe's Leaders Won't Welcome More Refugees."
22. Oikonomou and Papastergiou, "Update on the EU Response."
23. Gall, "Afghan Refugees Find a Harsh Border."
24. Bennhold and Erlanger, "Why Europe's Leaders Won't Welcome More Refugees."
25. Oxfam International, "Alleged Pushbacks at Greek Border."
26. Darvas, "Bold European Action Is Needed."
27. Johnnie Walker Storyline, "Ode to Lesvos."
28. Johnnie Walker Storyline, "Ode to Lesvos."
29. Orfanos, "Drops of Light into the Darkness."
30. Grobar, "*4.1 Miles* Doc Short Director Daphne Matziaraki."
31. Orfanos, "Drops of Light into the Darkness," 270.
32. McRostie, interview, April 5, 2018.
33. McRostie and Kosmetos, interview, April 23, 2018.
34. For more complete information on the current efforts being led by Starfish, go to the foundation website: http://www.asterias-starfish.org/en/.
35. Eric and Philippa Kempson, interview, April 9, 2018.
36. Eric and Philippa Kempson, interview, April 9, 2018.
37. Labous, "How Calm after the Storm?"
38. Derler, "We Are All Humans, Episode 4."
39. Robert and Robin Jones, interview, April 26, 2018.
40. Eric and Philippa Kempson, interview, April 9, 2018.
41. Vogt, interview, April 25, 2018.
42. Pasxouli, interview, April 23, 2018.
43. Adam, interview, April 21, 2018.
44. Kabanas, interview, April 24, 2018.
45. Kerwin, "Real Needs, Not Fictitious Crises."
46. Shear and Kanno-Youngs, "Surge in Migrants."
47. Jordan, "'No Place for a Child.'"
48. Kerwin, "Real Needs, Not Fictitious Crises."
49. Hernández and Leaming, "'People Will Always Come.'"

50. Mérancourt, Faiola, and Hernández, "Haitian Migrants."

51. Kerwin, "Real Needs, Not Fictitious Crises."

52. UNHCR, "Figures at a Glance."

53. Hernandez, "Humanitarianism without Humanitarians."

54. Orfanos, "Drops of Light into the Darkness," 273.

55. Kabanas, interview, April 24, 2018.

56. Ecclesiastes 11:1 (English Standard Version).

57. Rowland, "Refugee Crisis, Completed It."

BIBLIOGRAPHY

ABC News. "Aid Groups Create Peace Sign of Life Jackets on Greek Island of Lesbos in Tribute to Asylum." January 2, 2016. https://www.abc.net.au/news/2016-01 -03/aid-groups-create-huge-peace-sign-of-life-jackets-on-lesbos/7064788.

Al Jazeera America. "Dozens Missing after Refugee Boat Sinks in Aegean." October 29, 2015. http://america.aljazeera.com/articles/2015/10/29/at-least-11 -refugees-die-in-aegean-sea-hundreds-rescued.html.

Amnesty International. "Greece: Humanitarian Crisis Mounts as Refugee Support System Pushed to Breaking Point." Press release, June 25, 2015. https://www .amnesty.org/en/latest/news/2015/06/greece-humanitarian-crisis-mounts-as -refugee-support-system-pushed-to-breaking-point/.

Aurora Humanitarian Initiative. "Beacons of Safety." Aurora Prize for Awakening Humanity, 2018. https://auroraprize.com/en/aurora/article/heroes/9809 /beacons-of-safety/2018.

Banks-Anderson, Liz. "The Refugee Boats Keep Coming, but We're Making a Difference: How a University of Melbourne Law Student Was Moved by a Harrowing Image to Help Out on the Frontline of Europe's Refugee Crisis." *Legal Affairs*, Melbourne Law School, Melbourne, Australia, October 12, 2015. https://pursuit.unimelb.edu.au /articles/the-refugee-boats-keep-coming-but-we-re-making-a-difference.

Barnard, Anne, and Karam Shoumali. "Image of Drowned Syrian, Aylan Kurdi, 3, Brings Migrant Crisis into Focus." *New York Times*, September 3, 2015. https:// nytimes.com/2015/09/04/world/europe/syria-boy-drowning.html?_r=0.

Barnets, Nick. "Greek Islanders Strive to Help Refugees." Deutsche Welle, October 10, 2015. http://www.dw.com/en/greek-island-community-finds-private-ways -to-help-refugees/a-18578098.

———. "Refugee Crisis Heightens on Greece's Eastern Islands." Al Jazeera America, August 8, 2015. http://america.aljazeera.com/articles/2015/8/8/Refugee-crisis -heightens-on-Greeces-eastern-islands.

BBC News. "Moria Migrants: Fire Destroys Greek Camp Leaving 13,000 without Shelter." September 9, 2020. https://www.bbc.com/news/world-europe -54082201.

Bennhold, Katrin, and Steven Erlanger. "Why Europe's Leaders Say They Won't Welcome More Afghan Refugees." *New York Times*, August 18, 2021. https:// www.nytimes.com/2021/08/18/world/europe/afghanistan-refugees-europe -migration-asylum.html?referringSource=articleShare.

Bond, Kate, and Gordon Welters. "Help to Vulnerable on Lesvos Wins Efi Lat-soudi 2016 Nansen Award." United Nations High Commissioner for Refugees (UNHCR) USA, September 6, 2016. https://www.unhcr.org/en-us/news /stories/2016/9/57bafd3d4/help-vulnerable-lesvos-wins-efi-latsoudi-2016 -nansen-award.html.

Booth, William. "How the Refugee Crisis Turned Lesbos Waiters into Goat Herd-ers and Spread Ripples of Pain across Europe." *The Independent*, July 28, 2016. https://www.independent.co.uk/news/world/europe/how-the-refugee-crisis -turned-lesbos-waiters-into-goat-herders-and-spread-ripples-of-pain-across -europe-a7160021.html.

Canadian Broadcasting Corporation (CBC). "Syria's War Is 10 Years Old. It's the Only Life Its Children Know." March 10, 2021. https://www.cbc.ca/news/world/syria -anniversary-children-scroller-1.5944624.

CBS Interactive, Inc. "Volunteers Aiding Those Who Come Ashore." *60 Minutes Overtime*, October 18, 2015. https://www.cbsnews.com/news/volunteers-aiding -those-who-come-ashore/.

CBS News. "Seeking Asylum." *60 Minutes*, Anderson Cooper, correspondent, Octo-ber 18, 2015. https://www.cbsnews.com/news/seeking-asylum-60-minutes -anderson-cooper/.

Chase, Jefferson, and Rena Goldberg. "AfD: From Anti-EU to Anti-immigration." Deutsche Welle, October 28, 2019. https://www.dw.com/en/afd-what-you-need -to-know-about-germanys-far-right-party/a-37208199.

Chiovenda, Melissa Kerr. "Refugees in Athens: There Is No Humanity in This Place." *EuropeNow*, February 5, 2019. https://www.europenowjournal.org/2019/02/04 /refugees-in-athens-there-is-no-humanity-in-this-place/.

Cole, Diane. "The Aunt of the Drowned Syrian Boy Tells What Happened after the Tragedy." National Public Radio (NPR), August 31, 2018. https://www .npr.org/sections/goatsandsoda/2018/08/31/642952840/an-aunts-memoir -remembering-the-drowned-syrian-boy-on-the-beach.

Cooper, Belinda. "Trading Places." *New York Times Sunday Book Review*, September 17, 2006. https://www.nytimes.com/2006/09/17/books/review/Cooper.t.html.

Corrao, Ignazio (reporter). "Towards a New Policy on Migration: EU-Turkey State-ment & Action." European Parliament, Legislative Train Schedule, March 2016. https://www.europarl.europa.eu/legislative-train/theme-towards-a-new-policy-on-migration/file-eu-turkey-statement-action-plan.

Darvas, Zsolt. "Bold European Action Is Needed to Support Ukrainian Refugees." *Bruegel Newsletter*, April 6, 2022. https://www.bruegel.org/2022/04/bold-european-union-action-is-needed-to-support-ukrainian-refugees/.

DeLargy, Pam. "Europe's Humanitarian Response to Refugee and Migrant Flows: Volunteerism Thrives as the International System Falls Short." United Nations Office for the Coordination of Human Affairs (OCHA), September 1, 2016. https://reliefweb.int/report/world/europes-humanitarian-response-refugee-and-migrant-flows-volunteerism-thrives.

Digidiki, Vasileia. "Humanitarianism in Crisis: Lesbos, Greece April 2016." FXB Center for Health and Human Rights. Boston MA: Harvard University, April 2016. https://cdn1.sph.harvard.edu/wp-content/uploads/sites/2464/2020/01/humanitarianism_in_crisis-FINAL.pdf.

Drury, Flora. "Pictured: The Moment Walking Dead Star David Morrissey Helped Rescue Terrified Refugees from Flimsy Dinghy as Actor Demands Europe 'Open Its Eyes' to Migrant Crisis on Its Doorstep." *Daily Mail*, July 15, 2015. http://www.dailymail.co.uk/news/article-3162490/Pictured-moment-Walking-Dead-star-David-Morrissey-helped-rescue-terrified-refugees-flimsy-dinghy-actor-demands-Europe-open-eyes-crisis-1-000-arriving-Greece-day.html.

Edwards, Adrian. "UNHCR Viewpoint: 'Refugee' or 'Migrant'—Which Is Right?" United Nations High Commissioner for Refugees (UNHCR), Geneva, Switzer-land, August 27, 2015. https://www.unhcr.org/news/latest/2016/7/55df0e556/unhcr-viewpoint-refugee-migrant-right.html.

Eggink, Emma, and Melinda McRostie. "The Starfish Foundation: A Local Response to a Global Crisis." *Humanitarian Exchange Magazine*, no. 67 (September 15, 2016): 8. https://odihpn.org/publication/starfish-foundation-local-response-global-crisis/.

Eiseley, Loren. "The Star Thrower." In *The Unexpected Universe*. New York: Houghton Mifflin Harcourt, Brace & World, 1969.

Evans, Gareth. "Europe's Migrant Crisis: The Year That Changed a Continent." BBC News, August 31, 2020. https://www.bbc.com/news/world-europe-53925209.

Faiola, Anthony. "Anti-immigrant Golden Dawn Rises in Greece." *Washington Post*, October 20, 2012. https://www.washingtonpost.com/world/europe/anti-immigrant-golden-dawn-rises-in-greece/2012/10/20/e7128296-17a6-11e2-a346-f24efc680b8d_story.html.

Gall, Carlotta. "Afghan Refugees Find a Harsh and Unfriendly Border in Turkey." *New York Times*, August 23, 2021. https://www.nytimes.com/2021/08/23/world/europe/afghanistan-refugees-turkey-iran-taliban-airport.html?referringSource=articleShare.

Gatrell, Peter. "Europe, the 'Dark Continent,' Is the Stage for Another Great Migration." *New York Times*, March 14, 2022. https://www.nytimes.com/2022/03/14/opinion/ukraine-refugees-europe.html?referringSource=articleShare.

Geneva Academy of International Humanitarian Law and Human Rights. "Non-international Armed Conflicts in Syria." Rule of Law in Armed Conflicts (RULAC), May 29, 2021. https://www.rulac.org/browse/conflicts/non-international-armed-conflicts-in-syria.

Goodyear, Sheena. "She Survived the Syrian War, Came to Canada, Then Taught Herself English at Tim Hortons." Canadian Broadcasting Corporation (CBC), March 17, 2021. https://www.cbc.ca/radio/asithappens/as-it-happens-wednesday-edition-1.5953321/she-survived-the-syrian-war-came-to-canada-then-taught-herself-english-at-tim-hortons-1.5953325.

Gordon, Julie. "Canadian Government under Fire in Case of Drowned Syrian Toddler." Reuters, September 3, 2015. https://www.reuters.com/article/idUSKCN0R31DU20150903.

Grobar, Matt. "*4.1 Miles* Doc Short Director Daphne Matziaraki on Witnessing Firsthand the Reality of the Refugee Crisis." *Deadline Hollywood*, December 6, 2016. https://deadline.com/2016/12/4-1-miles-daphne-matziaraki-oscars-documentary-shortlist-interview-1201859038/.

Hamilton, Omar Robert. "Welcome to Lesvos: Two Weeks as a Volunteer at a Refugee Camp in Greece." *Guernica*, November 24, 2015. https://www.guernicamag.com/omar-robert-hamilton-welcome-to-lesvos/.

Harlan, Chico. "Migrants Wait in Bread Lines, While Tourists Dine on Grilled Octopus in Greece." *Washington Post*, February 23, 2020. https://www.washingtonpost.com/world/2020/02/23/moria-refugee-camp-migrants-waiting/?arc404=true.

Hernández, Arelis R., and Whitney Leaming. "'People Will Always Come': Inside a Haitian's Journey without End." *Washington Post*, October 7, 2021. https://www.washingtonpost.com/world/interactive/2021/haitian-migration-south-america-us-rio-grande/.

Hernandez, Joel. "Europe's Front Door: The Refugee Crisis on Lesvos Island." In *Fletcher Forum of World Affairs*. Medford MA: The Fletcher School of Law and Diplomacy of Tufts University, August 14, 2016. http://www.fletcherforum.org/multimedia/2016/10/19/europes-front-door-the-refugee-crisis-on-lesvos-island.

———. "Humanitarianism without Humanitarians: Refugee Relief in Lesvos, Greece." Harvard Humanitarian Initiative. Cambridge MA: Humanitarian Academy at Harvard (ATHA), September 4, 2015. http://archive-refugeeobservatory .ekt.gr/refugeeobservatory/bitstream/20.500.12037/253/1/Humanitarianism %20without%20Humanitarians_%20Refugee%20Relief%20in%20Lesvos%2C %20Greece%20_%20ATHA.pdf.

———. "Refugee Flows to Lesvos: Evolution of a Humanitarian Response." Washington DC: Migration Policy Institute, January 29, 2016. https://www .migrationpolicy.org/article/refugee-flows-lesvos-evolution-humanitarian -response.

International Committee of the Red Cross (ICRC). "The Geneva Conventions of 1949 and Their Additional Protocols." October 29, 2010. https://www.icrc.org /en/doc/war-and-law/treaties-customary-law/geneva-conventions/overview -geneva-conventions.htm.

———. "The Geneva Conventions of 1949 and Their Additional Protocols." January 1, 2014. https://www.icrc.org/en/document/geneva-conventions-1949 -additional-protocols.

———. "Protocol Additional to the Geneva Conventions of 12 August 1949, and Relating to the Protection of Victims of Non-International Armed Conflicts (Protocol II), 8 June 1977." https://ihl-databases.icrc.org/applic/ihl/ihl.nsf /INTRO/475?OpenDocument.

International Documentary Film Festival Amsterdam (IDFA). *4.1 Miles*. 2016. https://www.idfa.nl/en/film/2e454601-cdf4-4381-835f-71a9833e7ba4/4-1 -miles.

International Organization for Migration (IOM). "World Migration Report 2020." Geneva, Switzerland. https://worldmigrationreport.iom.int/wmr-2020 -interactive/?lang=EN.

International Rescue Committee (IRC) UK. "Learning from Lesbos: Lessons from the IRC's Early Emergency Responses in the Urban Areas of Lesbos." November 21, 2016. https://www.rescue-uk.org/report/learning-lesbos-lessons-ircs -emergency-response-urban-areas-lesbos.

———. "On Lesbos, Much-Needed Reception Centre Provides Crucial Services to Refugees." January 20, 2016. https://www.rescue.org/uk/article/lesbos-much -needed-reception-centre-provides-crucial-services-refugees-0.

Jackson, Bev. *A Month with Starfish: Volunteering with Refugees on the Greek Island of Lesbos*. N.p., October 2016.

James, Ella. "And When They Awoke . . . Their Precious Baby Was Dead. A Day in Lesvos." *HuffPost*, January 17, 2016. https://www.huffingtonpost.com/ella-james /how-to-help-refugees_b_8950492.html.

Jones, Robin, and Robert Jones. *The Refugee Crisis: Through the Eyes of the Children Lesbos, Greece*. Santa Barbara CA: Blue Point Books, 2016.

Jordan, Miriam. "'No Place for a Child': Inside the Tent Camp Housing Thousands of Migrant Children." *New York Times*, March 30, 2021. https://www.nytimes.com/2021/03/30/us/texas-border-facility-migrants.html.

Kadletz, Bruna. "Philoxenia: The Art of Expressing Love and Friendship to Strangers." *Kosmos Journal*, Fall/Winter 2016. https://www.kosmosjournal.org/article/philoxenia-the-art-of-expressing-love-and-friendship-to-strangers/.

Kanter, James. "Europe Nears Accord with Turkey to Stem Tide of Refugees." *New York Times*, November 12, 2015. https://www.nytimes.com/2015/11/13/world/europe/european-union-refugees-migrants-sweden.html?action=click&module=RelatedLinks&pgtype=Article.

Kempson, Eric, and Phillipa Kempson. "Phillipa and Eric Refugee Support Lesvos/The Hope Project." Facebook, March 22, 2018. https://www.facebook.com/thekempsons/.

Kempson, Philippa. "Our Story: The Hope Project." Facebook, July 25, 2019. https://www.facebook.com/HopeProjectKempsons/.

Kermeliotis, Teo. "*4.1 Miles*: Oscar Nod for Film Capturing Refugee Rescues." Al Jazeera, January 29, 2017. http://www.aljazeera.com/news/2017/01/41-miles-oscar-nod-film-capturing-refugee-rescues-170129173938040.html.

———. "Spurned, Hopeless and Attacked, Refugees' Drama Goes On." Al Jazeera, November 22, 2016. http://www.aljazeera.com/news/2016/11/spurned-hopeless-attacked-refugees-drama-161122183357579.html.

Kerwin, Donald. "Real Needs, Not Fictitious Crises Account for the Situation at the US-Mexico Border." Center for Migration Studies of New York, March 17, 2021. https://cmsny.org/publications/border-kerwin-031721/.

Khazan, Olga. "Meet Europe's Far-Right Groups." *Washington Post*, October 20, 2012. https://www.washingtonpost.com/news/worldviews/wp/2012/10/20/meet-europes-far-right-groups/.

Kingsley, Patrick. "Fire Destroys Most of Europe's Largest Refugee Camp, on Greek Island of Lesbos." *New York Times*, September 9, 2020. https://www.nytimes.com/2020/09/09/world/europe/fire-refugee-camp-lesbos-moria.html.

———. "Greek Island Refugee Crisis: Local People and Tourists Rally round Migrants." *The Guardian*, July 9, 2015. https://www.theguardian.com/world/2015/jul/08/greek-island-refugee-crisis-local-people-and-tourists-rally-round-migrants.

Kipling, Rudyard. "Recessional." *The Times* (London), July 17, 1897.

Kofou, Maria. "Lesvos Island—My Experience (Part I)." *T-Stories*, December 19, 2015. https://tstories.gr/en/lesvos-island-my-experience-part-i/.

———. "Lesvos Island—My Experience (Part II)." *T-Stories*, December 21, 2015. https://tstories.gr/en/lesvos-island-my-experience-part-ii/.

Larsson, Naomi. "'The Human Heart Is Surviving': The Woman Giving Sanctuary to Refugees in Lesbos." *The Guardian*, September 6, 2016. https://www.theguardian.com/global-development-professionals-network/2016/sep/06/lesbos-refugees-efi-latsoudi-unhcr-nansen-award-humanitarian.

Lee, Laurence. "Desperate Journeys: EU Liberalism Lost in Battle against Refugees." Al Jazeera, January 29, 2018. www.aljazeera.com/blogs/europe/2018/01/desperate-journeys-eu-liberalism-lost-battle-refugees-180126152936625.html.

Lindsay, Jenn. "Dispatch from the Lifejacket Graveyard near Eftalou Beach in Lesvos Greece." *State of Formation*. Boston MA: Center for Interreligious Learning and Leadership of Hebrew College and Boston University School of Theology, May 22, 2017. https://www.stateofformation.org/2017/05/dispatch-from-the-lifejacket-graveyard-near-eftalou-beach-in-lesvos-greece/.

Love, Brian. "Charlie Hebdo Stirs New Controversy with Migrant Cartoons." Reuters, September 15, 2015. https://www.reuters.com/article/idUSL5N11L2G820150915.

Magra, Iliana. "Greece's Island of Despair." *New York Times*, March 29, 2018. https://www.nytimes.com/2018/03/29/world/europe/greece-lesbos-migrant-crisis-moria.html.

Martin, James. "A 360 View of Lesvos' Refugee Life Jacket Graveyard." CNET *News*, October 11, 2016. https://www.cnet.com/news/greece-refugee-crisis-lesvos-life-jacket-graveyard-360-view/.

McElvaney, Kevin. "Rare Look at Life inside Lesbos' Moria Refugee Camp." Al Jazeera, January 19, 2018. www.aljazeera.com/indepth/inpictures/rare-life-lesbos-moria-refugee-camp-180119123918846.html.

McRostie, Melinda. "Melinda." *Molyvos Life*, February 8, 2015. https://molyvosevents.wordpress.com/tag/2015/02/08/melinda-mcrostie. (No longer accessible.)

———. "Our Father, Giorgos . . ." *Molyvos Life*, February 8, 2015. https://molyvosevents.wordpress.com/2015/02/08/our-father-giorgos/.

Médecins sans Frontières (MSF). "Greek Police Enforce Unwarranted and Cruel Quarantine of Moria Camp on Lesbos." September 3, 2020. https://www.msf.org/greek-police-enforce-unwarranted-and-cruel-quarantine-moria-camp.

Mérancourt, Widlore, Anthony Faiola, and Arelis R. Hernández. "Haitian Migrants Thought Biden Would Welcome Them. Now Deported to Haiti, They Have One Mission: Leave Again." *Washington Post*, October 1, 2021. https://www.washingtonpost.com/world/2021/10/01/haiti-deportees/.

Mesure, Susie. "Restauranteurs Launch Global Fundraising Drive to Help Syrian Refugees." *The Independent*, February 6, 2016. www.independent.co.uk/news

/uk/home-news/restaurateurs-launch-global-fundraising-drive-to-help-syrian
-refugees-a6858381.html.

Muller, Wayne. *How Then, Shall We Live? Four Simple Questions That Reveal the
Beauty and Meaning of Our Lives.* Penguin Random House, 1997.

National Herald. "Heroic Coast Guard Officer Papadopoulos, Who Saved Thousands at Height of Refugee Crisis, Dies at 44." October 12, 2018. https://www
.thenationalherald.com/heroic-coast-guard-officer-papadopoulos-who-saved
-thousands-at-height-of-refugee-crisis-dies-at-44/.

Nianias, Helen. "Refugees in Lesbos: Are There Too Many NGOs on the Island?"
The Guardian, January 5, 2016. www.theguardian.com/global-development
-professionals-network/2016/jan/05/refugees-in-lesbos-are-there-too-many
-ngos-on-the-island.

Niarchos, Nicholas. "An Island of Refugees." *New Yorker*, September 16, 2015. https://
www.newyorker.com/news/news-desk/an-island-of-refugees.

Oikonomou, Spyros-Vlad, and Vasilis Papastergiou. "Update on the EU Response in Lesbos." Greek Council for Refugees (GCR) and Oxfam Briefing, *Lesbos Bulletin*, June 17,
2021. https://www.gcr.gr/media/k2/attachments/June_Lesbos_Bulletin.pdf.

Orfanos, Spyros. "Drops of Light into the Darkness: Migration, Immigration, and
Human Rights." *Psychoanalytic Dialogues* 29, no. 3 (May–June 2019): 269–83.

Osmandzikovic, Emina. "The Drowning of Alan Kurdi." *Arab News*, April 18, 2020.
https://www.arabnews.com/node/1660926.

Oxfam International. "Alleged Pushbacks at Greek Border Are Persistent and Sys-
tematic." Press release, June 17, 2021. https://www.oxfam.org/en/press-releases
/alleged-pushbacks-greek-border-are-persistent-and-systematic.

Papadopoulou, Lambrini. "How Media in Greece Reported the Migration Crisis."
European Journalism Observatory (EJO), December 3, 2015. https://en.ejo.ch
/media-politics/media-greece-reported-migration-crisis.

Positive Action in Housing Ltd. "Notes on a Scandal—the Eric Kempson Tran-
script—4 November 2015." November 8, 2015. https://www.paih.org/eric
-kempson-transcript-4-november-2015-the-lighthouse-glasgow-scotland/#_ftn.

Reuters. "Greece Finds 35 COVID-19 Cases in Moria Migrant Camp." September 8,
2020. https://www.reuters.com/article/us-health-coronavirus-greece-migrants
/greece-finds-35-covid-19-cases-in-moria-migrant-camp-idUSKBN25Z2L5.

Ross, Melissa. "The ECO Warriors Are Back in Action on Lesvos." *Medium Lighthouse Relief*, September 7, 2018. https://medium.com/lighthouse-relief/the-eco
-warriors-are-back-in-action-on-lesvos-6aac2033b2db.

Rubin, Alissa. "Did the War in Afghanistan Have to Happen?" *New York Times*,
August 23, 2021. https://www.nytimes.com/2021/08/23/world/middleeast
/afghanistan-taliban-deal-united-states.html?referringSource=articleShare.

Saliba, Samer. "Learning from Lesbos: Lessons from the IRC's Early Emergency Responses in the Urban Areas of Lesbos between September 2016 and March 2016." IRC, November 16, 2016. https://www.rescue.org/sites/default/files /document/1175/learningfromlesbos.pdf.

Shear, Michael, and Zolan Kanno-Youngs. "Surge in Migrants Defies Easy or Quick Solutions for Biden." *New York Times*, March 16, 2021. https://www.nytimes .com/2021/03/16/us/politics/biden-immigration.html.

Shire, Warsan. "Home." Facing History and Ourselves, updated December 3, 2020. https://www.facinghistory.org/standing-up-hatred-intolerance/warsan-shire -home.

Skoufatoglou, Nelly. "From the Captain's Table to the Starfish Foundation." *Neos Kosmos*, March 7, 2016. https://neoskosmos.com/en/2016/03/07/news /greece/from-the-captains-table-to-the-starfish-foundation/.

Smith, Saphora. "Young Migrants Trapped in Greece Find That Life in West Isn't What They Hoped For." NBC News, April 15, 2018. https://www.nbcnews .com/news/world/young-migrants-trapped-greece-find-life-west-isn-t-what -n863801.

Smith, Timothy Jay. "Bank Closures, Refugees and Showers . . . an Update." *Tim's Blog*, October 31, 2016. http://www.timothyjaysmith.com/tims-blog/2016/10 /31/bank-closures-refugees-and-showers-an-update.

———. "Mister, They're Coming Anyway . . ." *Tim's Blog*, October 31, 2016. http:// www.timothyjaysmith.com/tims-blog/2016/10/31/mister-theyre-coming -anyway.

———. "Real Heroes, and Selfies." *Tim's Blog*, October 25, 2016. http://www .timothyjaysmith.com/tims-blog/2016/10/25/real-heroes-and-selfies.

———. "Reckoning . . . Helping Refugees in Greece." *Tim's Blog*, October 31, 2016. http://www.timothyjaysmith.com/tims-blog/2016/10/31/reckoning-helping -refugees-in-greece.

———. "A Tale of Two Toilets." *Tim's Blog*, October 25, 2016. http://www .timothyjaysmith.com/tims-blog/2016/10/25/a-tale-of-two-toilets.

Starfish Foundation. "Farewell Oxy." January 8, 2016. https://www.asterias-starfish .org/post/farewell-oxy.

Stevis-Gridneff, Matina. "Vigilantes in Greece Say 'No More' to Migrants." *New York Times*, March 7, 2020. https://www.nytimes.com/2020/03/07/world/europe /greece-turkey-migrants.html?referringSource=articleShare.

Stevis-Gridneff, Matina, and Patrick Kingsley. "Turkey, Pressing EU for Help in Syria, Threatens to Open Borders to Refugees." *New York Times*, February 28, 2020. https://www.nytimes.com/2020/02/28/world/europe/turkey-refugees -Geece-erdogan.html.

Stock, Dan. "Melinda McRostie of Starfish Foundation Is a Basque Culinary World Prize Finalist." *Herald Sun*, June 26, 2017.

Strickland, Patrick. "Protest in Greece as EU-Turkey Refugee Deal Nears Two Years." Al Jazeera, March 17, 2018. https://aljazeera.com/news/2018/03/protests -greece-eu-turkey-refugee-deal-nears-years-180317160611814.html.

Tarabay, Jamie. "For Many Syrians, the Story of the War Began with Graffiti in Dara'a." CNN *World News*, March 15, 2018. https://www.cnn.com/2018/03/15 /middleeast/daraa-syria-seven-years-on-intl/index.html.

United Nations High Commissioner for Refugees (UNHCR). "Convention and Protocol Relating to the Status of Refugees." Geneva, Switzerland, December 2010. https://www.unhcr.org/protection/basic/3b66c2aa10/convention-protocol -relating-status-refugees.html.

———. "Figures at a Glance." June 16, 2021. https://www.unhcr.org/en-us/figures -at-a-glance.html.

———. "Operational Data Portal, Refugee Situations, Mediterranean Situation." December 31, 2018. https://data2.unhcr.org/en/situations/mediterranean /location/5179.

Vickery, Matthew. "At the Captain's Table: The Restaurant Helping Refugees." Al Jazeera, October 13, 2015. https://www.aljazeera.com/news/2015/10/captain -table-restaurant-helping-refugees-151012133022206.html.

Voutsina, Katerina. "The Growing Refugee Toll on Lesvos: Volunteers Flood onto the Greek Island to Fill an Aid Void That Europe Is Unable to Address." *US News & World Report*, January 27, 2016. www.usnews.com/news/best-countries /articles/2016-01-27/the-growing-refugee-toll-on-lesvos.

Wall, Imogen. "The Humanitarian Caste System?" *Reliefweb*, United Nations Office for the Coordination of Humanitarian Affairs (OCHA), September 30, 2015. https://reliefweb.int/report/world/humanitarian-caste-system.

Westcott, Lucy. "'It Was Hell': Lesbos Volunteers Recount Harrowing Refugee Rescues." *Newsweek*, November 16, 2015. https://www.newsweek.com/it-was-hell -lesbos-volunteers-recount-harrowing-refugee-rescues-390837.

Whitfield, Peggy. "I Spent a Frenzied Night Saving Children Washed Up on a Greek Island." Vice Media Group, November 4, 2016. https://www.vice.com/en /article/7bddvx/diary-of-a-lesbos-refugee-aid-worker-822.

Witte, Griff. "On Greek Island, Tourists Come for the Sun and Stay to Help Refugees." *Washington Post*, August 5, 2015. www.washingtonpost.com/news /worldviews/wp/2015/08/05/on-greek-island-tourists-come-for-the-sun-and -stay-to-help-refugees/?utm_term=.8a3746112b4c.

Word Press. "The Refugee Crisis in Greece—The Human Toll." Wandering Star Monthly Archives, May 27, 2016. https://monadnomad.wordpress.com /category/refugees/.

———. "Volunteering with Refugees in Lesvos Greece." Wandering Star Monthly Archives, September 6, 2015. https://monadnomad.wordpress.com/2015/09/.

World Today. "A Week in the Life of Melinda McRostie: Starfish Founder Who Offers Refugees Support on the Greek Island of Lesbos." Royal Institute of International Affairs, February and March 2017. www.chathamhouse.org /publications/twt/melinda-mcrostie.

VIDEOS

AFP News Agency. "Volunteers Cry for Help on Greek Island's Tragic Shores." YouTube video, 2:00. November 5, 2015. https://www.youtube.com/watch?v= FZRaQU3M_O8.

Al Jazeera English. "Greece: Thousands Moved to New Refugee Camp." You-Tube video, 5:28. September 19, 2020. https://www.youtube.com/watch?v= 3FAVo75FEXw.

———. "Lesbos Refugees: Thousands Concerned about New Camp after Fire." YouTube video, 2:29. September 16, 2020. https://www.youtube.com/watch?v= VuVWt_fgbq0.

BBC News. "Lesbos: Tear Gas Fired as Migrants Hold Protest over Conditions." February 3, 2020. https://www.bbc.com/news/av/world-europe-51365502/lesbos -tear-gas-fired-as-migrants-hold-protest-over-conditions.

BBC *Newsnight.* "Lesbos: Who Started the Fire at Europe's Largest Refugee Camp?" YouTube video, 27:27. October 14, 2020. https://www.youtube.com/watch?v=1 -cjHUAxxNg.

Channel 4 News (UK). "The British Family Helping Thousands of Refugees on Lesbos." YouTube video, 8:07. September 17, 2015. https://www.youtube.com /watch?v=7UWa9u-W6eU.

———. "Lesbos Refugee Crisis Continues." YouTube video, 5:06. November 6, 2015. https://www.youtube.com/watch?v=zwXUEJXlFBI.

———. "Refugee Crisis: Lesbos Struggles to Cope as Winter Arrives." You-Tube video, 3:52. November 5, 2015. https://www.youtube.com/watch?v= Aseqik5V5qQ.

———. "Refugee Crisis: The Afghan Refugees Arriving on Lesbos." YouTube video, 3:37. November 7, 2015. https://www.youtube.com/watch?v=T09fQ7mr5bM& t=5s.

Crawford, Alex. "Joining Refugees on Perilous Boat Crossing | Special Report." YouTube video, 10:01. Posted by Sky News, September 11, 2015. https://www .youtube.com/watch?v=yjQMzEPASpU.

Deep Space Diver. "Way Out Home—Refugees in Lesvos, Part 03, Molyvos." YouTube video, 15:30. April 16, 2016. https://www.youtube.com/watch?v= fJu2euE6gHM&t=12s.

———. "Way Out Home—Refugees in Lesvos, Part 05, On Foot." YouTube video, 1:39. April 16, 2016. https://www.youtube.com/watch?v=-ij438KffUM.

———. "Way Out Home—Refugees in Lesvos, Part 07, Eftalou." YouTube video, 8:56. November 5, 2015. https://www.youtube.com/watch?v=TN7fPs2zTn0.

———. "Way Out Home—Refugees in Lesvos, Part 08, Eftalou-Sikamia Road." YouTube video, 2:56. November 8, 2015. https://www.youtube.com/watch?v=sr_KOZqUJW8.

———. "Way Out Home—Refugees in Lesvos, Part 10, Skala Sikamias." YouTube video, 25:37. November 27, 2015. https://www.youtube.com/watch?v=0T3 -JIF6O6w.

———. "Way Out Home—Refugees in Lesvos, Part 12, OxyCamp." YouTube video, 6:39. December 7, 2015. https://www.youtube.com/watch?v=C-22K4NRDoE.

Derler, Zack. "We Are All Humans: Troubled Waters, Lesvos Episode 4." January 22, 2016. https://www.youtube.com/watch?v=JUryd9RMSeo. (No longer accessible.)

———. "We Welcome You: Troubled Waters, Episode 3." December 30, 2015. https://www.youtube.com/watch?v=K9S3gWAm2nA. (No longer accessible.)

Dijksma, Mike. "Transit Refugee Camp Oxy Lesbos Greece in the Morning." October 17, 2015. https://www.youtube.com/watch?v=KGOew0hbsuQ. (No longer accessible.)

Flag, J. "Refugees Arrive in Skala, Lesvos 2015." YouTube video, 8:32. November 23, 2015. https://www.youtube.com/watch?v=m4zpOvubD2s.

Genauzeau, Franck. "Syrian Refugee Crisis: The Hardest Part of Their Journey to Europe." YouTube video, 1:11:56. Posted by "Tell Me Why?" October 18, 2015. https://www.youtube.com/watch?v=SN4fbiVTLLY.

Green, John. "Understanding the Refugee Crisis in Europe, Syria, and around the World." YouTube video, 9:20. Posted by "vlogbrothers," September 8, 2015. https://www.youtube.com/watch?v=KVV6_1Sef9M.

Guru-Murthy, Krishnan. "Refugee Crisis: New Boats Still Arriving on Lesbos Island." YouTube video, 4:15. Posted by Channel 4 News, September 9, 2015. https://www.youtube.com/watch?v=4DkZqXwhpok.

Howling Eagle. "Philoxenia Episode 1 Empathy—This Small Fishing Village Saved Thousands of Lives." YouTube video, 8:31. July 22, 2018. https://www.youtube .com/watch?v=SLlHfu8W8L0.

————. "Philoxenia Episode 2 Imagine Running—No One Leaves Home Unless Home Is the Mouth of a Shark." YouTube video, 11:06. October 1, 2018. https://www.youtube.com/watch?v=8dWDcWxaiU0&has_verified=1.

HuffPost. "Susan Sarandon with Refugees in Lesbos, Greece | The Crossing." YouTube video, 2:04. January 4, 2016. https://www.youtube.com/watch?v=dEI9ZgLFxe8.

International Rescue Committee (IRC). "Mandy Patinkin Visits Lesbos, Greece." YouTube video, 2:37. December 6, 2015. https://www.youtube.com/watch?v=tOwL89Tndk4.

Johnnie Walker Storyline. "Ode to Lesvos." September 20, 2016. www.youtube.com/watch?v=INkT00ewy48&index=1&list=PLxitlhQXKCQyzUWycTBoQ_7zvuYr22lj-. (This video is only available by subscription.)

Kempson, Eric. "Aid Agencies Deceiving the General Public!!" YouTube video, 15:25. November 7, 2015. https://www.youtube.com/watch?v=DWxBu9HcSfk.

————. "Angels & Demons." YouTube video, 15:43. June 9, 2015. https://www.youtube.com/watch?v=6ZBPJz53VKA.

————. "Another Tragic Day in Eftalou, Greece." YouTube video, 9:10. May 6, 2016. www.youtube.com/watch?v=GO3ounak64s.

————. "Another Tragic Morning on Lesvos Greece." YouTube video, 30:17. May 9, 2015. https://www.youtube.com/watch?v=Vd8w9-qvMqU.

————. "Appeal from Government Needed." YouTube video, 4:14. June 2, 2015. https://www.youtube.com/watch?v=ioCAoA_9tW0.

————. "Casualty & No Doctor!!!!!!" YouTube video, 3:03. June 9, 2015. https://www.youtube.com/watch?v=bt5cglIuu-0.

————. "Casualty & No Doctor!!!!!! Update." YouTube video, 7:06. July 9, 2015. https://www.youtube.com/watch?v=ykuVHKFZFhI.

————. "Desperate Calling from Lesbos." YouTube video, 4:14. October 24, 2015. https://www.youtube.com/watch?v=mP2ikMXbf3E.

————. "Disgusting Aid Agencies!" YouTube video, 9:17. October 28, 2015. https://www.youtube.com/watch?v=DJ4f8NBupog.

————. "Disgusting Behavior 30/09/2015." YouTube video, 9:11. October 10, 2015. https://www.youtube.com/watch?v=oTynm2ukFwQ.

————. "Dry Clothes for Wet Kids!!!!" YouTube video, 4:35. August 5, 2015. https://www.youtube.com/watch?v=zruI22ajjg8.

————. "8 Bodies Washed Up in Eftalou! 01/11/2015." YouTube video, 5:17. November 2, 2015. https://www.youtube.com/watch?v=3vO6AByd1mM.

————. "11 Year Old Girl Loses Family! 29/10/2015." YouTube video, 3:12. October 30, 2015. https://www.youtube.com/watch?v=Gc_WqWY9Wz8.

———. "Everyday Heroes!! Part One 01/09/2015." YouTube video, 3:44. September 2, 2015. www.youtube.com/watch?v=zhfxSYSJwe0.

———. "Everyday Heroes!! Part Two 01/09/2015." YouTube video, 8:19. September 2, 2015. https://www.youtube.com/watch?v=kJKGIReBWuI.

———. "Faith in Humanity Restored!!!!!" YouTube video, 20:09. May 22, 2015. https://www.youtube.com/watch?v=PLaJiMijjeg.

———. "Fourth Boat of the Morning!! 14th in 9 Hours." YouTube video, 9:26. July 17, 2015. https://www.youtube.com/watch?v=eH1k5ysdsPg.

———. "Get Off Your Arses and Help Us!!!!" YouTube video, 6:04. August 28, 2015. https://www.youtube.com/watch?v=NFA0rYj5wEA.

———. "Helicopter!!" YouTube video, 8:18. August 3, 2015. www.youtube.com /watch?v=h3BaFE07lsA.

———. "Heroes & Villains Part 1." YouTube video, 10:48. July 3, 2015. https://www .youtube.com/watch?v=3Vts9Mg6g3U.

———. "Heroes & Villains Part 2." YouTube video, 13:00. July 3, 2015. https://www .youtube.com/watch?v=5JocoTk0S98.

———. "Hot, Dusty, Dirt Road!!! 14/08/2015." YouTube video, 12:57. August 15, 2015. https://www.youtube.com/watch?v=uXUhGu7B6XA.

———. "In the Heat of the Afternoon!!" YouTube video, 4:20. September 9, 2015. https://www.youtube.com/watch?v=UWbogbK3MvY.

———. "Just Shows You the Scale of the Problem 01/11/2015." YouTube video, 7:33. November 4, 2015. https://www.youtube.com/watch?v=QmM2tw2gvhY.

———. "Landing on Lesvos!!!!" YouTube video, 19:41. June 26, 2015. https://www .youtube.com/watch?v=48_VB3uhIWI&t=949s.

———. "Lesvos Death March!!!!!" YouTube video, 8:02. May 22, 2015. www .youtube.com/watch?v=KSld5F7vjOY.

———. "Lesvos Death March Update." YouTube video, 25:13. May 23, 2015. https:// www.youtube.com/watch?v=VrJ-fUFOUjs.

———. "More Blood Spilled!!!" YouTube video, 13:07. June 3, 2015. https://www .youtube.com/watch?v=_iZC5XPduGI.

———. "Moving Forward Together." YouTube video, 14:05. June 16, 2015. https:// www.youtube.com/watch?v=P3LoPvrhKKU.

———. "Normal Landing." YouTube video, 4:05. August 31, 2015. https://www .youtube.com/watch?v=UkBPDfkgRnY.

———. "1 Month Old 08/08/2015." YouTube video, 5:52. August 9, 2015. https:// www.youtube.com/watch?v=e5GbgYn8MMQ.

———. "Our Country Is Being Destroyed!!" YouTube video, 7:40. August 28, 2015. https://www.youtube.com/watch?v=AJhKJH2Ja1I.

———. "Our House! 11/09/2015." YouTube video, 9:42. September 15, 2015. https://www.youtube.com/watch?v=UdOrCFPJDaE.

———. "Perfect Landing!!" YouTube video, 4:57. August 28, 2015. https://www.youtube.com/watch?v=Wbht_fY-a-0&t=187s.

———. "Real Greek Hospitality." YouTube video, 8:49. May 31, 2015. https://www.youtube.com/watch?v=kmzl9f1paII.

———. "Refugee Camp, Lesvos, Mytilene, Kara Tepe." YouTube video, 5:26. July 12, 2015. www.youtube.com/watch?v=f1K9CyHQFfs.

———. "Refugee Crisis in Lesvos." YouTube video, 14:15. May 21, 2015. www.youtube.com/watch?v=a1BLXb7eXtc.

———. "Refugee Landing, Skala Sikaminia, Lesvos, Boat 1." YouTube video, 10:39. July 27, 2015. https://www.youtube.com/watch?v=HhA1nf6sByw.

———. "Refugee Reception." YouTube video, 9:54. June 29, 2015. www.youtube.com/watch?v=WoFC4_FcUfk.

———. "Refugees in the Middle of Nowhere!!!" YouTube video, 4:33. August 1, 2015. https://www.youtube.com/watch?v=o3xBHHL3JFY.

———. "Resignations Needed." YouTube video, 14:59. June 1, 2015. https://www.youtube.com/watch?v=Wb9rYayWScc.

———. "Safe Landing Part 2." YouTube video, 6:58. July 5, 2015. https://www.youtube.com/watch?v=QiUYfPVWasU.

———. "Saints & Sinners!!!" YouTube video, 13:24. June 7, 2015. https://www.youtube.com/watch?v=egLX_gi7JmE.

———. "6th Boat of 19 That Landed!! 08/08/2015." YouTube video, 6:21. August 8, 2015. https://www.youtube.com/watch?v=GspMuiEfbi0.

———. "The Start of a Busy Day!! Refugees Lesvos." YouTube video, 3:12. August 1, 2015. https://www.youtube.com/watch?v=0KNchezVOko.

———. "The Struggle Continues." YouTube video, 8:10. June 11, 2015. https://www.youtube.com/watch?v=xkMvywG8etA.

———. "Super Jenni!! 04/09/2015." YouTube video, 11:34. September 5, 2015, www.youtube.com/watch?v=3xuk7rs3DUs.

———. "Tears for Suffering Refugees!!" YouTube video, 9:44. July 7, 2015. https://www.youtube.com/watch?v=ofL5A-yrAw8.

———. "They Tried to Kill Us!!!! 10/09/2015." YouTube video, 10:56. September 10, 2015. https://www.youtube.com/watch?v=KKN0JyLkwFY.

———. "This Is Not a Business!! 27/12/2015." YouTube video, 10:33. December 27, 2015. https://www.youtube.com/watch?v=p1zcLSTgL2I.

———. "To Stoop So Low!!!!" YouTube video, 5:18. June 12, 2015. https://www.youtube.com/watch?v=_pSSgOQXtRg.

———. "Tourism & Refugees in Greece." YouTube video, 27:46. May 25, 2015. https://www.youtube.com/watch?v=PQx0Ji6uv7E.

———. "UNHCR on Holiday in Lesvos." YouTube video, 6:38. June 17, 2015. https://www.youtube.com/watch?v=IYliEYOH3TM.

———. "We Do Our Best from Day to Day!! 5/09/2015." YouTube video, 7:36. September 8, 2015. https://www.youtube.com/watch?v=IkgNon8dMhw.

———. "You're Beautiful!!!" YouTube video, 4:31. August 28, 2015. https://www.youtube.com/watch?v=ef4nZtK8Wts.

Labous, Jane. "Lesvos: How Calm after the Storm?" YouTube video, 5:36. Posted by *Geographical Magazine*, May 2, 2017. www.youtube.com/watch?v=N-7ARwazvRI.

Matziaraki, Daphne. *4.1 Miles*. YouTube video, 21:21. Posted by *New York Times Op-Docs*, September 28, 2016. https://www.nytimes.com/2016/09/28/opinion/4-1-miles.html.

Media Line. "From Teacher to Award-Winning Filmmaker—Conversation with Hasan Oswald." April 29, 2020. https://themedialine.org/mideast-streets/from-teacher-to-award-winning-filmmaker-conversation-with-hasan-oswald/. (No longer accessible.)

NBC *Nightly News*. "Stirring Images of Syrian Boy's Body Now Symbol of Europe's Crisis." September 2, 2015. https://www.nbcnews.com/nightly-news/video/stirring-images-of-syrian-boy-s-body-now-symbol-of-europe-s-crisis-518263875644.

Newport, Kayla. "The Journey of a Refugee—Lesvos, Greece." YouTube video, 6:59. January 28, 2016. https://www.youtube.com/watch?v=DQYdixe_etQ&t=44s.

Nomikos, Alexandros. "In Transit—A Short Video about the Refugees in Lesvos." November 23, 2015. https://youtube.com/watch?v=qHuqrOjAcAO. (No longer accessible.)

Oswald, Hasan. "Refugees Welcome—Lesvos Greece." YouTube video, 9:37. December 22, 2015. https://youtube.com/watch?v=xViBBNDROag.

Psaropoulos, John. "Greek and European Reponses to the Refugee Crisis." YouTube video, 1:32:10. Einaudi Center's Foreign Policy Distinguished Speaker Series. Ithaca NY: Cornell University, November 18, 2015, posted November 23, 2015. https://www.youtube.com/watch?v=Q9QK9R92g9Q&app=desktop.

Rowland, Jack. "Afghan Dancing and Mental Breakdowns! Volunteering with Refugees at Camp Oxy, Lesvos, Greece." YouTube video, 5:19. December 9, 2015. https://www.youtube.com/watch?v=C_aC-vxw2as.

———. "Refugee Crisis, Completed It. Final Day Volunteering at Refugee Camp Oxy, Lesvos, Greece." YouTube video, 4:56. December 9, 2015. https://www.youtube.com/watch?v=EhUnkFEG0fA.

Samaritans Purse. "The Rising Tide: Europe's Refugees Wash Ashore in Greece." YouTube video, 5:54. October 8, 2015. https://www.youtube.com/watch?v=RBjZ7kpTLrs.

Sea-Watch e.V. "Eric Kempson the Hope Project." YouTube video, 7:04. August 24, 2017. https://www.youtube.com/watch?v=WTDipMVlLJk.

———. "Migrants Pulled from Sea between Turkey and Lesbos by NGOs (BBC News 16.12.2015)." YouTube video, 3:11. December 18, 2015. https://www.youtube.com/watch?v=miYe5uY6yMA.

Tanzania. "Lesvos Day 1, In Search of Refugee Boats." YouTube video, 19:35. April 10, 2016. https://www.youtube.com/watch?v=fFGeq_x0J_4.

———. "Lesvos Day 2—(Part 2 of 3) Food Distribution in Lesvos." YouTube video, 5:01. January 1, 2016. https://www.youtube.com/watch?v=F7WP2nibAto.

UNHCR, the UN Refugee Agency. "Greece: Boat Arrivals Continue." YouTube video, 2:26. October 2, 2015. https://www.youtube.com/watch?time_continue=6&v=ltHa9HCO45Y.

———. "Greece: Lesvos Coastguard Rescue." YouTube video, 3:50. June 17, 2015. www.youtube.com/watch?v=aHoKz75XNQo.

Wall Street Journal. "Drowned Syrian Boy: Story of Family's Plight." YouTube video, 2:04. September 4, 2015. https://www.youtube.com/watch?v=HSjhHRFaSA0.

Zahra Trust. "Zahra Trust in Lesvos, Greece." YouTube video, 3:25. Posted by Saarah Bokhari, November 19, 2015. https://www.youtube.com/watch?v=89Qj8l-H3K0.

INDEX

Ford Motor Company, 9
4.1 Miles (film), 67, 161, 221
Frontex, 141, 158, 200

gangs, prevalence of, 216–17
Genauzeau, Franck, 53, 54, 55, 169
Geneva Convention, 53, 69, 94, 142, 143, 204
Golden Dawn, 93
Greco-Turkish War, 34, 35, 92
Greek Coast Guard, 18, 19, 29, 37, 69–70, 76, 102, 138, 157–58, 161, 170, 175, 177, 186–87, 193, 194, 200, 219; Molyvos office of, 26, 31, 32, 33, 40, 42, 43, 44, 66, 70, 80, 88, 96, 101, 187; patrols by, 61, 67, 161; refugee boats and, 91; refugees and, 24, 29, 41, 44, 52, 66, 156, 205, 213; registration process and, 73, 101, 104, 110, 116; rescue efforts by, 36, 53, 56, 68, 71, 72, 88, 96, 112–13, 115, 132, 133, 159, 162, 187, 204, 206, 207–8
Greek Council for Refugees, 203
Greek Ministry of Welfare, 35
Greenpeace, 172
Grigorelli, Erasmia (Eri), 31, 67, 71, 77, 78, 160, 162, 185; animosity toward, 186–87; first aid and, 43; refugees and, 32, 33, 34, 35, 80, 219; rescue efforts and, 68–69
The Guardian, 56
Guernica, 150

Haitians, 9, 10, 217
Hamilton, Robert Omar, 150, 193
Harvard University, 11, 92, 195, 218
health care. *See* medical care
Hellenic Rescue Team, 211
"Help for Refugees in Molyvos" (Facebook), 74

Hernandez, Joel, 11, 13, 195, 218
Hilsum, Lindsay, 164
holding areas, 89, 116, 117, 133, 134, 138, 201; resistance to, 89, 90; temporary, 116, 118. *See also* parking lot; refugee camps
Holt, Lester, 123
Honegger, Michael, 2, 3, 4, 5, 7, 8, 85, 94, 108, 123, 130, 170, 178; help from, 86, 104, 173–74; postings by, describing refugee situation, 6; Red Cross and, 175; and transporting refugees, 87
Hope Project, 23, 164, 165, 166, 168, 188, 206, 210, 211; creation of, 22; resources for, 172; volunteers for, 170
hospitality, 3, 4, 83, 89
Humanitarian Academy (Harvard University), 11, 195, 218
humanitarian crisis, 76, 219–20
humanitarianism, 11, 92, 167, 187, 206
"Humanitarianism with Humanitarians" (Hernandez), 11
Human Rights Campaign, 178
Human Rights Watch, 178
human trafficking, 41, 168
Hungary, blockade by, 48
Hussein, Saddam, 36
hypothermia, 26, 43, 67, 157, 210

immigration, 27, 125, 142, 218; barriers to, 144; climate change and, 216; issues, 28, 93, 216, 217, 218
International Rescue Committee (IRC), 131, 139, 170, 171, 172, 174, 178, 210; and Camp Apanemo, 193; media personalities and, 176; refugee operations and, 200; report by, 177
Iranians, 25
Iraqis, 30, 36, 53, 62, 143, 160

222; independent, 165–66; local, 114, 173; refugees and, 140, 150, 166, 181, 191, 192; registration process and, 73; religious organizations and, 168; sandwich making and, 78; tourists as, 85, 131, 164, 218; transportation and, 107; "Western idea" of, 145–46

water, 122, 165, 167, 202, 216; distribution of, 104, 105, 106
WhatsApp, 132, 155
Whitfield, Peggy, 155, 156, 157, 158, 160
Women and Health Alliance International (WAHA), 138
World Trade Center, 25, 36